Web Stores Do-It-Yourself For Dummies®

Important Web Addresses

There are a number of companies that provide information, functions, and accounts that can help you build your Web store. This list features some of those companies that I mention in this book, and the URL Web addresses you would type in your Web browser to find these companies. Good luck!

Resource Web sites

✔ **Wiley Publishing, Inc.:** www.wiley.com
✔ **Small Business Administration:** www.sba.gov

Storefront Providers

✔ **Yahoo! Merchant Solutions:** smallbusiness.yahoo.com
✔ **ProStores:** www.prostores.com
✔ **1&1 Internet Inc.:** www.1and1.com

Vendor Web sites

✔ **PayPal:** www.paypal.com
✔ **Picasa:** www.picasa.com
✔ **eLance:** www.elance.com
✔ **GoDaddy:** www.godaddy.com

Marketing Web sites

✔ **Constant Contact:** www.constantcontact.com
✔ **Blogger:** www.blogger.com
✔ **WordPress:** www.wordpress.com

Shipping Companies

✔ **Federal Express:** www.fedex.com
✔ **United States Post Office:** www.usps.gov
✔ **United Parcel Service:** www.ups.com

Tips for Web Store Success

✔ **Know your products:** Your customers are coming to you for advice and guidance in finding a solution to their problems. It helps if you are familiar with the products you are selling, so you can suggest and promote the correct products in each situation.

✔ **Know your customers:** In this age of technology, it is much easier to track your customers' orders and get an idea of what they want, so you can serve their needs better. Not only will watching customer orders give you a better idea of what to stock in your store, but being able to suggest or cross-sell new products to your existing customers will definitely keep you in business or grow your Web store.

✔ **Know your competitors:** Unfortunately, every niche that exists on the Internet typically has more than one Web store serving that niche. You need to always be on the lookout for potential and actual competitors, and see how they're reaching their customers. You don't have to steal, but learn from their techniques, and be ready to adopt new methods or change direction if necessary.

✔ **Know your financial numbers:** It's one thing to create a Web store and get orders coming in. It's another thing to run a *profitable* Web store that is making money. Hire a CPA or accountant to help you keep track of your financials, or use an accounting software program like Quickbooks so you can figure out your cash flow situation, profit and loss statement, and be able to come up with a basic balance sheet. The days of burning money every year in hopes of a big buyout or IPO are over.

BESTSELLING
BOOK SERIES

Web Stores Do-It-Yourself For Dummies®

Cheat Sheet

Important Terms to Know

Term	Definition
Bandwidth	Amount of information being sent from your Web store server to your customers' computers. Text is low bandwidth, audio/video is high.
Cookie	Text file that resides on a customer's computer and stores information that a Web site can access when that customer uses that Web site. Cookie files store information so Web sites can track how customers use that site.
CSS	Cascading Style Sheets; an advanced Web design programming language that allows a Web designer to build Web pages whose style can be centrally updated regardless of page length or content.
Disk space	Hard drive space on an Internet server that stores your Web store page information, digital photographs, product descriptions, and more.
Domain name	An alphanumeric name that refers to a unique, particular Web site on the Internet. Company owners actually "rent" the right, on a yearly basis, to use a domain name for their Web site. They do this by going to a domain name registrar, like GoDaddy.
FTP	File Transfer Protocol, a system to transfer files between your computer and another computer on the Internet. For example, you may FTP files (such as Web pages, graphics, or logos) from your home computer to your Web server.
PPC	Pay Per Click, where you pay a search engine every time a new visitor clicks on your advertisement from the search engine results screen.
RSS	Really Simple Syndication, a newer technology that automatically sends updates of your Web store to interested customers.
SEO	Search Engine Optimization, refers to a field of study that tries to determine what to include or connect to your Web site to influence your Web site's positions in a search engine's rankings or results.
Shopping Cart	An online program that acts as a holding bin for a customer's intended purchases until that customer checks out and pays for those items.
SKU	Stock Keeping Unit, a term used to indicate a unique ID number or letter sequence that refers to a particular item. For example, a UPC code (for commercial products) or an ISBN number (for books) could be used as a SKU.
SSL	Secure Sockets Layer, allows your customers to safely transmit sensitive information like credit card numbers to you over the Internet.
URL	A World Wide Web address that represents a specific Web site or Web page on the Internet.

Things to Have in Place Before You Start

- **Business paperwork:** If you're planning to open a new Web store, you should consider getting a Reseller's Permit from your state government, a Business License from your city hall, and perhaps a Fictitious Business Statement (also known as a d/b/a) from your county government.

- **Business bank account:** Unless you want the money from your Web store to be mixed in with all your other revenue and expenses, you should probably set up a new bank account for your Web store. This will allow you to accept checks made out to your Web store name, and you can use this account to order a debit card, which you can use to buy items for your Web store that require a credit card.

- **An idea of what you want to sell:** If you want to open a store, hopefully you have your initial product line in mind. Understand, however, that you don't necessarily have to sell tangible, "stuff-in-a-box" products. You can open a store that sells other people's products by joining their *affiliate* programs and reselling their products. You could sell information in the form of e-books, audio, or video files. You could put a lot of information on your Web site and sell the advertising space on your site.

- **Time:** It's the one commodity we never seem to have enough of, but if you bought this book, that means you should have the time to construct your Web store, polish it up, launch it, and maintain it as you receive orders. Don't forget to budget some time once you launch your store, as you will need to update your store regularly.

For Dummies: Bestselling Book Series for Beginners

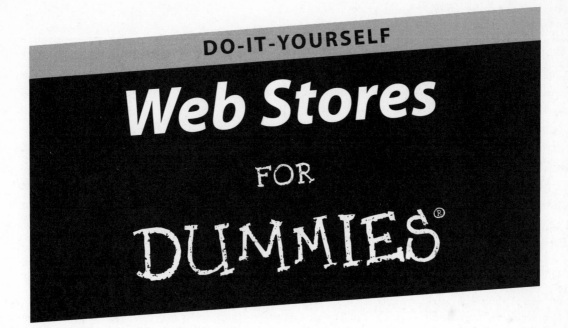

DO-IT-YOURSELF

Web Stores

FOR

DUMMIES®

by Joel Elad

WILEY

Wiley Publishing, Inc.

Web Stores Do-It-Yourself For Dummies®

Published by
Wiley Publishing, Inc.
111 River Street
Hoboken, NJ 07030-5774
www.wiley.com

WILEY

About the Author

Joel Elad is the head of Real Method Consulting, a company dedicated to educating people on how to sell on the Internet, and eBay in particular, through training seminars, DVDs, books, and other media. He holds a Master's Degree in Business from UC Irvine, and a Bachelors Degree in Computer Science and Engineering from UCLA.

Joel has written several books in the field of e-commerce, including *Starting an Online Business All-In-One Desk Reference For Dummies*, *eBay Your Business*, and *How to Sell Anything on Amazon . . . and Make a Fortune!* He has contributed to *Entrepreneur* magazine and Smartbiz.com, and has spoken at regional and national conferences on the topic of eBay and/or e-commerce. He is the lead eBay instructor for the Learning Annex in New York City, Los Angeles, San Diego, and San Francisco. He has taught at institutions like the University of California, Irvine. He is an Educational Specialist trained by eBay and a proud member of eBay's Voices of the Community.

Joel has previously worked for companies like IBM Global Services, where he was a project manager and software developer working for Fortune 500 clients. He operates several e-commerce sites, including NewComix.Com, which has quickly become a low-priced leader of comic books, toys, and action figures to US and international customers. While he was the Marketing and Sales Director at Top Cow Productions, Joel implemented an eBay sales channel and helped revamp their e-commerce operations. He continues to consult for various clients to add or improve their e-commerce operations.

Joel lives in San Diego, California. In his spare time, he hones his skills in creative writing, Texas Hold 'Em poker, and finance. He is an avid traveler who enjoys seeing the sights both near and far, whether it's the Las Vegas Strip or the ruins of Macchu Picchu. He spends his weekends scouring eBay and local conventions for the best comic book deals, catching the latest movie with friends or family, and enjoying a lazy Sunday.

Dedication

I hereby dedicate this book to two dear friends, Anthony Choi, and Michael Wellman, who help make my dreams a reality and make my reality that much more enjoyable. They have defined my success with my online ventures and I wouldn't be where I am without their help, knowledge, patience, dedication, and drive. You two are my inspiration!

Author's Acknowledgments

I have to give a BIG thanks to the superb team at Wiley for making this book a reality and trusting me to guide the way. I have to especially thank Blair Pottenger for his infinite patience, advice, and steady guidance, as well as Steven Hayes for his encouragement and faith. I also have to thank Michael Bellomo for keeping me on the straight and narrow, an exhausting job to be sure. And where would I be without the editors at Wiley, like Jenn Riggs, to make me sound so clear and grammatically correct?

Secondly, I'd like to acknowledge the various e-commerce store owners, IT professionals, and friends who gladly gave their time, advice, and opinions to help me craft this book: Anthony and Yvonne Choi, Lynn Dralle, Phil Dunn, Joshua MacAdam, James Marchetti, Chandler and Sharon Rice, and Joshua Schwartz. Also, I have to thank several assistant managers at the San Diego Kinko's locations for helping me as I holed up there for weeks and weeks to get this book written. (Thumbs up to Christine Seliger and Dan Chandler.) The Napa and Point Loma locations are ACES in my book, and the 24-hour Hazard Center Mission Valley location was my lifeline!

Lastly, thanks to my family for putting up with my late-late-night writing sessions and frequent seclusion to get this book ready for publication. Your support is always invaluable.

Publisher's Acknowledgments

We're proud of this book; please send us your comments through our online registration form located at www.dummies.com/register/.

Some of the people who helped bring this book to market include the following:

Acquisitions, Editorial, and Media Development

Project Editor: Blair J. Pottenger

Executive Editor: Steven Hayes

Copy Editor: Jenn Riggs

Technical Editor: Michael Bellomo

Editorial Manager: Kevin Kirschner

Media Project Supervisor: Laura Moss-Hollister

Media Development Specialist: Angela Denny

Editorial Assistant: Amanda Foxworth

Sr. Editorial Assistant: Cherie Case

Cartoons: Rich Tennant (www.the5thwave.com)

Composition Services

Project Coordinator: Kristie Rees

Layout and Graphics: Carrie A. Cesavice, Stephanie D. Jumper

Proofreaders: Laura Albert, Linda Quigley

Indexer: Potomac Indexing, LLC

Publishing and Editorial for Technology Dummies

Richard Swadley, Vice President and Executive Group Publisher

Andy Cummings, Vice President and Publisher

Mary Bednarek, Executive Acquisitions Director

Mary C. Corder, Editorial Director

Publishing for Consumer Dummies

Diane Graves Steele, Vice President and Publisher

Joyce Pepple, Acquisitions Director

Composition Services

Gerry Fahey, Vice President of Production Services

Debbie Stailey, Director of Composition Services

Table of Contents

Introduction

● ●

You're not a dummy, even if you think you are. But starting your own business can be a challenge — and then, when you add the computer part to it . . . well, the whole thing can seem so overwhelming that you avoid it. (What? Never crossed your mind?)

Okay, now that you're looking at this book, you probably decided that you've avoided it long enough, and now you're going to do it — bite the bullet and build your Web store. I want to help you get the job done as quickly as possible with the least amount of pain. You've got lots of other things to do, after all, because running your business will be the most important part.

About This Book

Web site programming isn't exactly a fun subject — unless, of course, you're a programmer . . . and even then it might not really be all that much fun, because of all the options and things you could do that might not work down the road. Some people would rather set up a cardboard table in front of their house and try to sell things than organize their efforts with a Web store. I'm here to help you get past the ugly part so that you can start enjoying the benefits of being a store owner.

What benefits? Well, when you have your Web store, you have your own business, with a set of customers, cash flow, and a brand. Yes, every Web store has their own brand (maybe not as recognizable as Coca-Cola or IBM) that is defined by how they present themselves, treat their customers, and operate as an Internet entity. Many Web store owners have given up their day jobs and have the freedom to work from home, raise their kids, and set the course of their own future. Some people keep their day jobs, but make a nice secondary income from their Web store to help them and their families. Then, there are the retail store owners who are joining the 21st century and putting their operations online to reach a whole new market segment; that's got a global reach, by the way.

Web Stores Do-It-Yourself For Dummies shows you how to set up your Web store and all the steps you should think about before, during, and after the setup process. I take great pains to give you step-by-step instructions whenever possible to get you up and running. But it's also a real-life-situation kind of book. I show you what to consider as a Web store owner without forcing you to pick one specific Web store-front provider. I throw out some business techniques and give you options for how you want to build your Web store and interact with your customers. As you'll see, there are a lot of things you can sell, and a lot of ways you can build your Web store. This book is designed to be your guide, with flexibility and assistance throughout these pages.

What You Can Safely Ignore

Throughout the book, I include Web store tips — you can probably ignore those unless you're interested in that kind of stuff and want to make your life easier.

Oh, and the gray boxes that you see throughout the book? Those are sidebars, and they contain extra information that you really don't *have* to know but that I thought you might find useful and interesting. So feel free to skip the sidebars as well.

Foolish Assumptions

I'll be honest — I had to assume some things about you to write this book. So, here's what I assume about you:

✔ You already know a little something about the day-to-day stuff that you need to do to run your store — you know, figure out that you want to sell something, come with a list of products to sell, take orders, pack and ship your products, and so on. I *don't* assume that you know how to do all that on a computer.

✔ You have a personal computer (that you know how to turn on) with Microsoft Windows 2000, Windows XP, or Windows Vista. I wrote this book by using Windows XP.

How This Book Is Organized

Every great book needs a plan. I divided this book into six parts, each made up of chapters so that you can easily find the information that you need.

Part 1: Planning and Gathering

If you've never operated your own store or business, you probably want to read this part. I first go into the different kinds of things you can sell on your Web store. While many of you would think, "Duh, you sell stuff," the answer is actually more than that. I talk about how you can sell products at a higher margin, or how you can sell other people's products, as well as information, advertisements, or your own homemade products. Then, I talk about all the different policies your Web store should have in place before that first order comes in. Nowadays, the privacy policy is considered a requirement, but there's also the matter of your shipping policy, return policy, and payment policy. Even if you don't set them in stone at this phase, you should think about them before building your store.

Part II: Constructing Your Web Store

In this section, I cover the essential building blocks of getting your Web store up and running:

- ✔ How to select the right Web storefront provider (what features should you look for, and what should you pay for).

- ✔ How to sign up with a payment processor so you can accept credit cards on your Web store.

- ✔ How to design your store on paper so it's easier to build the right sections.

We go into some massive detail by actually opening a Web store account with three main providers: Yahoo! Merchant Solutions, ProStores, and 1&1 eShops. For each of these, I show you exactly how to open an account, create your Web store, and fulfill the basics to get it operational. (For Parts 3–5, I use Yahoo! Merchant Solutions as my storefront provider when showing you examples. Understand, however, that the concepts I present in this book work for any storefront provider.)

Part III: Filling In the Blanks (and Shelves)

In this section, I cover the steps you take after constructing the basic Web storefront. First and foremost is your catalog of products, so I spend an entire chapter helping you get the catalog created in an efficient and correct manner. Next, I talk about the images and descriptions that will make up your product catalog, and tips and tricks to make those as professional and appealing as possible. Then, I open up the discussion about functions you can add to your Web store to engage your customers and keep them coming back for more, from a discussion board so they can chat with each other to a Web store specific search engine and customer accounts. (For specific ways you can enhance your Web store, check out Web Sites Do-It-Yourself For Dummies, by Janine Warner, as she focuses on the non-commerce ways to improve your Web store.) Finally, I talk about the importance of tying your Web store operations to the "back end," so shipments get out correctly. I walk you through the main shipping companies and how to set up your own store account with each service.

Part IV: Finalizing Your Web Store

In this part, I cover a variety of steps that you should take before you start taking orders on the Internet. Yes, you've worked hard to get to this part, building a Web store from scratch and filling it with products, functionality, and a great look and feel. But a polished Web store goes through some finalization, so here I talk about putting your store at the hub of your sales by integrating your Web store URL into every single thing you do in your business. I then talk about an extensive site-wide review of the Web store, looking for any outdated or incorrect information, cleaning up any spelling or grammatical errors, and making sure that each page is correctly linked to each other. Finally, I have you check to make sure every section of your

Web store is "talking" correctly with every other section, and how to put your Web store up on the Internet early to have friends and family check it out first and place sample orders (or real orders, whatever you prefer).

Part V: Promotion and Outsourcing of Your Web Store

In this section, I cover all the all-too-important tasks of promoting your store, once you've worked so hard to build and perfect it. I talk about ways you can build "buzz" online through different marketing efforts like creating a blog, having a customer newsletter, or selling on other sites, like eBay, to gain attention for your Web store. I then move into the area of paid advertising, where you can take out pay per click advertising ads on search engines like Google and Yahoo! to drive traffic to your Web store. I even talk about how to send your Web store information directly to the search engines. Finally, I discuss that "next step" in Chapter 18, when you should be thinking of hiring employees or independent contractors to handle the "fun" stuff like packing and shipping, or maybe even a redesign of your Web store. I even talk about using the Internet, through sites like Prosper.com, to get additional funding or financing for your Web store expansion plans.

Part VI: The Part of Tens

If you've ever read a *For Dummies* book, you've seen the Part of Tens. This part contains a collection of ten-something lists. My Part of Tens comprises the following:

- ✔ Ten elements every Web store should have, from a good contact information page to clear product descriptions.

- ✔ Ten simple design tips to make your Web store stand out from the legions of "beginner" Web stores that savvy customers like to skip over.

- ✔ Ten common mistakes that Web store owners make and how to avoid those traps and not infuriate your visitors and potential customers.

Icons Used in This Book

Throughout the book are symbols in the margin. These symbols, or *icons,* mark important points.

This bull's-eye appears next to shortcuts and tips that make your work easier.

When you see this icon, something could go wrong, so make sure that you read the paragraph. This icon warns you of common mistakes and ways to avoid them.

This icon marks any point that you want to be sure to remember. You might want to reread paragraphs that are marked with this icon.

This icon relates to geeky computer stuff that might interest you, but really has little impact on you. You can safely skip them.

Where to Go from Here

Just getting started with building a Web store? Turn the page. Do you have a specific topic of interest? Use the index or the Table of Contents to find the topic and turn to that page.

Part I
Planning and Gathering

The 5th Wave   By Rich Tennant

"You know, it dawned on me last night why we aren't getting any hits on our Web site."

In this part . . .

In this part, I cover the first steps and thoughts you should undertake when trying to build your own Web store. Chapter 1 talks about the different types of products or services you could sell on your Web store, and provides a few examples. I then talk about the "back-office" elements that any Web store owner should have, as well as some Web sites that help provide these services for you, and how to enroll with these services.

I then talk about an often-overlooked part of operating your Web store, which are the policies and rules that make your Web store function. I give examples about elements like a privacy policy, return policy, and other policies that should be defined before you open for business so every-one knows the rules of your business.

Chapter 1

Web Stores Overview: Discovering Your Purpose

Tasks performed in this chapter

- ✔ Determining what to sell in your Web store
- ✔ Finding products to sell in your Web store
- ✔ Establish your store information
- ✔ Getting a Skype phone number

When you think of opening your own store, you usually have to consider a game plan that involves scouting out a retail location, negotiating a price per square foot, buying fixtures, carpeting, and lighting, assembling shelves and stocking tangible merchandise, and planning for a grand opening campaign that could involve balloons, a big ribbon to be cut, and lots of festivities.

Today, you can open your own store on the World Wide Web, without physical rent costs or high-capital investments. In the United States, as of 2007, over 211 million Americans have Internet access, according to Internet World Stats (www.internetworldstats.com).

More importantly, as of September 2007, Pew Internet & American Life Project reported that 50% of U.S. Internet users had broadband or fast Internet access at their home.

Consumers are overwhelmingly using the Internet to do their personal and holiday shopping, which presents a great opportunity for Web stores to take advantage of this growing population. Worldwide, Internet access is growing in practically every country, with shipping companies making Beijing as likely a customer target as Boston.

So, the question is raised: How can you take advantage of this growing, eager market? In this chapter, I begin to walk you through some of the steps you should take in the planning stages of building your own Web store. Later in the book, I walk you through the steps of actually building, filling, and promoting your Web store successfully.

Deciding What to Sell

It's very common to be in this situation: You know you want to build a Web store, but you're unsure exactly what to sell in your store. Perhaps you own a physical retail store and you want to add a Web store to offer multiple ways for your customers to reach your products. Perhaps you want to close down your physical store and only offer your products through a Web store. In these cases, your question is not *what* to sell, but rather, which of your items would sell best in a Web store? After all, if you sell heavy items, the shipping cost may make it prohibitive for your customers to save money and for you to make money. (One of the reasons Pets.com filed for bankruptcy was having to ship 50 pound bags of dog or cat food for free or very little money.)

Let's assume, however, that you don't currently have a physical store and you're trying to decide what it is that you want to sell. One way to get started is to ask yourself a few questions:

- ✔ **What do you know?** Can you turn information or experience from a hobby into your own store? Can you identify a rare antique? Do you know what the hottest toy should be next year? Do you know where to get all the different types of remote-controlled cars, airplanes, and boats? Do you know the difference between an amplifier and a subwoofer? Your experience in the area will help you identify the manufacturers or product sources, spot the latest trends, and understand the nuances of that particular market, plus you can identify with your customer so you know what they'll be looking for and what questions they might ask.

- ✔ **Who do you know?** It's like the old saying goes, "It's not what you know, it's who you know." With so many e-commerce stores going up (and some of them closing) you need to have an edge, and one way to gain a competitive advantage is to know the right people. Perhaps you know a local business that hasn't sold their products online yet and needs a good partner. Maybe you have a connection or knowledge of a wholesale source, or a good way to get products cheaper than the average person. Sometimes, it's as simple as having an old college roommate who works or lives near Factory X or ABC Distributors.

- ✔ **What do you like to do?** Here's another saying, "You have to love what you do." If you're going to open your own Web store, don't do it if you hate the product you're selling, or you simply don't believe in it. It'll become a rough enterprise if you do. Ask yourself what you enjoy doing in your spare time. Maybe you like to work with your hands and create things. You could open your own store selling handmade jewelry, crafts, or apparel. Your focus could be customization, offering a one-stop shop to customize your customer's motorcycles, cars, or RVs.

- ✔ **What are people asking you, or what are you good at?** Sometimes, the best market research can come from your immediate network. One question I ask people is this, "Is there anything you know, better than most people, where people are always coming to you and asking you questions about it?" Maybe you're the foremost expert on how to beat a traffic ticket. Not only can you turn that knowledge into an informative product to sell, but you can create a Web site with lots of great advice and sell advertising space and related products as an affiliate member.

- ✔ **What do you think will sell well?** Ok, you've read the slogans, you've thought about my previous questions, but deep down, this is the one question some of you want to focus on. You want to pick a winning product (hopefully, it's a winning category — stores rarely do well on a single product) that will have a healthy profit margin and sell well. Use your knowledge as a consumer, do some research online, and ask around to see if others agree with your assessment. I don't think there is one "magic" product that is 100% guaranteed to work, but I do think that if you pick the right area, like the Apple iPod after that was first released, the success of that product could carry you far.

If you want to draw from the experience of other small business owners, here are a few online sources (like the U.S. Small Business Administration shown in Figure 1-1) you can check out for ideas, research, and inspiration:

- ✔ **The U.S. Small Business Administration (SBA;** www.sba.gov)
- ✔ **SCORE (Service Corps Of Retired Executives;** www.score.gov)
- ✔ **Your local Chamber of Commerce** (www.uschamber.com)
- ✔ *Entrepreneur* **magazine** (www.entrepreneur.com)
- ✔ **National Federation of Independent Businesses** (www.nfib.com/page/toolsHome)

Figure 1-1: The SBA has lots of tools to help new business owners.

In addition to the questions to ask yourself above, you also need to consider your options for what to sell:

✔ **Tangible products:** This is the most common type of thing to start selling online, as most people understand and need physical products. Your goal here is always the same — buy low, sell high. You focus on keeping your costs down, and earning a healthy profit margin with each sale. Remember that your costs are more than just the price you paid for the item in the box. You need to factor in your overhead costs, keeping your Web store running, your time and effort, the cost of any employees you may hire, and so on.

✔ **Homemade products:** I make the distinction between tangible products and homemade products because the former is something you order from a manufacturer or distributor, while in the latter case you're the manufacturer, distributor, wholesaler, and retailer. Here, the term accountants love to use, *Cost of Goods Sold (COGS),* isn't just the cost of the raw materials used to put together your product, but your time (or your employee's time) in assembling and finishing the product. In this case, your profit margin definitely has to cover the cost of your time, because in a homemade goods business, without you, there is no business (unless you train someone to replace you).

✔ **OPP (Other People's Products):** There are many businesses out there that have products or services they're eager to sell, but they need a sales force of people to help them sell it. You can become an affiliate and sell other people's products in exchange for a commission you earn from brokering the sale. This allows you to offer a wide range of merchandise without investing in lots of inventory, stocking, packing, and shipping the merchandise.

✔ **Information:** As I mentioned earlier in this section, maybe you know something better than most people, or are always asked to explain a certain procedure or solution. You can turn that information into an eBook or informative product that you sell on your Web store. In today's age of technology, you have several options to package your information product:

  • eBook (PDF file)

  • Audio file (CD, MP3, `.wav`)

  • Audio/Video file (DVD, `.mov`, `.mp4`, `.avi`)

  • Physical book

  • Subscription to a newsletter (PDF or DOC file, via e-mail)

  • Monthly subscription to an information Web site (all of the above)

✔ **Advertisements:** If you can build a Web site that people enjoy going to, whether it's full of informative content, fun games and activities, or the latest news and columns, you can earn money by selling the advertising space on your site. Typically, you want the ads on your Web store to reinforce the categories you offer on the store, but if you become part of a network of stores, you can exchange advertisements to encourage people to shop at multiple stores.

- ✔ **Services:** Sometimes, the best thing you can sell is your experience. You can use your Web store to sell your services, whether you have a professional talent (accountant, lawyer, PR guru), creative talent (graphic designer, artist), technical talent (software developer, electrical engineer), or any other kind of service that you can provide remotely. You can sell your services by the hour or by the assignment, and use your Web store to show off your portfolio, give away sample tips in exchange for leads, and perhaps build an additional revenue stream by selling products you know your clients will definitely need.

- ✔ **Combination of some or all of the above:** Hey, why limit yourself? Feel free to combine a few of these ideas and build multiple revenue streams for your business. You should probably pick one to focus on first and build up. Once you have one revenue stream rocking, think of expanding to the next area. You can't wake up one day and create a fully functioning site like Amazon.com, with 41 categories, an affiliate program, and tons of extra features. Take one at a time.

Finding Products to Sell

Okay, you have an idea of what you can sell online, now you need to find them! For many entrepreneurs, the act of *product sourcing,* or getting the merchandise they want to sell in their Web store, is not only their first big challenge, but for some of them, their competitive advantage as well. Your goal is to find a reliable, renewable source of quality merchandise that you can order, add a markup, and resell to your customers at a higher price.

There are multiple options when it comes to product sourcing, so let's look at the most common and hopefully, the most fruitful.

Start with what you own

When I teach people how to start their eBay business, one of the core bullet points I cover in every class is this: Most people started selling on eBay by cleaning out a room in their house, whether it was a closet, garage, attic, or the living room. This makes sense for an eBay business — there are over 50,000 distinct categories to put your stuff for sale, a built-in audience of 244 million members around the world who already come to shop on the site, and you can start your eBay sales with one or two items.

When it comes to running your Web store, however, I don't feel this principle universally applies. Let me explain: If you plan on opening a coin store, and you want to use your personal coin collection as your startup inventory, great. If you plan on starting a "Whatever I can find" store, and just stuff it with things in the garage so you have something available to sell, not so good. Your Web store needs to have a consistent set of categories that your customers can depend on, and a steady base of core products to fill your catalog. You don't want to be constantly writing descriptions and taking pictures for your Web store if your products change on a whim.

Pound the pavement

Unless you're sitting on a mountain of boxed-up products ready to be sold, you'll need to get out and start looking. Depending on what you decide to sell, you can go out and search for your products and buy them in whatever quantity they're available in. Some people call this "the thrill of the hunt" because they're looking for that undervalued product to add to their store inventory and sell for a higher margin. If you're selling products that are rare, unique, one-of-a-kind, antique, vintage, or collectible, you can fill your inventory by going to one or more of these places:

- ✔ Flea markets
- ✔ Thrift shops (such as Goodwill and Salvation Army stores)
- ✔ Secondhand or consignment stores
- ✔ Local auctions
- ✔ Estate sales
- ✔ Garage sales
- ✔ Merchandise outlet or closeout stores

You can find a lot of these events and more by searching sites such as Craigslist (www.craigslist.org) in your city or state, and going to their For Sale section, as shown in Figure 1-2.

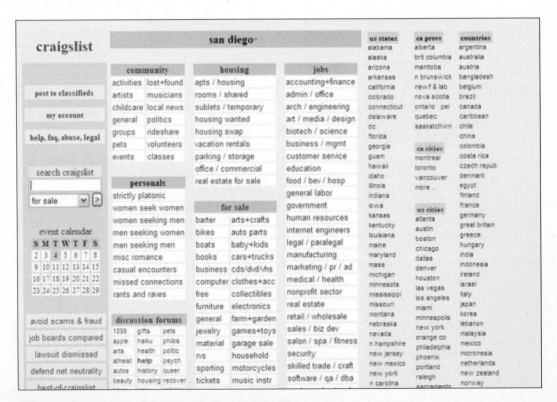

Figure 1-2: Find lots of local products through Craigslist.

What if you're looking for more common items, more "commodity," regular everyday items like apparel, electronics, gifts, or something similar? Thankfully, depending on where you live, there are places you can go. Sometimes they're called *merchandise marts* or *districts* where wholesalers in a certain category congregate and have offices and warehouse space. In Los Angeles, for example, there's the Fashion District in downtown LA (shown in Figure 1-3), where you can buy wholesale from different apparel manufacturers.

Figure 1-3: Find deals at places like the Fashion District.

The other big source of products that you can go and visit are trade shows. Every industry has their own version of a trade show, convention, or national (or regional) events. Many times, you can order products directly from the wholesalers or manufacturers that attend these events. Merchants gather at these trade shows to meet the manufacturers, learn from their colleagues, and get product information. Once you've identified your market or industry, you can look for trade shows in that industry through several mediums:

✔ **Newspapers and magazines:** Most industries have their own magazines or newspapers dedicated to their genre, from *Antiques Weekly* and *Frame Building News* to *Military Trader* and *Needlepointers Magazine.* The big trade shows will advertise in these newspapers and magazines, and typically, columnists will write articles about how to approach these shows and make the most of your experience.

- **Trade Associations:** If you think slogans like "got milk?" and "Beef. It's what's for dinner" were invented by one dairy or meat company, you'd be mistaken. Most industries have organized a trade association that furthers the interest of everyone in that industry, from the National Milk Producers Federation to the National Cattlemen's Beef Association. Do an online search for your industry plus the words "trade association."

- **Physical retailers:** Walk into your local retail store that carries products in your targeted industry, and ask the manager or employees if there are any local or regional trade shows that they know about which would interest you. While some of them may not say anything for fear of losing a customer, others may be advertising the show in their shop.

If you're planning to walk into Best Buy to ask about electronics, let me save you a trip. The biggest electronics convention is the Consumer Electronics Show in Las Vegas in early January. It's a great show, I have a lot of fun when I go there, and it's where all the retailers go to figure out what to stock in their stores for the next year. Go to http://www.cesweb.org for more information.

Work on the wholesale

As you work your way up the "food chain" of products, your ultimate goal as a Web store owner is to purchase your inventory via wholesale channels and pay a lower price than the common person, so you can afford to re-sell it at retail (or a fraction thereof) and make money for your store. As your volume increases, you'll get used to ordering from a wholesaler or distributor to re-stock your inventory.

When you order direct from a wholesaler, you enjoy several advantages:

- **Lower prices:** Because you are ordering a larger quantity from someone who doesn't have to cater to lots of individual buyers, you usually get a great discount on the suggested retail price.

- **Steady inventory source:** As you sell out of your merchandise and place re-orders, you want to know that you can get a steady supply of this inventory. You're building a name for yourself in this category, and you don't want to earn a pool of customers only to tell them, "Oops, I can't get any more of this category X. Try back in a week or two." I guarantee you, they'll be off in search of the next deal . . . far away from you.

- **Access to newer products:** When you have a relationship with a good wholesaler, you'll find out about new product lines first, and typically have the chance to stock them as soon as possible, so you can keep your customers coming back to you.

- **You control the buyer experience:** Because you're ordering the products directly and warehousing them, you can make sure that your customers are getting the correct order, properly packaged, and with any additional sales information you care to put in the box. You handle the returns directly, so customers get a quicker response time.

Of course, there are some downsides to going the wholesale route:

- **Up-front investment:** Typically, you have to buy a sizable quantity in advance to get the big discount. Oh, and typically, that merchandise is *non-returnable,* which means if you can't sell it, you're stuck with it.

- **Storage space required:** Once you order it and receive it, you have to provide a place to store or warehouse the goods until your customers can order it and you can ship it out to them. The more you have to order, the more space you'll need to keep it all.

- **You control the buyer experience:** Yes, you're reading it right, it's both a pro and a con. While you ensure a good experience, it means you also have to coordinate the packing and shipping of these products as well, which is an additional cost.

The other main option is something called *drop-shipping.* In drop-shipping, the company that holds the merchandise simply provides you with the information needed to make the sale, like product descriptions, photos, and a wholesale price. You go out and make the sale, and collect the money from the customer. You notify the drop-shipper, pay them the wholesale price, they pick it from their warehouse, and ship it *directly* to the customer, so you never get in the middle of that process. You keep the difference between what you charged and the drop-shipper charged you, as your profit margin.

When it comes to the benefits versus drawbacks on this one, it's somewhat the opposite of wholesaling. There is no up-front investment, and no need to warehouse, pack, or ship the item. However, the prices sometimes aren't low enough, they control the experience (which means if the drop-shipper is late, runs out of the product, or packs the item poorly, you get blamed, not them), and you rely on them to provide a steady supply of the product. In addition, you're typically competing against other members of their "wholesale clubs" for some drop-shippers, and the only criteria left to bargain with is price. This means you're at risk of someone undercutting you to gain business. When there is a price war, economics teaches one basic truth: In a price war, profits typically go to zero.

When it comes to product sourcing, here are a few Web sites to help you get on the right track:

- **Worldwide Brands (**www.worldwidebrands.com**):** They sell up-to-date directories of information, and have a OneSource program for helping you connect with the right wholesale companies for your needs. You can see more of what they offer in Figure 1-4.

- **WhatdoISell.com (**www.whatdoisell.com**):** This site is similar to Worldwide Brands, but is a bit more eBay-focused. They have a great library of information, courses, research, and suggestions that many Web store owners could benefit from.

- **Liquidation.com (**www.liquidation.com**):** They auction off lots of business surplus goods, but usually in small enough quantities to appeal to many small businesses.

- **DMOZ Wholesale Trade (**www.dmoz.org/Business/Wholesale_Trade**):** The Open Directory project has a directory of different wholesale sources in various categories.

Figure 1-4: Wholesale directories and more at Worldwide Brands

TIP

If you want to buy wholesale, you'll typically need (as a minimum) a resale certificate or sales and use tax permit that shows you're a business. Contact your state government's secretary of state or type "resale license" and your state into a search engine for more information on how to get one. Beware of middlemen helping you get this license — go directly to a state government Web site for more information.

Establishing Your Store Information

When you set up your store, you typically need to have some contact or business information to provide when signing up for everything. If this is a home business, you could simply provide what you already have — your home address, telephone number, e-mail address, credit card number, and so on. Many store owners, however, set up their own business identity, so their business and personal information don't get mixed together.

Here are some thoughts for what to set up:

✔ **P.O. Box or private mailbox service:** For as little as $48 per year, you can have a separate address to receive all your business mail and correspondence. The Post Office offers P.O. Boxes for rent that you can sign up for to help establish your business. You can also go to a private mailbox provider, like the UPS Store (formerly Mail Boxes Etc.) and local pack-and-ship stores, to get a private mailbox. The advantages of a private mailbox include

- Your own street address (instead of P.O. Box 1234) which gives a better professional image of your company.

- The ability to receive packages from any shipping company, including UPS and FedEx (some shipping companies can't deliver to P.O. Boxes).

- The ability to have someone available during normal business hours to sign for all your incoming packages.

When it comes to your e-mail address, you should always get one that matches your domain name and storefront provider. We discuss storefront providers in Chapter 3, so don't worry about business e-mail accounts until then.

✔ **Fax number:** Despite the explosive growth of the Internet and e-mail, the fax machine hasn't been made obsolete enough, as the need to transmit documents continues every day. Rather than purchase your own fax machine and pay for a dedicated phone line (or share the fax machine with your answering machine), you can sign up for an online service that gives you a fax number and allows you to retrieve your faxes from their Web site, or they can e-mail you a copy of each fax as they come in. You can e-mail or upload documents that they can fax out for you as well. Some services to check out include

- **eFax** (www.efax.com)

- **MyFax** (www.myfax.com)

- **jConnect** (www.j2.com)

- **uReach Consumer Solutions** (www.ureach.com)

Two other sources for your own local fax number are your private mailbox shop (whether or not you have a mailbox there) and your local FedEx Kinko's locations. Both of them will send and receive faxes for you based on a $1–2 per page average rate.

✔ **Telephone number:** It's true that most people today have at least two phone numbers, their home (landline) telephone number, and their cell phone number. But do you really want customers calling your house or cell phone at 2am to ask a question? Many small business owners get an extra line to handle their business calls, or at least get a number with voicemail to field customer concerns until the owner can call back on another line.

There's a newer development which offers an affordable solution that's easy to use. Internet telephony has been booming the last few years, and one of the leading companies in that area is Skype. Purchased by eBay in 2005, Skype helped lead the way for people to make free phone calls, using their computers and the Internet, anywhere in the world. In the next section, I go through the steps needed to create your own SkypeIn number.

Creating a Skype Phone Number

Stuff You Need to Know

Toolbox:
- Business credit card or PayPal account
- Business contact information

Time Needed:
10–15 minutes

Skype has developed a new feature called SkypeIn, which offers you a personal telephone number with voicemail included. Anybody can call this number and either reach you (when you're logged in to Skype) or leave a message in your voicemail, which you can retrieve online. It costs approximately $5–6 a month, as of this writing, and is a great way to separate business from personal calls. In addition, you can use your Skype account to make all your business calls, whether your customer, vendor, or supplier is in Boston or Beijing.

It's free to download and free to call other people on Skype

1. Go to the Skype home page at `www.skype.com` and sign up to be a member. Click on the Download option. In order to get a SkypeIn telephone number, you have to join Skype's system first and download the software onto your computer. You can see from their homepage that you can use Skype to call anyone around the world.

2. When you get to the Download page, you see the various programs that Skype offers their members. Once you install the software, you'll come back to get the personal number for your business, also known as SkypeIn. For now, just click the Download Now link to start the download process.

Click this link.

3. When you see the SkypeSetup warning pop up on your computer, either Save the file to your computer and then run the application, or click Open to run the installation program from their Web site. If you have a fast, broadband connection, you can click Open to start the installation program from Skype dynamically. If you're unsure about your connection, click the Save button to save the setup software onto your computer. Once it has fully saved onto your computer, run the program from your computer by double-clicking on the file or, for Windows users, use the Start button and the Run command, and find the `SkypeSetup.exe` file by clicking the Browse button from the Run window.

4. Click Install to start the process. The first window you'll see when the setup software starts running will ask you for your Language preference, and to agree to their End User Licensing Agreement. Review the terms, and click the check box to agree. At that point, the Install button will become clickable, so click that button to start the installation.

5. Once the Skype software has fully installed on your system, click the Start Skype button to create your account. You'll see a flurry of activity as Skype installs their user software on your computer. When that process is done, you'll see a confirmation screen. Click the Start Skype button to start creating your account.

6. In the first step to establish your Skype account, you have to give Skype your full name, and come up with a unique Skype Name (or userid) and a password to control access to your account. Review their Terms of Service and Privacy Agreement, click the check box to agree to those terms, and then click the Next button, which should now be clickable, to proceed.

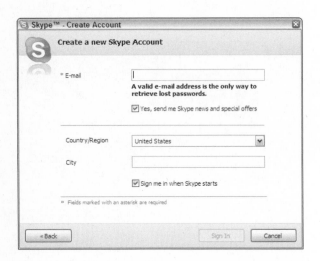

7. In order to establish your Skype account, they need a valid e-mail address on file for you, as well as your city and country information. Provide those in the boxes provided and the Sign In button should become clickable. Click that button to send the information to Skype and create an account for you.

8. Go back to the Skype Web site, click on Download or Skype Credit, then click on SkypeIn. You should be taken to the SkypeIn product page. This page explains the functionality behind your SkypeIn phone number. Scroll down and click the Get a SkypeIn number link to start this process.

9. Since all SkypeIn numbers have to be associated with a Skype account, log in to Skype with your newly created account. Click the Sign Me In button to proceed.

10. You'll see a list of countries that Skype offers phone numbers in. Peruse through the list and pick the country where you want your SkypeIn phone number to be based out of, and click that country's flag or designated link.

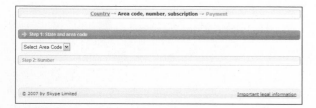

11. You'll be prompted to pick from a list of area codes derived from your country selection. Click the drop-down list and select the area code that you wish from the list provided.

If there is any sort of local component to your business, you'll probably want an area code where most of your customers or vendors reside, so it's only a local phone call for them to reach you.

12. Once you pick your area code, Skype will update the screen with a list of potential phone numbers in that area code that you can choose from. If you want a specific set of digits, use the combination box provided to look for available phone numbers with your requested set of digits. If you don't like any of the numbers presented, click the Show Ten New Suggestions link to present ten new numbers.

13. Once you see the number you want to use, click on that number. Skype will select it for you and assign it to your account. Then click the blue Buy Selected Number button to continue the process.

14. You'll see the subscription payment. Decide if you want to try this system for 3 months, or order 12 months of service. Then, complete the fields as prompted and click Next to proceed.

15. Follow the prompts to complete your billing information. As of this writing, Skype gives you multiple ways to pay for your SkypeIn number: PayPal, Visa, Mastercard, bank transfer, or Click & Buy. Pick the payment method you would like to use, and review the bill and Terms of Service. Then, follow the prompts, depending on your payment method, to get the correct information to Skype.

16. Your order is complete! Start using your SkypeIn number for any business transactions, and once you get the e-mail, log in to your account so you can format your voice-mail system to receive calls for you when you're not at your computer.

Chapter 2

Developing Your Store Policies

Your Web store isn't simply about the items you have to sell. Your customers are a big reason why you're in business, and many store owners simply assume that customers will show up as expected, buy your goods, and leave without an issue. It's easy to forget that the customer interaction can get complicated. The best way to reduce most of these issues is to come up with a set of rules and guidelines in advance, so you and your customers know what to expect.

In this chapter, I walk you through some of the basic policies any Web store owner needs and I go step by step into the decision-making process that goes into crafting these policies so you can focus later on your biggest asset — your customer.

Putting the Service in Customer Service

As you begin your journey as store owner, you need to make a lot of decisions. You decide which products you want to carry and how much inventory to stock, what marketing budget to create and implement, and hopefully develop a full-functioning business plan to guide your efforts. Another element to think about is the level of customer service you wish to provide to your customers.

As a Web store, you don't have the luxury of meeting your customers face to face and physically handing them the merchandise on the way out the store. You're relying on electronic means and partners (such as shipping companies) to complete the experience for you. In addition, depending on the model you choose to make money, your Web store may be solely focused on low price and can't afford to give a high level of customer service. Therefore, you need to think about what level of customer service you give and express that with a Customer Service policy.

Finding your level of customer service

Your goal should always be to provide the best kind of customer service that you can afford. When I think of excellent customer service, I think of companies that make the shopping experience as effortless and pleasant as possible. However, costs are involved when you offer constantly staffed telephone support lines, a no-questions-asked Return policy, and awards of discounts or gifts to handle any complaint regardless of who is at fault.

Your level of customer service is defined by certain elements, such as

- ✔ What forms of communication can customers use to contact you?
- ✔ When can customers contact you for any issue?
- ✔ Who will handle your customers' issues and where are those customer service representatives located?
- ✔ What can your employees offer the customer when a problem occurs?
- ✔ How quickly do you promise to respond to customers' issues?

There are some elements of your Customer Service policy that are better addressed in other documents — your Return policy for example, which addresses when and how people can return their purchases. The main goal of the Customer Service policy is to give your customers a concrete idea of what they can expect from doing business with you and the guidelines you want them to follow in communicating their issues.

Don't expect all your customers to follow the policy blindly. When there's an issue, some customers yell, scream, and e-mail everyone in your company to get a solution. Be prepared internally to handle concerns that don't come through the normal channel, and in your response to the customer, refer them to the preferred method specified in your policy.

Writing your Customer Service policy

So, how do you actually create your Customer Service policy? Here are some steps to get you going:

1. Your introductory paragraph introduces your store name and indicates your level of customer service to your customers. Many companies use this space to express the company mission, whether that mission is to be the low price leader or the service leader.

2. You can organize the body of your policy several different ways:

   - You can use headers to separate the sections of your policy, such as Services Offered, Hours of Operations, and Ways to Communicate a Problem.

- You can organize your policy as a series of questions and answers with the title of Frequently Asked Questions (FAQ) at the top of the page.

- You can use a combination of sections that begin with a clear identifying header, where the top of the page contains a hyperlinked list of the various sections, so customers can click through to the section they need without reading through the entire page. An example of this is provided in Figure 2-1.

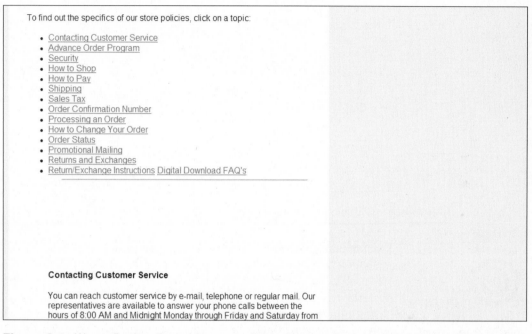

Figure 2-1: Warner Brothers Record Store organizes its Customer Service policy by headers and sections.

3. You need to decide the method(s) that customers will be allowed to communicate with you. You must offer at least one method of communication, but you can decide to offer one or more of the following:

- **E-mail:** Definitely the most cost-effective method and considered the standard when it comes to Web operations. One example is how Circuit City uses e-mails and, more specifically, Web forms to have customers relay issues, as shown in Figure 2-2. You can emphasize that this option is available 24 hours a day, 7 days a week.

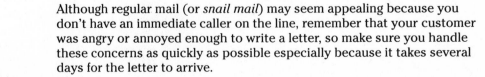

Contact Us

Welcome to Circuit City's email support page. Simply choose a topic from the menu below, fill out the required fields and click send. A customer service associate will review your email and reply to your request with a personal response.

Sometimes our emails get filtered out as spam, so be sure to check the junk folder of your inbox.

Figure 2-2: Circuit City uses e-mail to have their customers stay in touch.

I recommend creating a dedicated e-mail address specifically for customer service issues. This way, customer concerns don't get mixed in with daily business issues, and you can assign someone to monitor this account specifically to handle customer issues.

• **Telephone:** This is the most-preferred form of communication for customers because it's immediate and most customers have access to a phone. You can choose to pay for a toll-free telephone number (to limit your customers' costs) or offer a regular phone number, which would be a long-distance phone call for most of your customers. The other decision to make is whether this phone is staffed by a live person or whether it goes straight into a voicemail system, where you or your employees review the calls within a specific period of time and then return the customer's call.

• **Mail:** This is probably the least-preferred method for customers but a cost-effective way for you to receive customer concerns. You can post an address or, in some cases, a P.O. Box (if you don't want to give out your home address) that customers can write to and express their concerns.

Although regular mail (or *snail mail*) may seem appealing because you don't have an immediate caller on the line, remember that your customer was angry or annoyed enough to write a letter, so make sure you handle these concerns as quickly as possible especially because it takes several days for the letter to arrive.

- **Multiple methods:** If you plan to offer multiple methods of communication, you can create a section of your Customer Service policy that reads like the following example:

Contacting Customer Service

You can reach customer service by e-mail, telephone, or regular mail. Our representatives are available to answer your phone calls between the hours of 9:00 a.m. and 5:00 p.m. Monday through Friday, and Saturday from 9:30 a.m. to 3:00 p.m., Eastern Standard Time (except holidays).

E-mail address: `custserv@yourcompanyname.com`

Phone Number: (866) 555-1234

Regular Mail:

Your Store

P.O. Box 12345

Anytown, CA 12345-6789

4. After you tell your customers how to get in touch with you, it's helpful to give them an idea of the response time they can expect. Your options here can be as quick as "We promise to get back to you within 24 hours," whereas other companies offer response times, like "We pledge to respond to your issue within 2 business days." If you're unsure or can't promise a specific response time, be general but state that you'll respond in a timely manner or as soon as possible.

5. The next area to address is the technical support or product support of the items you sell in your store. As a retailer, usually you can refer the customer to the manufacturer for a limited warranty on their end if the product is defective or has any technical issues. However, you do need to state that, as a retailer, you offer no additional or concurrent warranty with the product if that's the case. A simple one- to two-sentence paragraph should suffice.

   If you do offer warranties on your item, you need to provide at least one paragraph explaining the time period, type of warranty (for example, do you offer a 30-day limited warranty, a 90-day complete warranty, or a lifetime guarantee on the product), and how the customer should contact you to take advantage of the warranty. This can include, but isn't limited to, using e-mail or a specified phone number to report the problem and ask for a return label or providing the address to mail in the defective unit.

   Also, post information about your warranty policy in your store Return policy, which I discuss in the next section.

6. Finally, your Customer Service policy can include any other disclaimer, copyright, or company information that would be helpful to your customers. If there's any important information or features about your company that help you stand out from the competition, talk about that information here to inform the customer of your exciting opportunities. Perhaps you offer online help or chat with the company founder or CEO every quarter, or you want to communicate any specific service guarantee you wish to provide to your customers.

Writing Your Return Policy

After you've laid out your main Customer Service policy, think about other policies that affect how you do business with your customers. First and foremost is your store's Return policy. We all dream of the situation where every item you ship to your customers is perfectly assembled, packaged, and in working order. In the business world, however, that's not always the case, so you need to think about what level of Return policy you offer your customer.

The extreme cases are easy to quantify:

- A customer places an order and it never arrives. As the retailer, you have to either replace the order or refund the customer.

- The customer receives the item, but the item is completely smashed, destroyed, and/or unusable. As the retailer, you either ship a duplicate item as a replacement or refund the customer.

- The customer orders a Widget RX200 and receives a Widget TR500. As the retailer, you ship the correct item and pay to have the incorrect item shipped back, or offer a deal to the customer where they keep the incorrect item in exchange for some compensation.

Here are some other cases that aren't so obvious to handle:

- The customer orders the item and after it arrives, he either decides that he doesn't want the item anymore or he dislikes the item based on a cosmetic or non-technical issue.

- The customer claims that the item never arrived, but you have tracking or delivery confirmation that shows the item was delivered successfully.

- The customer orders the item, receives it, uses it for several weeks, and then wants to return it because he never needed it for the long term or bought one cheaper from another retailer.

There are lots of reasons why a customer would want to return part or all of a purchase he made with you, and it is up to you, the business owner, to decide how many of these reasons become part of your Return policy. If you craft your Return policy up front and display it clearly on your Web site, your customers can't claim ignorance after the order is completed and they ask you to change the rules. (Okay, they'll ask you, but you can decide on a case-by-case basis whether you want to honor that request.)

The Return policy comes down to a business decision that you have to make, based on the costs you incur and the level of service you wish to provide. Web stores are out there (especially those that deal with used and liquidation merchandise) that can't afford to take back any merchandise and simply state "NO RETURNS ALLOWED" and enforce the All Sales Are Final rule. On the opposite end of the spectrum, you could take back all purchases, no questions asked, for a finite period of time (known as the *return window*) and pay for return shipping as well.

One way to decide what type of policy to implement is to look at your online competitors. Go to a few Web stores that sell your type of merchandise and look at their Return policy. Do they take items back? How long of a return window do they offer? Who pays for return shipping? This helps you develop your own policy because you want to know what your competition's offering.

The goal of your store Return policy is to offer something useful or appealing to your customers while limiting the store's potential loss of revenue. Therefore, make sure that in your Return policy you address the following issues:

1. Your first paragraph should clearly state whether you accept returns or you don't allow any returns. If not, the policy is very simple. If so, will you accept returns on all merchandise, or are some items ineligible for returns? State which products are non-returnable. Also, you can allow only *exchanges* — the product can be returned only to receive another copy of the same product.

2. If you do allow returns, make sure that your second paragraph clearly states the Return window; in other words, how many days does the customer have before he has to return the item? You should clarify whether the Return window starts from the day of purchase or the day the product arrives. Set a maximum number of days the customer has to report the issue or return the item.

You may want to check with your suppliers and find out what their window is for you to send back items as well. For example, if you have 30 days to send something back to the supplier, perhaps you can give your customers 15 to 20 days to return the item so you can send the returned merchandise to the supplier.

3. Your second or third paragraph should also clarify the Conditions of use for a product. You need to state that the item has to be returned in the same (or reasonable) condition as it was sent to them. Put a note in this paragraph that you reserve the right to reject any return if the condition of the returned item is clearly different and/or unsellable based on the condition when the product was sent.

4. An optional part of your Return policy is whether you want to impose a Restocking fee on your customers when they return something. If you take back an item and charge a Restocking fee, the customer has to pay a small percentage to cover your costs. These costs can include resealing the item and integrating the return back into your own inventory. You see this term used frequently at electronics stores, for example, because those electronics have to be retested and resealed for a future purchase. Typically, retailers charge anywhere from 5–20 percent of the purchase price as a restocking fee. Make sure this fee is stated clearly in your Return policy.

5. Your next paragraph should address the matter of return shipping, specifically who pays for the item to be mailed back to the store — you or the customer? If there are conditions where the store pays and other conditions where the customer pays, state those conditions in your policy. Typically, the retailer pays for shipping when he makes a mistake on the order, and the customer pays when he voluntarily chooses to return the product with no technical fault.

6. Don't forget to clarify in a paragraph the exact Payment form of the refund. State how the refund is issued to the customer. Will you post a credit on his credit card account? Will you mail him a check? Will you issue him store credit? Most importantly, does the customer have a choice as to how he'll receive his refund or will you offer only one method? Finally, state approximately how many days he has to wait to receive his refund.

7. Your final paragraph of the return policy should address any Exceptions to your stated rules. If there are certain exceptions in your Return policy (such as addressing seasonal, liquidated, used, or timely merchandise), state that clearly as your final paragraph in your policy.

Remind your customers that this Return policy covers only items that you sell directly. If you're selling any items for a third-party vendor, check with him to see if he offers differing rules or has strict requirements for returns that you have to honor as a vendor.

In the end, you'll see from your sales and customer reports how your Return policy is working. Many big retailers talk about having return rates of 1–3 percent and feel that their customers' confidence in their Return policy allows them to earn more money from their customers and, ultimately, pays for the cost of their Return policy. However, if you're experiencing high return rates or the same complaint is coming up repeatedly, you may need to alter your Return policy to reflect the business issue you're facing.

If you alter your Return policy for any reason, you need to notify your existing customer base that a new Return policy will be in effect and pick a starting date for the new policy to take effect. Typically, give 2–3 weeks notice to your customers so they can decide if this new policy will affect their orders with you.

Making Your Privacy Policy Public

Given all the problems with identity theft and online fraud, its now required for every Web retailer to state a Privacy policy on their Web site. This policy is intended to inform your customers as to exactly what customer information you collect, what you plan to do with their information, and how you protect that information from falling into the wrong hands. This policy applies to all customers and visitors to your Web store, especially regarding any *cookies,* or information files that Web servers may create for you on your visitor's computers. Your policy, like the sample policy from this book's publisher, Wiley Publishing, Inc. (see Figure 2-3), lets your customers know who sees their information and that you, as the retailer, are keeping that information as private as possible.

The Federal Trade Commission (FTC) has mandated that all online businesses in the United States carry a Privacy policy that's accessible from the home page and properly identified. You can go to `www.ftc.gov/privacy` to read up on more of its privacy initiatives.

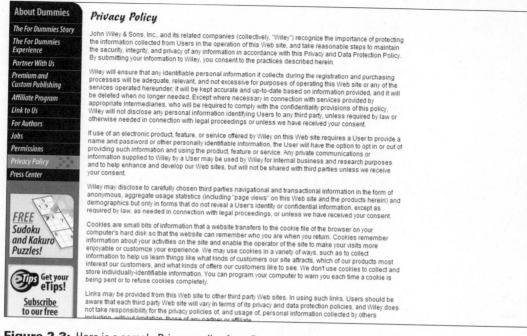

Figure 2-3: Here is a sample Privacy policy from Dummies.com.

Preparing your Privacy policy

You want to provide a clear, concise Privacy policy that people can read and understand as well as details on the collection of data, the use of that data, and the protection of that data, typically in that order. Therefore, here are the elements you need to think about when writing your privacy policy:

1. In the first section of your Privacy policy, you need to state, very specifically, what kind of information you'll be collecting from your Web store visitors and/or customers. Do you require a ZIP code from every visitor, like Radio Shack asks when you buy batteries from them? Does the customer have to give all her personal information when she registers on your site? You definitely need address and contact information for your customers, but some sites go further and ask for things, like birthdate, Social Security number, driver's license number, or other criteria, like shirt size, height, and weight. Finally, what financial information are you collecting? If you take credit cards, do you also ask for the billing ZIP code or the three digit card verification value (CVV) security code on the back of the card, on top of the card type, number, and expiration date?

2. In the next paragraph, you need to state how you're collecting this information. Do customers have to enter all their information on a Web form? Are you using technology, like the Secure Socket Layer (SSL), to protect that information? (We discuss SSL further in Chapter 3.) Can the customer phone in some information, like credit card numbers or bank account data?

3. In the second section of the Privacy policy, you need to state how you're storing this information? You don't want to be too detailed as to how and where you store your data. The point of this section is to relay that the information is protected with some form of security and that the data is stored safely. You can even state that very few personnel will have access to your data at all. Finally, if you're using cookies to store information on the customer's machine, talk about what information is being stored, whether the customer can opt out or block the cookie from being created, and the impact of doing so on their order.

4. In the third section of the Privacy policy, you need to state if you're sharing any customer data with any other business or company. This section is meant to inform the customer whether you're sharing, selling, or relaying customer data to any other party. In many cases, retailers who work with promotional partners share customer data gathered during a promotion for use by both parties. In other cases, retailers build up customer lists for specific products and sell that data outright to other companies. Even if you group together your customer data and sell or share only anonymous statistics that can't be traced back to individual users, state that in your policy. Be as specific as possible even if you're stating that customer data is seen only by employees in your company.

5. In the last section of the Privacy policy, you need to provide information that will allow the customer to contact you. Based on the type of information you collect, you have to provide a method where customers can change their records, block access from any third parties receiving their information, and delete or opt out of your customer database at any time.

Writing your Privacy policy using the Direct Marketing Association

A handy tool helps you create your own Privacy policy, courtesy of the Direct Marketing Association (DMA). If you want them to create your policy, think about the points discussed in the preceding section and then follow these steps:

1. Using your Web browser, go to `www.the-dma.org/privacy/creating.shtml` and you'll see the instructions for using the form, as in Figure 2-4.

2. Click the bulleted link for the DMA's Privacy Policy Generator to go to the beginning of the form, as shown in Figure 2-5.

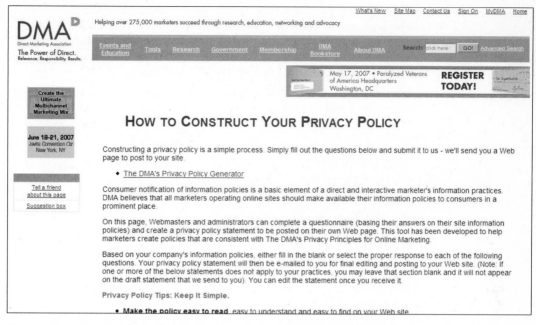

Figure 2-4: The Direct Marketing Association offers a Privacy Policy Generator.

---

1. Identity of the Web site Administrators
(Fill in the blanks)

This is the Web site of	*Company Name*
Our postal address is	*Address*
Our location	*City, State, Zip*
We can be reached via e-mail at	*e-mail*
Or you can reach us by telephone at	*Phone*
*This Policy is effective on	*Insert effective date of policy*

2. For each visitor to our Web page, our Web server automatically recognizes...
(choose one)

○ the consumer's domain name and e-mail address (where possible)
○ only the consumer's domain name, but not the e-mail address (where possible)
○ no information regarding the domain or e-mail address
○ other [   ]

***3. We collect...**
(choose all that apply)

☐ only the domain name, but not the e-mail address of visitors to our Web page
☐ the domain name and e-mail address (where possible) of visitors to our Web page
☐ the e-mail addresses of those who post messages to our bulletin board
☐ the e-mail addresses of those who communicate with us via e-mail
☐ the e-mail addresses of those who make postings to our chat areas
☐ aggregate information on what pages consumers access or visit
☐ user-specific information on what pages consumers access or visit
☐ information volunteered by the consumer, such as preferences, survey information and/or site registrations
☐ name and address
☐ telephone number
☐ fax number

Figure 2-5: Select your Privacy policy options.

3. Fill in the appropriate blanks and select the appropriate options based on how your site will operate. You're asked 16 different questions, such as the type of data you collect, different potential usage of that data, how the customer can be contacted, and so on. Most questions give you multiple options via check boxes, so check all conditions that apply for each question.

4. After you complete all 16 questions, you're at the bottom of the form, as in Figure 2-6. You have three choices to collect your generated policy:

   • **Generate HTML Page:** The policy is generated as a Web page, which you can then save to your computer and upload to your store.

   • **E-Mail Me HTML:** Your policy is e-mailed to you as a Web page, which you can save to your store's Web site. If you select this option, be sure to provide your e-mail address in the e-mail Address box.

   • **E-Mail Me Plain Text:** Your policy is e-mailed to you as plain text, which you can then copy and paste into a Web page on your Web store labeled as your Privacy policy. If you select this option, be sure to provide your e-mail address in the e-mail Address box.

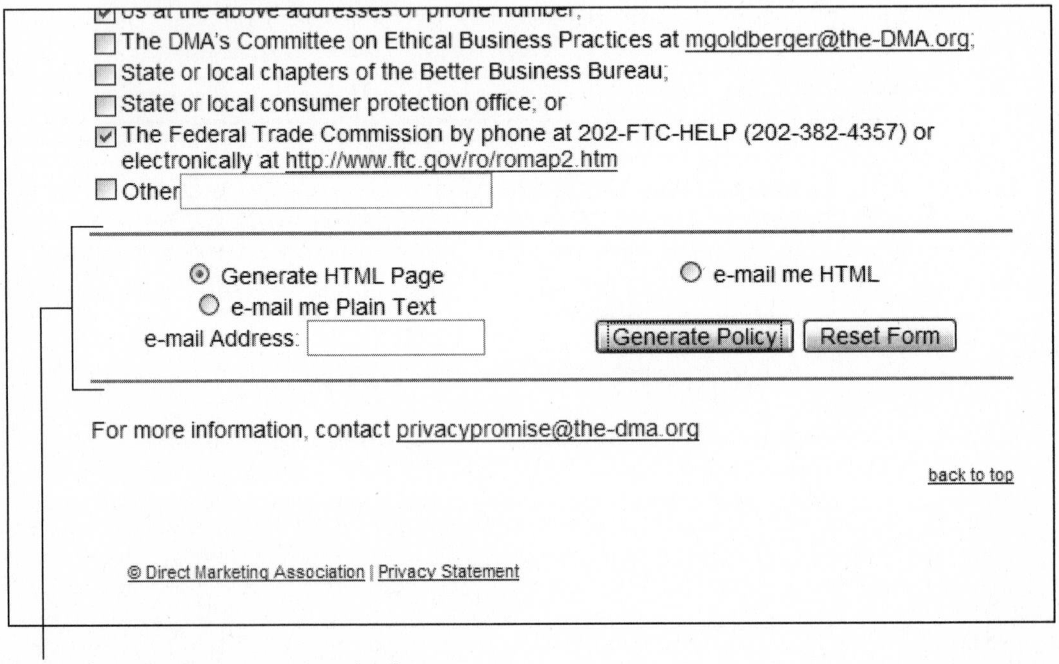

Options for collecting your generated policy

Figure 2-6: You can generate your policy online or have it e-mailed to you.

5. If you want to see your policy and make sure you completed the form correctly before you collect it, click the Generate Policy button. The DMA Generator will take all the options you checked and build the appropriate paragraphs to construct a very thorough privacy policy. Check out the sample policy I created in Figure 2-7 to get an idea of what the policy looks like.

Privacy Policy Statement

This is the web site of **Your Web Store**.

Our postal address is
**PO Box 1234
Anytown, US 10001**

We can be reached via e-mail at privacy@yourstore.com
or you can reach us by telephone at 800-555-HELP

For each visitor to our Web page, our Web server automatically recognizes the consumer's domain name and e-mail address (where possible).

We collect the e-mail addresses of those who post messages to our bulletin board, the e-mail addresses of those who communicate with us via e-mail, aggregate information on what pages consumers access or visit, information volunteered by the consumer, such as survey information and/or site registrations, name and address, telephone number, fax number, payment information (e.g., credit card number and billing address).

The information we collect is used for internal review and is then discarded, used to notify consumers about updates to our Web site, shared with other reputable organizations to help them contact consumers for marketing purposes, not shared with other organizations for commercial purposes.

With respect to cookies: We use cookies to store visitors preferences, record session information, such as items that consumers add to their shopping cart, record past activity at a site in order to provide better service when visitors return to our site .

If you do not want to receive e-mail from us in the future, please let us know by sending us e-mail at the above address, calling us at the above telephone number, visiting us at http://www.yourstore.com/unsubscribe.html.

From time to time, we make the e-mail addresses of those who access our site available to other reputable organizations whose products or services we think you might find interesting. If you do not want us to share your e-mail address with other companies or organizations, please let us know by calling us at the number provided above.

From time to time, we make our customer e-mail list available to other reputable organizations whose products or services we think you might find interesting. If you

---

Figure 2-7: See a sample policy generated by the DMA Privacy Policy Generator.

After the generated policy is displayed, save the page to your computer or Web site and feel free to update it with any headers, logos, or color schemes to make this page match the overall look and feel of your Web store.

Writing Your Shipping Policy

One of the benefits of customers shopping over the Web is the immediate gratification of placing their order. That benefit comes with responsibility, however, as the retailer has to get that order shipped to the customers, many of whom want the gratification of holding that package in their hands as soon as possible. Therefore, it's important to detail how and when you handle the shipment of customer orders so you can properly set the expectation of when the order is fulfilled and delivered.

If you're a Web retailer in the United States, you're required to follow the rules of the FTC's Mail or Telephone Order Rule, which can be found at www.ftc.gov/bcp/conline/pubs/buying/mail.shtm, and an example is shown in Figure 2-8. Many of the guidelines stated have to do with the time frame of shipping, notices to be sent if an order can't be completed, and what to do with unsatisfactory goods and services.

Shopping by Phone or Mail

Produced in cooperation with the Direct Marketing Association and AARP

Shopping by phone or mail is a convenient alternative to shopping at a store. The Federal Trade Commission's (FTC) Mail or Telephone Order Rule covers merchandise your order by mail, telephone, computer, and fax machine.

Mail or Telephone Order Rule

By law, a company should ship your order within the time stated in its ads. If no time is promised, the company should ship your order within 30 days after receiving it.

If the company is unable to ship within the promised time, they must give you an "option notice." This notice gives you the choice of agreeing to the delay or canceling your order and receiving a prompt refund.

There is one exception to the 30-day Rule: if a company doesn't promise a shipping time, and you are applying for credit to pay for your purchase, the company has 50 days to ship after receiving your order.

Fair Credit Billing Act (FCBA)

You're protected by the FCBA when you use your credit card to pay for purchases.

Billing Errors

If you find an error on your credit or charge card statement, you may dispute the charge and withhold payment on the disputed amount while the charge is in dispute. The error might be a charge for the wrong amount, for something you did not accept, or for an item that was not delivered as agreed. Of course, you still must pay any part of the bill that is not in dispute, including finance charges on the undisputed amount.

If you decide to dispute a charge:

- Write to the creditor at the address indicated on the monthly statement for "billing inquiries." Include your name, address, credit card number, and a description of the billing error.
- Send your letter in a timely fashion. It must reach the creditor within 60 days after the first bill containing the error was mailed to you.

The creditor must acknowledge your complaint in writing within 30 days after receiving it, unless the problem has been resolved. The creditor must resolve the dispute within two billing cycles (but not more than 90 days) after receiving your letter.

Unsatisfactory Goods or Services

You also may dispute charges for unsatisfactory goods or services. To take advantage of this protection regarding the quality of goods or services, you must:

Figure 2-8: Make sure your shipping policy falls within FTC guidelines.

When you're developing your Shipping policy, you definitely need to think about what shipping company (or companies) you'll partner with to build your business (I discuss this in depth in Chapter 12). Depending on the company you choose, you may have to come back and update this policy later. For right now, include the goals you wish to accomplish with your Shipping policy.

Here are the specific issues to address when you are writing your Shipping policy:

1. In the first section of your Shipping policy, give your customers an estimate of how long until their order will be sent. Here, you should talk about a general *turnaround* time, or the length of time between the submitted order and the shipping of the order. Many retailers describe this as "We ship out our orders within two to three business days." Sometimes, different products have different turnaround times, and if so, state that here. (For example, small consumer electronics may have a 2–3 day turnaround, whereas big screen TVs may have a 7–10 day turnaround time.)

2. You should also address, in the first section of your policy, whether the customer can get same-day shipping, and if so, provide details as to how the customer should request this option. Remember that some customers need (or want) their orders ASAP. If you offer Express shipping, be sure to include

a disclaimer that states when in the day the order must be received to qualify for express shipping (for example, "All orders with Express shipping selected must be received before 11:45 a.m. Pacific time to be shipped out the same day.")

3. In the second section of your shipping policy, you should detail the different shipping options your customers have available. If you ship all your orders using one company and one method of shipping (perhaps, USPS Priority or Media Mail), simply state "All orders will be shipped using USPS Media Mail." If you offer customers a choice of companies and/or a choice of shipping methods, describe those choices in a paragraph.

   Any exceptions or special considerations should also be detailed in this section. One of the most famous examples of this is from Amazon.com and states that certain orders over $25 receive Free Super Saver Shipping from the company.

   Even though the customer should see these options in the checkout form, it never hurts to detail her options here in case she's reading up on your store before deciding to order.

4. As part of your second section on shipping options, you should provide details as to whether you solely offer domestic shipping or allow for domestic and international shipping for your orders. The global nature of the Internet gives your Web store an instant potential base of customers around the world. However, the products you sell may not lend themselves easily to international sales. For example, if you're selling metal anvils, the shipping cost is probably too prohibitive to offer international shipping on them. If you do offer international shipping, create an International Shipping subsection that details what countries you ship to, what shipping options and rates are offered for overseas buyers, and any pertinent information regarding taxes, customs duties, or import fees.

   If you're a Web retailer in the United States, there are some items (like software with 128-bit encryption) that you're not allowed to sell outside the United States. Check with the U.S. Department of Commerce at `www.bis.doc.gov/DeemedExports/DeemedExportsFAQs.html` for up-to-date information on what's allowed.

5. In your next section, you should address the issue of whether the customer will be able to track their order on your Web site. You may not be able to answer this question until you decide how many advanced functions you're going to build into your Web store. If you know that your users will be able to create accounts and monitor the status of their orders, state that capability here. Otherwise, you may want to state that customers will automatically receive an e-mail when their order is shipped or offer a phone number where they can call your store and inquire on the status.

6. In your final section, you should mention any shipping restrictions a customer may encounter based on their address. If you use companies, like UPS or FedEx, to handle your shipments, you can't accept an order where the shipping address is a U.S. P.O. Box. Therefore, if you use one of those companies, enforce getting a valid street address from your customers. In addition, if you don't want to ship to Military (APO/FPO) addresses or any other special addresses, state that in your policy.

Writing Your User Agreement

If you plan to offer a lot of functionality with your Web store, where users can log in to their own customer account and perhaps access different store functionality or additional functions, games, or applications that you provide to your customers, you might want to consider crafting a User Agreement to set the terms and conditions for how users can interact with your business.

Although you want your users to take advantage and use the functionality provided, you probably want to establish some guidelines so these users know what acceptable behavior is and what conditions cause their account to be suspended, blocked, or deleted. The benefit of creating this early in the process means that users have to agree to this right away and they can't claim ignorance if a problem occurs in the future.

Typically, a User Agreement has to be reviewed during the registration process a user follows on your Web site. Not only do you have to provide all the terms, you should make the user acknowledge that he or she has read the terms and agrees with all the provisions. This can be done by having the user click a check box or enter his initials in a specified text field.

Here are some of the specific points you should address in your User Agreement:

1. Section 1 of your User Agreement should state how a site visitor can regularly use your Web site. Start with the basics of what functionality you provide, and whether the site's a free or paid service or whether certain functions are available only to paying customers instead of all visitors.

2. Section 2 of your User Agreement should state any restrictions you are imposing on customers who use or view your site. Do you have to impose any age restrictions based on the type of products you're selling (for example, do users have to be 18 or 21 years old)? Do they have to pay a certain membership fee, perform certain actions every month, or order a certain amount to get access or discounts?

3. Section 3 of your User Agreement should state any copyright or legal issues with your Web store. Do you allow your visitors to copy and paste your site content on their Web site? Are customers giving up their copyright protection by posting on your message boards or submitting entries to one of your contests? If you think that there may be a legal issue, consult an attorney for advice in this area.

4. Section 4 of your User Agreement should state any restrictions on user-generated content, if your Web store has user-generated content. If you use message boards, chat rooms, or other ways to solicit and display customer information, like customer-written reviews and guides for example, you need to state some basic guidelines on how each area is operated. Mainly, this section is to clearly state that no offensive, vulgar, pornographic, copyrighted, or illegal information can be posted onto your site by anyone, including your own employees. You're encouraged to give some examples of inappropriate material (without being too specific, of course) and the situations when you would remove or censor this material.

5. You should create a section of your User Agreement to discuss any extra terms or conditions you need to create for your customers based on the functionality you offer through your Web store.

6. You will need a section in your User Agreement entitled Notices that explains how you will communicate any changes, updates, or cancellations of this User Agreement to your customers, such as "Notice will be given by e-mail to the e-mail address provided during the registration process at mystorename.com. Alternatively, we may deliver notice through certified mail to the address provided in the registration process."

7. You will need a section in your User Agreement entitled Arbitration that details how you will handle any claims or controversy caused by the agreement between you and your customer. You should consult the laws governing arbitration and business in your state, as laws vary by state. You can also consult the American Arbitration Association at `www.adr.org` for more information.

8. Finally, you should have a section in your User Agreement entitled General that includes statements like these: This agreement shall be governed in all respects by the laws of the state of (insert your state here) as such laws are applied to agreements entered into and to be performed entirely within (your state) between (your state) residents. This agreement sets forth the entire understanding and agreement between us with respect to the subject matter hereof.

Policies — The Final Word

Depending on your type of business, you may need to add additional policies, like how you handle spam, deal with affiliates, or interact with third parties. The main policies detailed in the preceding sections are enough to get you started. In the end, these policies are all meant to be a guide, not literally written in stone. As time progresses, you may see the need to update, revise, or even eliminate one or more of these policies.

The key is having a communication channel open with your customers. If a policy is either too strict or too lenient, you need a mechanism where you hear about it and can make changes. When changes need to be made, follow these steps:

1. Create a Web page that shows the old policy language, the new policy language, and a clear explanation as to why the change is made.

2. Assign a date in the near future when the new policy will be in effect.

3. Use one or more communication methods (e-mail, phone, or mail) to update your customers and visitors on the new change.

4. Place a notice on the home page, or one of your main product pages, informing them of a policy change, with a hyperlink to the detailed policy explanation page you create in Step 1.

5. If possible, offer a way to gather customer feedback on the new policy change and update accordingly.

Part II
Constructing Your Web Store

The 5th Wave   By Rich Tennant

"Just how accurately should my Web site reflect my place of business?"

In this part . . .

In this part, I cover the heavy lifting of constructing your Web store from scratch. I start by discussing the necessary elements you should evaluate from an e-commerce storefront provider in order to pick the company that will put your Web store on the Internet and maintain the store's operations.

I then discuss three different store-front providers in Chapters 4, 5, and 6, and show you the essential steps for creating an account and building the essential Web pages to get a Web store up and running with those providers. I picked three of the leading companies in this space, including Yahoo! Merchant Solutions, ProStores, and 1&1 eShops.

Finally, I end this part by talking about other necessary pieces of building your Web store, like enrolling with a payment processing firm like PayPal, and laying out your Store Design on paper before diving into the details in Part III.

Chapter 3

Finding Your Storefront Provider

Tasks performed in this chapter

✔ Assessing Web storefront providers

✔ Deciding your store's domain name

✔ Registering your store's domain name

✔ Finding a domain name's current owner

✔ Exploring other domain name options

When you want to open a retail store, your first steps toward opening the doors are to find those doors . . . and walls and floors, locating the perfect retail space, and then filling the space with fixtures, inventory, and signage. When you're opening a Web store, one of the first big steps to making your dream a reality is to find your "virtual" space — the *virtual* or *Web storefront*.

Luckily for you, there are dozens of providers out there that will provide you with all the virtual bells, whistles, and everything else you need to get set up. Because of all the variety and different costs out there, let's start by taking a look at what features you need to build your Web store.

In this chapter, we evaluate what features are available (and necessary) from the storefront provider that you'll need to select. We then talk about how to reserve that other important aspect of your Web store — the domain name. Finally, we discuss the options you can take if your perfect domain name is taken already.

Evaluating Web Storefront Providers

Thousands of people are out there that will offer you a place to build a Web site. What you're looking for, however, is an e-commerce account, or something e-commerce capable or ready. An *e-commerce account* is a specific account you open with an Internet Service Provider that has the capability to accept orders for products and process the payment electronically for those product orders. Let's compare this with opening a brick-and-mortar retail store.

You can rent all kinds of space on the Web — *residential space* (like the apartment or house you live in), *industrial space* (where you can warehouse all your inventory or equipment), *commercial space* (all those shiny office buildings that reach for the sky and offer clean, carpeted, air-conditioned paradise while you work), and *retail space* (which is space specially designed for retail activities, like selling goods to customers). You wouldn't expect to see a Wal-Mart in an office building or someone's garage, just like you wouldn't want to get a generic Web site provider to host your e-commerce Web store. You want to establish an account that matches the goals of your business, and for Web stores, that's an e-commerce account.

E-commerce accounts differ from many of the other packages primarily because of three components:

- Shopping Cart technology
- Secure Socket Layer (SSL) technology
- Credit card processing capability

Many of the elements we discuss in the next section are available on regular Web site plans, but the ability for customers to add items to a virtual basket, check out securely, and pay for those items, is the essence of e-commerce, which makes these three elements very important to your Web store future.

Evaluating storefront accounts

When it comes to picking an e-commerce account, you need to figure out the basics of your account in terms of how many products you hope to sell, how many pictures, audio, and video you plan to include on your site, and how many features your customers will have on your site. When you go to the Web site of a Web storefront provider, look for a link about account packages that allow you to sell online. Click that link and then look for a link that discusses features and/or benefits. This should let you pull up the specifics of any Web storefront provider, and when you do, be sure to look at these aspects of the account(s) they provide:

- **Shopping Cart technology:** If your customers can't shop in your store, they can't become customers. Find out what kind of shopping cart program comes with the account. At a minimum, you want a shopping cart that can allow the customer to add at least 2-5 products to their basket at one time, and check out using a credit card or PayPal account. Questions to ask include

  - How many products can be added to the catalog?
  - Is there a maximum number of items I can sell in my store?
  - How is customer information stored for future use?
  - What payment solutions are integrated with your shopping cart software?
  - How are orders transmitted to you or your staff?
  - How easy is it to set up?

- **Disk space:** Think of disk space as the storage space for your Web site. Typically, accounts start in megabytes (MB), but many accounts give a minimum of 1 gigabyte (GB). If you plan on having mostly text descriptions and very little in the way of pictures, audio, or video, disk space isn't an issue, and anywhere from 100 MB to 500 MB for a basic site is plenty. If you do need to present a lot of pictures, audio, or video, go for a plan with a lot of disk space, at least 1 or 2 GB. Questions to ask here include

  - How many regular JPG images could fit on my disk space (ballpark figure)?
  - Can I add additional disk space if needed to my monthly account?
  - How much is additional disk space and how do I order it, if necessary?
  - Do I get an automatic warning if I'm running out of space?

✔ **Bandwidth:** If you think of your Web store as a real store on the road, *bandwidth* is the amount of traffic flowing in and out of your store. Every time someone looks at your Web pages, all that information has to flow over the Internet to and from your Web server. Too much usage may cost you in the end, as most Web storefront providers have a limit when it comes to the bandwidth of your site. On one end, if a simple text-only site has a few visitors, it has low bandwidth. YouTube, which serves up millions of video clips a day, has very high bandwidth. If 6 million people had to drive up to one store to get their video clips, imagine the traffic jams and problems that would cause. An unprepared Web store can have the same catastrophe on the Internet.

Most of the time, the bandwidth limits set by your storefront provider are enough to do business, whether it's 1 GB or 10 GB per month. The only concern should be if you plan to offer a lot of rich data, like audio and video, regularly on your site. Then, you may look for a plan that has 50–100 GB per month or more. Questions to ask here include

- On average, how many people a day can go to your store given your bandwidth limit?

- Can you pay for additional bandwidth if needed?

- How much is additional bandwidth and how quickly can it be available?

- Do I get any automatic warnings if I start to hit my bandwidth limit?

Another term related to bandwidth is *data transfer*, which is the specific Internet traffic of sending a file (whether it's a picture, audio WAV file, or video clip) from your Web storefront to a customer or visitor's computer. Some storefront providers put daily, weekly, or monthly limits on the amount of data transfer to and from your Web site. If you plan to use a lot of multimedia on your Web store, ask your provider the same bandwidth questions mentioned previously, but substitute data transfer for bandwidth.

✔ **E-mail accounts:** You can't do business without communication, and any good Web storefront provider includes a way for you, as the store owner, to create e-mail accounts that match your storefront name and work in conjunction with your store. Options here range from a few accounts to thousands or unlimited numbers of e-mail accounts. You should have a minimum of at least 2–5 accounts, so you and at least one other employee (or function, like customer service) can have an e-mail account with your store name to interact with customers, partners, and vendors.

It's always helpful to establish dedicated e-mail accounts for issues, like customer service, affiliate relations, marketing, sales, and for employees in your company to communicate with each other and the customers.

Questions to ask here include

- How many e-mail accounts can you create?

- What is the size limit of each mailbox?

- How can people access their e-mail accounts (*POP, or Post Office Protocol,* a popular way for e-mail applications to retrieve e-mail from a server; WebMail, where the e-mail owner uses an Internet Web browser to retrieve and read their e-mail; and so on)?

- How easy is it to create or suspend any particular e-mail account?

- Can I set up an e-mail address where any incoming e-mail goes to a list of accounts instead of just one account?

✔ **Programming extensions:** A lot of functionality is out there for e-commerce operations that are written in various programming languages. For those functions to work, your storefront provider's computer servers have to be able to understand the *scripting language,* or the set of instructions that make up the functions. This ability is commonly expressed as *programming extensions offered* or *languages allowed.* Questions to ask here include

- What programming languages or functions does the storefront provider support?

- Do I need to do anything special in configuration to turn on this extension support?

- Is it possible to add support for an extension, like *PHP (Hypertext PreProcessor,* a popular Internet programming language) or Microsoft FrontPage (a popular Web function authoring software tool)?

- Is there a limit to the size or number of scripts that can run on your site?

- Are there any templates or sample code that you can download for these extensions?

✔ **Application integration:** Typically, your business needs more than just a shopping cart software tool to help you manage all the day-to-day issues. For example, you need accounting programs, marketing programs, online shipping and postal tools, and possibly, systems to manage operations and inventory management. Given all the data that your Web storefront is generating, you want the ability for your Web storefront to communicate automatically and correctly with the other software programs you'll use to run your business. Therefore, you want to see if the storefront provider provides any application integration tools for you to use or plan to implement. Questions to ask here include

- Which accounting programs does the storefront provider integrate sales with (QuickBooks, Microsoft Money, Excel, and so on)?

- Which order-processing software, if any, does the storefront provider system link with (UPS WorldShip and so on)?

- Can you hire someone to write and implement a custom application integration tool, if needed?

- What options does the storefront provider offer to link with my payment-processing system (credit card processing, PayPal, and so on)?

✔ **Additional features:** Usually, each provider provides various options for your Web storefront account, and picking these really depends on how you like to do business or how your programmers or employees need to do business. Sometimes, the way to decide is to go with the provider that offers the most of what you need with a nice assortment of functions you could use or want to use. Questions to ask here include

- *What operating system will your account run on?* If your programmers use Windows development tools, ask for a Windows account. Otherwise, a UNIX or Linux account runs lots of programming options but doesn't offer the same graphical user interface that Windows gives you.

- *What databases are supported on your account?* If you plan for your customers to have accounts on your system, you'll need a database to store all that information. Typically, the shopping cart program coordinates the inventory and order databases, but if you want to build additional functionality, you need to know if your account can handle supporting the database system you need.

- *What reports and features come with your account?* Because your storefront is gathering all your Web sales, why not ask if the provider can offer a way for automatic reports to be generated so you can see your sales, potential, and problems. Also, any e-commerce provider should have some functions, templates, or code they can offer their customers.

Evaluating storefront services

You've found the account of your dreams, with all the sizes, functions, and everything else that you need built into your account. However, before you sign on the dotted line, here are some areas you should look into with the specific provider. Just like landlords who can offer excellent or poor service, storefront providers need to provide acceptable levels of security, reliability, and service to handle your needs.

Consider asking or researching some of these questions in the following areas:

✔ **Security:** Your goal here is that the provider protects your customer data, your store catalog data, and of course, your store sales and order data. You need to provide a secure experience for your customers to pay you so that they can be sure their information won't end up in a crook's hands down the road. At a minimum, you should be able to offer Secure Socket Layer (or SSL) security for your customers. Questions to ask here include

  - Does your provider offer SSL security for your customers? If not, do they offer assistance in getting you an SSL certificate for your Web store?

  - How does the storefront provider protect your data from hackers or intruders?

  - What policies does the storefront provider have in place to protect your servers?

  - What security measures are in place to guard your physical servers?

  - Who has access to your account besides your site administrator?

✔ **Reliability:** If there's a problem with the Web server running your store, no one can see or order from your store, which means you're losing sales every minute. You're looking for a Web storefront provider that cares about the reliability of its machines and has processes or systems in place to keep its customers (meaning you and your store) up and running. At a minimum, you should be able to expect 99% uptime or better. Questions to ask here include

  - What was the provider's *uptime* in the last year? In other words, out of 100 percent of the year, what percentage of time were their servers available and on the Internet? If it's not 99 percent or better, keep looking.

  - What backup procedures does the provider use to protect and restore your data?

- What processes are in place to notify you of any hardware or software failures?

- How quickly will someone respond to a call regarding the availability of your account?

- Does the provider have multiple data centers and are they linked?

✔ **Service:** Your storefront provider is providing you with a service, so in case there are any issues, you need to know how to contact the provider, which method to use, and what to expect in terms of a response. There are some providers that charge more but provide additional levels of service, coaching, and/or support; based on your needs, pick an appropriate provider with the right level of service. At a minimum, you should have at least e-mail and phone support available for your account. Questions to ask here include

- How do you contact the provider in case of a technical problem (via e-mail, phone, and so on)?

- What are the provider's customer service hours of operation?

- Do you have an account manager assigned to your account? If so, how do you contact that person and what issues does he handle?

- How quickly can you expect your first response to any problem inquiry? How quickly are problems typically solved?

- What help functions or guides does your provider provide online? Are there any tutorials you can download and watch?

Picking Your Storefront Domain Name

When Shakespeare said, "What's in a name?" he could have been talking about your storefront domain name. A domain name is the URL Web address that your customers will have to type to get to your Web store. If you already have a name for your business, such as ACME Widgets, then you should select a domain name like acmewidgets.com to preserve your business identity and bring that business name online.

If you don't have a business name yet, then it is time to sit down and think of a good name for your business. Some owners tackle this problem by researching available domain names first, and when they find a domain name they like, they reserve that name and adopt that name for their business, like drugstore.com. It's generally a good idea to include a reference to what you're selling in your store name so customers know what your store offers. This isn't a requirement, though. After all, before 1995, when people thought of the word Amazon, they thought of a river in South America, not Earth's Biggest Bookstore. You can develop your own brand if you have a store name that you like, as long as you understand that challenge when you begin to market your store.

Registering Your Domain Name

Stuff You Need to Know

Toolbox:
- Computer
- Internet connection
- Credit card

Time Needed:
10 minutes

After you've decided on a domain name you need to pick a domain registrar. A *domain registrar* handles all the administrative issues regarding your domain name, so you can file for the exclusive right to use your chosen domain name for your Web site. The domain registrar will create a record with the main organization that manages all Internet domain names (known as ICANN, or Internet Corporation for Assigned Names and Numbers), and that record will link people who type in your domain name with the Internet address of your e-commerce Web site. Originally, there was one registrar, Network Solutions (www.network solutions.com), but several years ago the U.S. government allowed competition in the industry, which means that dozens of competitors have sprung up offering the same service as Network Solutions. Although Network Solutions has stayed in business by offering lots of additional services, some low cost providers, like GoDaddy.com, have sprung up and gathered a lot of customers. For this example, I use GoDaddy.com to sign up a domain name.

1. Go to the GoDaddy.com Web site at www.godaddy.com.

2. On their home page, look in the top-left corner for the Start a Domain Search text box. In that text box, type the name you want to register — without the preceding www. or the extension .com.

3. Next to the text box, select the extension you want to use. The traditional extension for e-commerce is .com, but if the name you want is taken, you may consider using .net, .org, .biz, or .info.

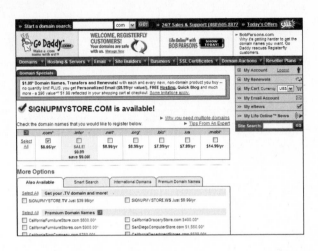

4. Click the Go! button to start your search and have the results displayed. If your name is available (like my example, `signupmystore.com`), you see the accompanying statement and the costs associated with reserving that name. If you want to hold the same name with more than one extension, click the appropriate check boxes to add any or all these options (`yourname.info`, `yourname.biz`, `yourname.org`, `yourname.net`, `yourname.name`, or `yourname.mobi`) to your registration. If your domain name is unavailable but you really want it, check out the next section.

5. After you pick all the extensions you want to use, scroll down and click the orange Continue button. Be warned that you'll probably see some screens trying to sell you additional extensions. One thought here is that if you build a good brand name, you want to reserve all the different extensions up front so someone else can't use your brand name to build a store with a similar name and different extension.

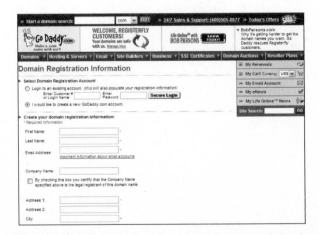

6. After you select all your extensions for your domain, it's time to create your GoDaddy.com account. Fill in all the appropriate fields of information and be sure to complete any field with a red * next to it because those fields are required for registration. Scroll down and click the orange Continue button when you're ready to continue.

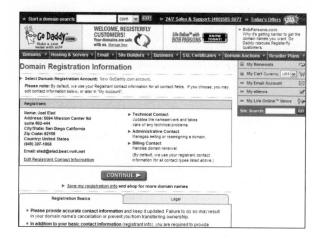

7. Now you have to define the contact information for your registration. In this step, click the Edit Registrant Contact Information link if you want to assign a specific person to handle the administrative, billing, or technical aspects of your registration. If you do nothing and click Continue, GoDaddy.com uses your contact information for all three categories. You can always log in to your GoDaddy.com account to change this contact information later.

8. GoDaddy.com asks you to confirm the length of your registration and makes one last attempt to sell additional services. The minimum length of time for registration with any registrar is one year, and the maximum that GoDaddy.com (or any domain registrar) offers is ten years. If you don't want your information linked publicly with this domain name, consider adding Private Registration to your registration.

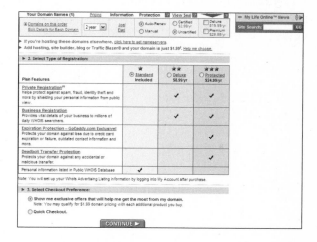

WARNING!

The standard option that GoDaddy.com offers is a two year registration. If you only want to reserve the name for one year, be sure to change the Registration Length by clicking the drop-down box and picking the 1 Year option.

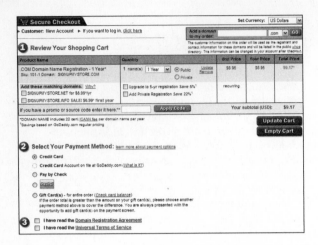

9. After you pick all your options, you see the Secure Checkout screen and are asked to enter your billing information to confirm the order. Go through the Registration Agreement and Terms of Service to make sure you don't have any issues (for example, their requirement that you update GoDaddy within 5 days of any account change, or their rules for accepting payments via check) and then click the check boxes to acknowledge your understanding of those terms. You can pay by credit card, check, PayPal, or a GoDaddy.com gift card.

10. You see a screen with confirmation of your order and you get an e-mail confirmation with your order as well. The e-mail contains instructions on how to access your GoDaddy.com account for future usage.

Using WHOIS to Find a Domain Owner

Stuff You Need to Know

Toolbox:
- Computer
- Internet connection

Time Needed:
5 minutes

Let's say that you find the domain name of your dreams. For this example, I use www.realecommercesales.com; this is the name you believe takes your Web store to the next level. You have to have it. But when you go to register it, the registrar tells you that the name is unavailable! What do you do? Typically, the first response is to type the URL (Uniform Resource Locator) or Web address into a Web browser and see if contact information is available.

In many cases, you see a *parked page*. When someone signs up for a domain name but he doesn't have a Web site created for that domain name, he usually creates one page to hold the space until the Web site is created. Typically, these parked pages contain advertisements so the domain holder can make some money if people click the ads or links to move on, as shown in the figure. However, there's usually no contact information or e-mail address to contact the owner(s). Thankfully, most domain names have a public record that you can access for free to contact the owner.

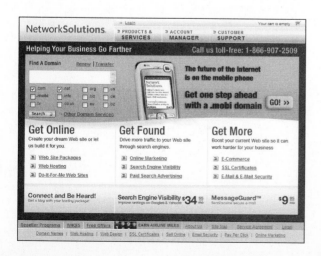

1. Using your Web browser, go to www.network solutions.com; you see the home page. They maintain the WHOIS database that contains the contact information for thousands of domain name owners.

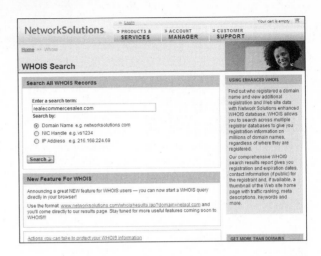

2. Click the WHOIS link from the home page. This takes you to the WHOIS search page. From here, you can either search by the domain name itself, by the *NIC handle* (a username some domain name owners have created through Network Solutions), or by a specific IP address.

3. Type the name of the URL you're researching in the text box provided. You do *not* need to put the initial `www.` before the URL name. Simply put the name and extension (in this case, `realecommercesales.com`) in the box and click the green Search button.

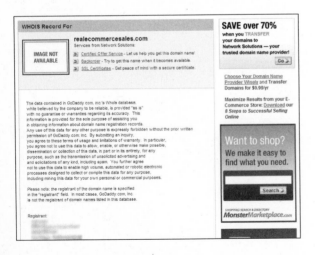

4. On the results screen, scroll down until you see the Registrant and Contact information. When the results screen is displayed, you see one of two different types of screens. In some cases, the owner has chosen to make his or her registration private, and therefore, the WHOIS results page has no helpful information. (Think of it as someone who has an unlisted telephone number.) In most cases, you see that the registration information is *public* — you get a mailing address, e-mail address, and (sometimes) a phone number for the person who registered the name. Simply scroll down past any disclaimer information from the registrar used to reserve the domain in question. (In this case, the text is from GoDaddy.com.)

5. Scroll down farther to get the Administrative
    and Technical Contact information. While you
    scroll down the page, notice several pieces of
    information. The first section of data contains
    the Registrant information. This information is
    tied to the person who owns the domain and
    paid to have it registered in the first place. The
    person listed under Registrant is considered
    the legal owner of the domain name. However,
    when you scroll down past the Registrant sec-
    tion, notice other information associated with
    the domain name record. A domain can have a
    different person as the Administrative Contact
    and yet another person as the Technical
    Contact. Specifically, you're looking for the
    information listed in the following table.

Result Screen Information	
Section	**Description**
Registered Through	In this section, focus on the Expires On date. This is the date that marks the end of the Registrant's subscription to the domain name. If the Registrant chooses not to extend or renew his contract to this domain name, you could come in and register the name for yourself!
Administrative Contact	This is the person who receives notices from the domain name registrar about any questions the registrar has. Sometimes, the Administrative Contact is the same as the Registrant, other times it isn't. The best person to present with an initial offer for the domain is the Administrative Contact.
Technical Contact	This is usually the person who links the domain to the Web server for your business, so it is usually someone who works for your storefront provider. In this case, it points to GoDaddy.com, who is handling the technical aspects for this domain name because the parked page for this domain also sits on their site. If you can't contact anyone in the Registrant or Administrative Contact sections, you can always try to reach the owner through his Technical Contact.

Researching Other Domain Name Options

You've probably heard the expression "What's in a name?" For a store owner, a recognizable and easy-to-remember name can be critical to future growth. If you're spending most of your time trying to remind customers how to spell the precise name of your Web store or the URL is so long it doesn't fit on your business cards, you may want to look at other options. Here are some different methods you can use to see what domain names are for sale or what different domain extensions you can try:

✔ **Look for domain names on sale at various domain name resellers:** There's a business market of people who purchased domain names specifically to resell those names to companies who will use them properly. Think of it as the World Wide Web name grab, like the land grab of the Wild Wild West. By going to these resellers, you can estimate the value of certain names, and perhaps get the idea of which domain best suits you, and probably figure out which domain most fits your budget.

Some of the values that you see for these domain names have been created purely by the seller as their goal. Any appraisal doesn't automatically mean that the domain is worth that much on the open market. The domain name has to lend value to your Web store in order for you to pay for it. Remember that principle if you see a domain name you like but that may be too highly priced . . . and never be afraid to negotiate!

Some of the leading domain name resellers include

- *AfterNIC* (www.afternic.com)
- *OnDomains* (www.ondomains.com/sales.htm)
- *The Domain Name Aftermarket* (www.tdnam.com)
- *DOTCOM Agency* (www.dotcomagency.com)

Say that you want to build a Web store for exercise equipment, but you can't find a domain name that you think is sufficient. You can go to one of these sites and see what names are up for sale. For example, you can go to AfterNIC (as shown in the figure) and see all the domains they have for sale.

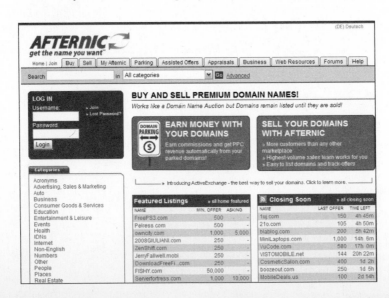

If you want to get more specific, you can click the Health subcategory, for example, and get a more focused list of domains, as shown in the figure. You can click any of the domain names listed to read more about their asking price and offers. You can also use the search box at the top of the page to type the keywords you want for your domain, which in this figure is exercise equipment.

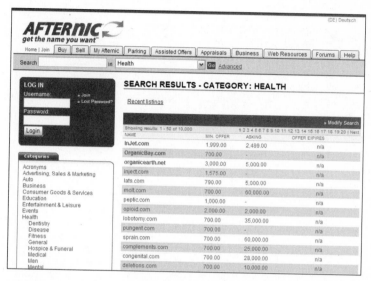

When you do that, you get a list of suggestions that match your keywords and their database of names, as in the figure. You can go through the list, see which domain names you like, and make offers on the names you want to purchase. You can also type different keywords or start with one keyword to get more selections.

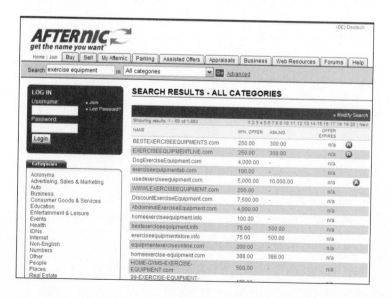

Let's say that you have tons of sources for getting used exercise equipment at a cut-rate price, and you want to be known as the Used Exercise Equipment store. If you look at the list in the figure, you'll see that usedexercise equipment.com is available. Click the URL to see detailed information about it and what these resellers feel is the market value for the name. You can make an offer, but the minimum offer for this particular domain name is $5,000.

If you make an offer and it's accepted, the domain name reseller coordinates the legal exchange and lists you as the Registrant for the domain name. From there, you can assign your own Administrative and Technical Contact and do what you wish for that name.

✔ **Try different extension names for your domain:** When it comes to domain names, .com is still considered the gold standard for commerce, and it's the first extension that people think of when it comes to e-commerce. However, a growing list of other extensions can be used for e-commerce purposes as well. Some people have heard of the .net extension, and the .org is typically for non-profit organizations, though sites like Craigslist and the U.S. Postal Service actively use the .org extension. The .tv and .us extensions are growing in popularity, but most of these extensions are rarely used. If *yourname*.com is taken, consider some of these other options:

- *yourname*.net
- *yourname*.biz
- *yourname*.org
- *yourname*.info
- *yourname*.name

- *yourname*.mobi
- *yourname*.tv
- *yourname*.us
- *yourname*.bz
- *yourname*.cc

You can back order your domain in case it becomes available: Even though you're the owner of the domain name, you have to pay a yearly fee to keep your domain name. Many people have signed up for a domain name, found no use for the name, and let their registration expire. So, if you want to wait until the registration has expired, you could then sign up for that domain name with your new registration.

The domain name registrars saw a new stream of revenue by providing a service where they'd watch the domain name registrations, and if a particular name has expired without being renewed, the registrar would automatically register the person who back ordered the name. *Back order* reflects the fact that you're placing an order for something that may become available in the future.

If you're going to back order a domain name, do your research with WHOIS (see the preceding section) and try to back order the domain name with the same registrar that currently registered the domain name. This way, your back order doesn't have to check external databases every day for the expiration date.

✔ **Invent an entirely new name or concept for your store domain name:** No one had ever heard of Google, Yahoo!, or eBay before the Internet craze made these companies household names. Therefore, maybe your store will want to take an avant-garde look and create a unique name, which you could turn into your own brand.

Web sites are out there to help you. MakeWords.com (as shown in the figure) is an example of a Web site that offers name generators based on rules or keywords that you give it. MakeWords.com tells you whether its newly generated names are available for registration or whether you have to approach the owners, using methods like the ones we discussed earlier.

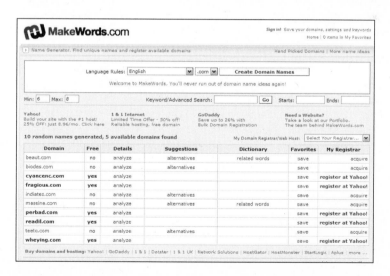

✔ **Go long (with hyphens, extra words, and numbers):** Yes, we all want the short and sweet domain name that's easy to remember, easy to spell, quick to type, and reinforces your core product. However, with so many domain names being registered every day, the newest trend is to go for the longer domain names because you're allowed to use letters, numbers, and the dash (–) character. The domain name can be up to 63 characters long, which gives you some options:

• **Put dashes between the keywords in your desired domain name.** Although `yourname.com` may be taken, try `your-name.com`.

  You can't start or end your domain name with a dash, but the dash can go anywhere else in your name, and you can use multiple dashes in your name as well.

• **Add an extra word or two to the end of your domain name.** Instead of `yourname.com`, try `yournamecompany.com`, `yournamebusiness.com`, `yournamesales.com`, and so on.

• **Use numbers to create variations of your desired domain name.** Instead of `yourname.com`, try `1yourname.com`, `4yourname.com`, `8yourname.com`, `1your4name.com`, and so on.

• **Use a combination of the above techniques to create a name that may be long, but have well-defined keywords.** (An example of this is `this-is-a-really-long-1-Web-store-name.com`.) As I discuss in Chapter 19, well-defined keywords help your store get better search engine results.

In Chapter 4–6, I create three different example storefronts, complete with step-by-step instructions. The three different Web storefront providers I use are Yahoo! Merchant Solutions (`http://smallbusiness.yahoo.com`), ProStores (`www.prostores.com`), and 1&1 eShops (`http://1and1.com`). These example storefronts are meant as illustrative only, as many providers work in a similar way. But if you choose one of these three Web storefront providers, you'll get the specific how-to on storefront creation.

Chapter 4

Yahoo! Merchant Solutions

Tasks performed in this chapter

✔ Reviewing the features and benefits of Yahoo! Stores

✔ Creating an e-commerce account with Yahoo! Stores

✔ Designing your store using pre-defined templates

✔ Defining your catalog items

✔ Finishing the Yahoo! checklist to open your store

The first Web store we're creating involves one of the oldest and widely known providers of Web stores, namely Yahoo!. Specifically, it's *Yahoo! Small Business,* which offers different Merchant Solutions based on the size and sales volume of the store you wish to create. They've been in business for over a decade and have created several levels of storefronts that are full of helpful advice, from the telephone consultants available during the first 60 days, to the hundreds of pre-programmed templates you can use to instantly construct a slick store design, to the additional functionality, reports, and e-mail marketing tools that Yahoo! offers its customers based on the fact that Yahoo! represents so many e-commerce storefronts.

According to market studies that Yahoo! generated a few years ago, approximately one out of every eight e-commerce Web sites was using Yahoo! to power their site. Although I'm not sure how many customers Yahoo! has today, Yahoo! Small Business clearly powers thousands of merchants with its easy setup, stable environment, and feature-rich Web storefronts. A quick look at the featured Customer Stores (see Figure 4-1) shows a variety of clients, including the Lance Armstrong Foundation!

In this chapter, I start from the beginning: You'll sign up for a Merchant Solutions account, configure the account for your new Web store, pick a store design, add at least one inventory item, and complete Yahoo!'s handy checklist for opening a Web store.

Because Yahoo! offers a lot of benefits too numerous to mention in one chapter, a good companion book to this one (if you choose Yahoo! to host your storefront) is *Starting a Yahoo! Business For Dummies* by Rob Snell (Wiley Publishing, Inc.).

This chapter gives you the core set of instructions to get up and running with Yahoo! Small Business Merchant Solutions. There are a lot of extra functions you should take advantage of when building and operating your Yahoo! store, some of which are covered in other chapters. Just remember to log in to your account and go to the appropriate Control Panel when needed.

Figure 4-1: From furniture to foundations, Yahoo! Stores powers them all.

Why Yahoo?

Before I get into the step-by-step instructions, I talk about some of the benefits that a Yahoo! storefront can provide you. Here's some qualities of Yahoo!'s accounts, which I discuss in Chapter 3, and how they apply to you:

✔ **Shopping Cart technology — Check!**

- You can add an unlimited number of products to the shopping cart, including information products for digital download.

- You can manage up to 50,000 different products.

- Customer information is stored in your system based on their Yahoo! ID.

- Yahoo! integrates with PayPal or your own Merchant account (via Chase Paymentech) with no additional gateway fee, and built-in verification tools are provided to double-check the customer's payment information.

- Orders can be transmitted via e-mail and, for Yahoo's Standard or Professional level accounts, via fax.

- It's very easy to set up! Phone and online support are available.

✔ **Disk space and bandwidth — Check!**

- Each Yahoo! store comes with at least 20 GB of disk space per store, which is enough for tens of thousands of product pictures and descriptions.

- The 500 GB data transfer limit means that tens of thousands of visitors can be browsing your Web store at the same time!

- Yahoo! has the capability to add extra disk space, bandwidth, or data transfer whenever needed.

- Yahoo! just unveiled unlimited storage for their e-mail accounts, so I suspect disk space will *not* be an issue for their storefront customers.

✔ **E-mail accounts — Check!**

- Yahoo! offers each store owner up to 1,000 unique e-mail addresses.

- Each e-mail account has an unlimited amount of storage space.

- People can access their e-mail through a *POP (Post Office Protocol)* or *SMTP (Simple Mail Transfer Protocol)* service, or through Yahoo!'s WebMail service at `mail.yahoo.com`.

- Each account comes with Norton AntiVirus screening and SpamGuard Plus protection.

✔ **Programming extensions — Check!**

- Yahoo! supports Adobe Dreamweaver, Adobe GoLive, and Microsoft FrontPage to help you build custom Web stores as well as a special Dreamweaver extension that works directly with your stored product information.

- Yahoo! has built-in support for programming languages and databases, like Perl, *PHP (Hypertext PreProcessor programming language),* and MySQL.

- Yahoo! has hundreds of templates available and an extensive dealer network of third-party providers to help you build any additional functionality that you need or want.

- **Application integration — Check!**

- Yahoo! has a built-in exporting tool to send transaction information to QuickBooks for your accountant.

- Yahoo! can integrate with OrderMotion for order management and fulfillment.

- Yahoo's Order Manager can export orders into UPS WorldShip for easy label creation and shipment tracking.

- Yahoo! works with Chase Paymentech to coordinate payments going into your credit card Merchant account.

- Yahoo! integrates with Stone Edge Order Management software to coordinate inventory management and order fulfillment.

✓ **Additional features — Check!**

- Yahoo! runs their storefront accounts by using the FreeBSD (UNIX) computer system with Apache servers, which are considered among the most popular and stable in the industry.

- Yahoo! offers up to 40 reports and graphs to show everything from customer and order information to the actual path of Web pages each customer sees when he uses your Web site (known as *customer navigation paths*) and the most frequently searched topics in your store.

- Yahoo! offers Inventory alerts — you get automatic e-mails if any product inventory falls below a certain level.

✓ **Security, reliability, and service —Check!**

- Yahoo! supports Secure Socket Layer (SSL) technology with 128-bit encryption to keep your customers' information private.

- Yahoo! has customizable risk tools to help you identify fraud in your orders before the products are shipped out and to help keep out unwanted visitors from bringing down your Web store.

- Yahoo! reports that their servers had 99.9 percent uptime from mid-2005 to mid-2006 for their store servers — their stores were almost always on and available!

- Yahoo! backs up your Web store automatically every day (locally and at a remote site) and allows you to easily switch between older and newer versions of your account. If you accidentally lose data, Yahoo! can help you restore the most recent version quickly.

- Yahoo! has a 24/7 toll-free phone and an e-mail support hotline, along with the first 60 days free support via telephone with a store specialist to help build your store. Large customers (over $500,000/year) may qualify for their own account manager.

- Yahoo! has built an extensive online help section (`http://help.yahoo.com/help/us/store/`) with a Getting Started guide plus built-in tutorials on basic and advanced topics.

Yahoo! Account Types

Yahoo! offers three basic account plans, all of which come equipped with a very strong foundation for building your Web store. Yahoo! has created a plan comparison chart (see Figure 4-2) so you can compare costs and benefits of each plan.

See all features	Starter	Standard	Professional
	Sign Up	Sign Up	Sign Up
Recommended plan if you expect sales of:	Up to $12K/mo.	$12K-$80K/mo.	More than $80K/mo.
Monthly price	~~$39.95~~ $25.97/1ˢᵗ 2 mos.¹	~~$99.95~~ $64.97/1ˢᵗ 2 mos.¹	~~$299.95~~ $194.97/1ˢᵗ 2 mos.¹
One-time setup fee	~~$50~~ WAIVED	~~$50~~ WAIVED	~~$50~~ WAIVED
Transaction fee	1.5%	1.0%	0.75%
▶ No transaction fees for six months when you use PayPal Express Checkout† Learn more			
Product Promotion			
Cross-selling	No	Yes	Yes
Gift certificates	No	Yes	Yes
Coupons	No	Yes	Yes
Order Processing			
Real-time integration with backend systems	No	Yes	Yes
Notification of new orders by fax	No	Yes	Yes
Shipping			
Export orders to UPS Worldship®	No	Yes	Yes

Figure 4-2: Use this chart to find the right Yahoo! plan for your Web store.

Starter

At the core, every account offered by Yahoo! has the features and tools of the Starter account. This includes the shopping cart that supports up to 50,000 products easily, the templates, the customer service, and the marketing program discounts to help you build and grow your business as well as basic reports to gauge your success.

For the Web store I create in this chapter, I select a Starter account. Unless you're a big, established retailer or you're planning a major presence to open your Web store, the Starter account is more than enough to handle your needs. You can always upgrade your account later, so use the Starter account to get your Web store up and running.

The cost of the Starter account includes a $50 setup fee, a $39.95 monthly fee, and a 1.5 percent transaction fee based on sales volume every month. Yahoo! recommends that after you reach $12,000 in monthly sales, upgrade to a Standard account because of the lower transaction fee in that package.

Standard

After you achieve at least $12,000 in monthly sales or you have a need for additional functionality, upgrade to a Standard account. This account takes the basic features of the Starter account and adds more advanced features to help you run your growing business more smoothly.

You can expect to receive these benefits by upgrading to Standard:

- ✔ Orders can be automatically faxed to you as well as e-mailed. (With Starter, it's e-mail only.)

- ✔ Your databases have real-time access to your order data.

- ✔ You can use UPS WorldShip to coordinate your shipments and package labels.

- ✔ You receive advanced reports, showing paths taken by customers and frequently used search terms.

- ✔ You can create and distribute special Web links to have your own affiliate program with other resellers.

- ✔ You can offer the use of electronic coupons and gift certificates on your Web store.

- ✔ You can specify cross-selling opportunities for each product in your catalog.

The cost of the Standard account includes a $50 setup fee (waived if you're upgrading from Starter), a $99.95 monthly fee, and a 1 percent transaction fee based on sales volume every month. Yahoo! recommends that after you reach $80,000 in monthly sales, you upgrade to the Professional account because of the lower transaction fee in that package.

Professional

When Web stores exploded in popularity and sales, Yahoo! had to offer bigger packages to handle the growing needs of these now-large e-commerce merchants. Therefore, the Professional package was born, focusing more on the scalability needs of a large merchant than the functionality. This means that Yahoo!'s servers act quickly to provide additional disk space, bandwidth, data transfer, and other backend services to keep the Web site running through busy, peak demand times. The features and benefits of this account are similar to the Standard package, but the transaction fee is lower.

The cost of the Professional account includes a $50 setup fee (waived if you're upgrading from Starter or Standard), a $299.95 monthly fee, and a 0.75 percent transaction fee based on sales volume every month. At this point, you have Yahoo!'s highest package and best deal as far as sales transaction volume goes.

Special Promotions: Get that Setup Fee Waived!

As of this book's writing, Yahoo!'s offering several promotions for new customers of their Merchant Solutions accounts. You might want to try one of these avenues first before signing up:

✔ Establish your PayPal account first. (Go to Chapter 7 for detailed instructions on how to do this.) After you log out of your PayPal account, scroll down to the bottom of the page and look for a link like the one circled in the figure. Click that link to go to Yahoo! Merchant Solutions. The discount offered is reflected in the prices displayed.

Shops Resources

Register for Shops free! Online sellers who accept PayPal can register for PayPal Shops, at no cost, or learn more about PayPal Shops in the Shops Resource Center.

PayPal is the safe way to pay online. Learn how we help safeguard your privacy, protect you against unauthorized payments sent from your account, and help prevent fraud.

Special offer from ProStores: Create your own branded storefront at your own web address. ProStores, an eBay Company, offers everything you need including free domain registration, shopping cart, and easy set-up and design wizards. Get a 1 month FREE trial and pay NO SET UP FEES.

Yahoo! Merchant Solutions. Save $50.00 in setup fees, and get 25% off the first 2 months of Yahoo! Merchant Solutions. Build, manage and market your online store easily—complete with 24/7 customer support and 60 days free consulting!

Want something you don't want to pay for right now? Get it with PayPal Buyer Credit.

The merchants listed on PayPal Shops operate independently from PayPal, and PayPal does not endorse any merchant or assume responsibility for transactions conducted with them.

About | Accounts | Fees | Privacy | Security Center | Contact Us | Legal Agreements | Developers | Jobs | Mobile | Plus Card | Referrals | Shops | Mass Pay

Copyright © 1999-2007 PayPal. All rights reserved.
Information about FDIC pass-through insurance

(continued)

(continued)

✔ Do a search on Google or Yahoo! with the keywords `web stores`. Your search results screen (as shown in the figure) should contain an ad for Yahoo! stores that offers a discount and free setup.

When you click the link, you're taken to Yahoo! Merchant Solutions, where the discount price is reflected in the options, as in the figure.

Signing up with Yahoo! Merchant Solutions

Stuff You Need to Know

Toolbox:
- Computer
- Internet Connection
- Domain name
- Credit card

Time Needed:
15 minutes

This section takes you step by step through signing up for your Yahoo! Merchant Solutions Starter account.

1. Go to the Yahoo! Small Business home page at `http://smallbusiness.yahoo.com` and click the Merchant Solutions link under the Sell Online header to sign up.

2. Click the yellow Sign Up for Starter button in the Merchant Starter Plan box.

REMEMBER

You can also use the techniques that I describe in the sidebar, "Special Promotions: Get that Setup Fee Waived!," to see if there are any promotions for signing up. You must follow the techniques above and click the promotional link to get the discount because you can't apply for a credit after your account is created.

3. Pick the domain name for your Web storefront. If you haven't yet reserved your domain name, enter the domain name you want in the box provided and click Search. If you've already reserved your domain name, click the yellow Use It with Your Order button and follow the instructions to link your domain to your new account.

4. If your domain name is available, you see a message similar to the one in the figure on the left. If your first domain name choice isn't available, you see a message similar to the one in the figure on the right and you're asked to enter another domain name in the box provided. (If your first choice for a domain name isn't available, read Chapter 3 and research other methods of obtaining a good domain name for your store. Also consider opening another Internet Web browser window and trying different options until you find an available domain name, then come back to this screen and enter your name.)

5. Click the Continue button to reserve your chosen domain name. You're then asked to log in to Yahoo!. If you have a Yahoo! ID already, simply provide your User ID and password, and your Merchant account is tied to the existing ID. If you don't have a Yahoo! ID (or want to keep your business Yahoo! ID separate from your personal Yahoo! ID), click the Sign Up for a New Account link and provide your information. Click the Continue to Yahoo! Small Business button when you're done.

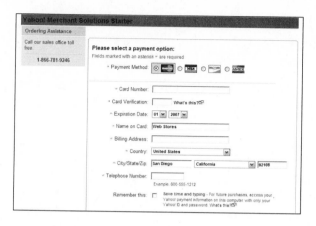

6. You're asked for your billing information. In order to have a Merchant Solutions account, Yahoo! must be able to bill a Visa, MasterCard, American Express, or Discover card on file each month for your fees. If you just signed up for Yahoo!, you're asked to verify your billing address as well.

7. Review your order information and click the Continue button to place your order. You can hide your registration information from the general public by selecting the Private Registration option. For $0.75 per month, Yahoo! doesn't provide any public information regarding the WHOIS record for your domain name. If you're interested, select the check box next to that option. Scroll down the page to click Continue and place your order.

Creating Your Store Design

You did it! You have a Yahoo! Merchant Solutions Web storefront. When you log in to your account at `http://smallbusiness.yahoo.com`, you see your control panel of functions, as shown in the figure.

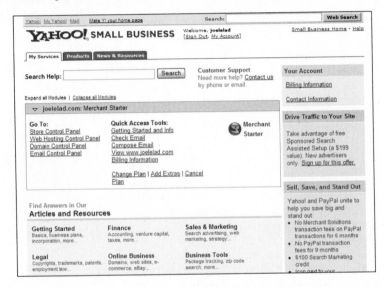

The four main aspects of your account are as follows:

- **Store Control Panel:** You click this link when you want to design, build, and manage your actual Web store. I use this link later.

- **Web Hosting Control Panel:** You click this link to alter any aspects of the Web hosting space you now own and to see your available space left on the account. You also click this link to get the SiteBuilder tool for a custom design of your Web site and to activate the blogging capabilities of your Web store.

- **Domain Control Panel:** You click this link to handle any administrative aspects of your custom domain name. If you ever need to add additional URL domain names, re-direct any other domain names, or create subdomains for your Web site, start here.

- **E-mail Control Panel:** As I mention in the section, "Yahoo! Account Types," earlier in this chapter, you get up to 1,000 different e-mail accounts with your package. Click this link to create and manage your business e-mail accounts as well as to establish a *catchall e-mail address,* which receives any message addressed to your domain name but not to a specific user.

In this section, I concentrate on the Store Control Panel functions. First, you need to create a design for your new Web store:

1. Log in to your account and go to your main control panel. (Refer to the figure earlier.)

2. Click the Store Control Panel link to start your Open for Business checklist. When you first sign up for Yahoo! Merchant Solutions, you see a five-part checklist that walks you through the process of opening a store. After you complete every step, your store is published on the Internet and ready for your customers!

3. Click the Design Your Site link to go to the Store Editor. When you click the link, you're taken to the Design Your Site overview page (expect to see one of these overview pages for each step in the process). This page lets you know of any requirements you need before getting started and an estimated time for completion.

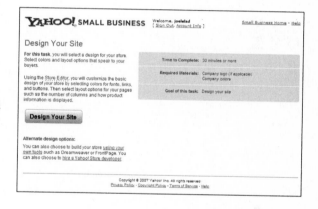

4. Click the Design Your Site button to get started. After you click the button, you're asked to select either a generic template or a pre-defined template for your store. If you have a very specific color scheme in mind for your store and you already have many of the images for your store design, select the generic template so you can insert your colors and pictures when needed. Otherwise, a pre-designed template provides your layout and matching color scheme, along with lots of pre-defined images you can use within your store without worrying about copyright infringement or paying a graphic designer thousands of dollars for your unique look. For your purposes, I select the pre-designed template.

5. After clicking the Pre-Designed Templates button, review the various templates available and click the Select Template button when you've decided on one. At press time, 12 different pre-designed templates are available for your Web store. You can always customize a template after you select one, so don't think you're forced to adopt the entire template. Each template is displayed with a paragraph of notes, an example of the home page, and the author who designed it. You can move between templates by clicking the thumbnail of another template from the blue Select a Template box at the top of the page.

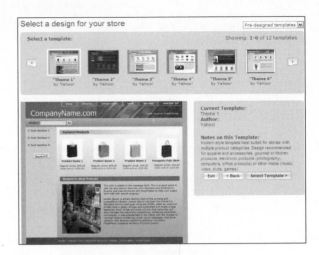

6. After you pick your template, Yahoo! asks you to design your site header by either providing your store name or logo. At this stage, you're presented with two choices (as shown in the figure on the left) on how to proceed. If you've designed a company logo, pick the radio button Upload Your Own Logo and follow the instructions to upload the logo from your computer to Yahoo!'s servers. If you just want your store name stated as the header, pick the radio button Use Plain Text and click Next to enter your store title in the box provided (as shown in the figure on the right).

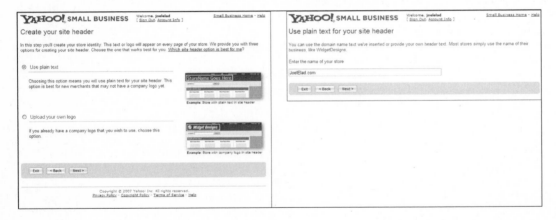

Read the product notes for each template because Yahoo! recommends different templates, depending on the category of products you're selling. For example, "Theme 1" is recommended for stores with multiple product categories, like home and garden, sports and outdoors, toys and games, or health and beauty. These are only suggestions, as most templates work fine for practically every store.

7. After you pick your header, click the Next button, and Yahoo! presents a branding Web page asking for some basic information to fill in your store template: your home page message, your About Us contact info and greeting, your Privacy policy, and your Copyright information. At this stage, you're asked to fill in several boxes that correspond to different pages of your Web store. Each section comes with an illustration of where the information will reside. You can always go back and enter more information later, but spending the time now to write a quality introduction saves you time down the road when you're close to opening and have no time to write something fit for general consumption.

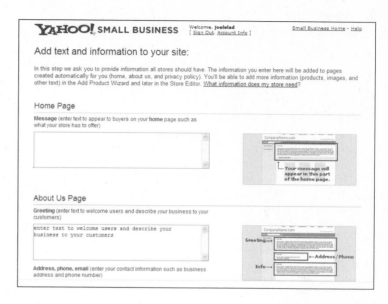

8. When you scroll down the page, you see a box for your information. This includes any Shipping policy, Return/Refund policy, and Frequently Asked Questions. See Chapter 2 for steps on how to develop your own policies or use the standard text provided to create your own policies. After the Information box, you're asked to provide a Privacy page. See Chapter 2 for tips on building a Privacy Policy, but note that Yahoo! gives you a template you can follow. Simply read through their text, change some fields when prompted, and *voilà!*, your Privacy page is ready.

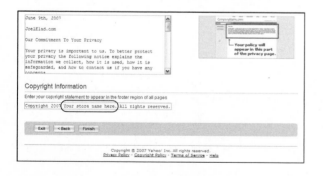

9. The last field to complete is the Copyright Information field. You can simply substitute *your store name here* with your store name in the box provided to protect your store design and text, or you can write your own Copyright header, depending on the content you plan to display in your Web store.

10. After you're done, click the Finish button and you're taken back to your Open for Business checklist screen, with Step 1, Design Your Store, complete!

Adding an Item to Your Store

Stuff You Need to Know

Toolbox:

- Item or product names
- Item/product detailed information (SKU, price, cost)
- Item/product descriptions
- Item/product photos

Time Needed:

3–5 minutes per product

You've created the outside look of your Web store through the Design phase; now it's time to fill the shelves by adding items, or products, to your Web store.

1. Click the Add Products link on your Open for Business checklist. You're taken to the Add Products overview screen.

2. Click the Start Adding Products button to get started. You're taken to the first step of a 4-step process to add a product to your store. In the first step, you need to provide the product information. This includes the product name, description, picture, price, sales price (if applicable), and the shipping weight. After you fill in the basic information, click the Next button.

Although you could gather the elements you need during the Add process, if you plan on adding multiple products in one session you save time and effort by having everything ready beforehand with a list handy for review.

If you plan to add a lot of items, you may want to create a Comma Separated Values (CSV) text file of all your products and upload them at once to your Yahoo! store. Click the Batch Upload link in the Advanced Users section for more information on how to do this.

When inputting your product description, do *not* use the single quote mark (') because Yahoo! interprets that as the end of your description. Every time you need to use a single quote, put two quotes (") instead.

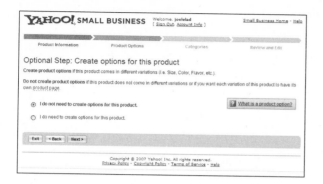

3. (Optional) You can define any product options. This is designed for products that have multiple options, like colors, sizes, or styles. You can either define a general product, like a T-shirt, and then define ordering options for that product, like different sizes (S, M, L, XL) or colors (red, blue, black, white, and so on), or you can create specific product entries, like a blue L T-shirt, a blue XL T-shirt, a red L T-shirt, and so on. If you're defining specific products with no options, leave the I Do Not Need to Create Options for This Product radio button selected. If you leave this button selected, go straight to Step 5.

4. If you determine in Step 3 that you do want to offer different options, select the I Do Need to Create Options for This Product radio button and click the Next button. When you do that, you're prompted with a blue pop-up box to define your option. Give your option a name and define your option in the fields provided. Click the + Add Another Option Value button if you need to have more than two options available. Click the I Need to Make Price Changes for Each Option Value check box if you have to charge more or less money based on the option selected. For example, you may want to add $2 to the cost if someone orders an XXL T-shirt, instead of a L or XL T-shirt. After you're done with this option, click the Create Option button. Repeat this process if you want to create multiple options for this product; after you're done creating options, click the Next button to proceed.

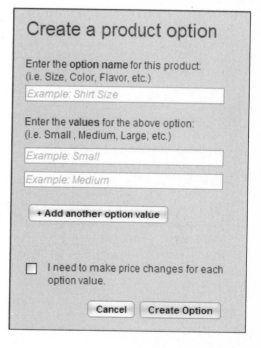

5. After you have (or haven't) created any product options, you must assign your product to a store category. Every product in your store should be associated with a store category. In the beginning, you have one default Home category for your products (as shown in the figure on the left). You can create a product category by clicking the blue + Create Category button and completing the Category Name and Category Description (as shown in the figure on the right). After you create a category, Yahoo! assigns your product to that category. You can repeat this process to create all your categories and then select the category for your product. *Note:* Each product can only belong to one category or sub-category.

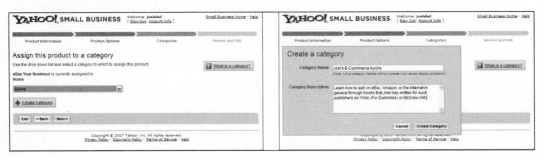

6. After you select your category, the final step is to review all the information and either edit your product info or submit it to your store. You see a summary screen for your item; look over the information and make sure everything is correct, from the spelling, to the price, to the category. You can make any changes by clicking the Review and Edit link on the right side of the screen. If everything looks good, click the Next button to finalize your entry.

7. Repeat Steps 2–6 for any additional products you want to add to your store; click the Create Another Product button to walk through the 4-step process of adding another product to your store (you can always return to this section later through your Catalog Manager). Click Finish when you're done. After you create your first product, you see a summary screen, showing the default table of items in your new Web store

Completing the Open for Business Checklist

You've designed your store template and added products that are available for sale. Think you're finished? Not quite — Yahoo! has a few more steps for you to complete before you can open your virtual doors, like establishing payment methods, tax information, and shipping methods and rates for your products.

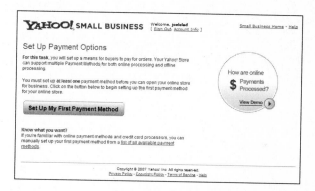

1. Click the Payment Methods link on your Open for Business checklist. You're taken to the Payment Methods overview screen. Because Yahoo! doesn't own a partner that can handle credit card transactions, they rely on you to go out and get at least one company that can act as your payment processor. Therefore, you may need to skip to Chapter 7 and find out how to join PayPal or set up your own Merchant account for credit card purchases. After you've set up at least one account, come back here and continue with the steps.

2. Click the Set Up My First Payment Method button. You're taken to a screen where you're asked if you're currently able to collect payments electronically. If you aren't currently able to collect payments electronically, select the No option and click the Next button (if you are able to currently collect payments electronically, skip ahead to Step 3). You're taken to an options screen that asks you if you want to sign up your Merchant account through Chase Paymentech, use a PayPal Merchant Solutions account, or use PayPal Express with a regular PayPal account and have your purchases processed on PayPal's Web site instead of your own. Consult the table for the processes to set up these accounts. To find out more about the accounts and how they compare to each other, click the blue How Are They Different button.

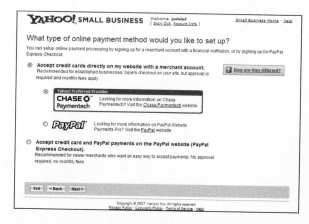

Online Payment Method	
Account Type	*Process*
Merchant account	Pull out your account information, select Chase Paymentech from the Accept Credit Cards Directly on My Website with a Merchant Account section, and click the Next button. You're given specific instructions on what information to give your bank and what information to ask for in order to create a link to your Yahoo! Web store. *Warning:* Allow a few days for the Merchant account process to complete. Your bank has to add the information about Yahoo! Merchant Solutions and create a special ID that Yahoo! and Chase uses to charge your customers' orders through your Merchant account.
PayPal Web sites Payments account	Select PayPal from the Accept Credit Cards Directly on My Website with a Merchant Account section and follow the instructions to link up that account with your Web store.
PayPal Premier or Business	If you've created a PayPal Premier or Business account account to handle payments (like getting paid for eBay auctions), but haven't applied for the Web site Payments program, select the Accept Credit Card and PayPal Payments on the PayPal Web site (PayPal Express Checkout) radio button and click the Next button. This is by far the easiest process to set up so you can get going. You see a summary screen that explains the process of completing this application.

 3. If you've already created a payment account, select the Yes option and then click the Next button to input your specific account information. Yahoo! links to that account for your Web store so customers are taken to the correct checkout page to pay you for their order. Depending on whether you're using PayPal or your own Merchant account, it takes up to a few business days to link the accounts.

 4. Repeat Steps 1–3 to add any additional payment methods to your store. Yahoo! Merchant Solutions has a minimum of one payment method, but there's no maximum. If you already have a Merchant account and want to offer your customers a choice of going through your existing Merchant account or your PayPal account, add both accounts to your store. Otherwise, one of these methods is sufficient to run your customers' credit cards.

 5. Now, you need to define your Tax Rate information. Click the Set Up Tax Rates link on your Open for Business checklist. Here, Yahoo! recommends that you know the tax status of your business as well as the states and accompanying tax rates for those states that you have to charge. Typically, if you're running a one-location home business for your Web store, you need only to charge sales tax for customers in the same state as you, at the tax rate of the county you're doing business in (which is usually the county where you reside).

6. Click the Start Tax Wizard button and you're taken to the Tax Setting window. You're asked whether you need to collect sales tax online and you have three options: I'm not required, I'm required, or I'm not sure.

7. If you're required to collect sales tax, select the I am Required to Collect Tax on Taxable Goods Purchased from My Online Store radio button and then click the Next button. You're asked to create sales tax rules for each state where your business operates. Yahoo! shows you a map of the U.S. Simply click each state where you have a physical business presence and you see your state appear in the States Selected list on the left. Then click the Next button to create the rule for that state.

8. Yahoo! automatically creates a rule for each state selected and shows you the base formula it created (as shown in the figure on the left). If you need to update the rule created, simply click the Edit link next to that rule, and in the box provided (as shown in the figure on the right), put in your business operations ZIP code and the correct tax rate you have to charge and then click the Update button to save your changes.

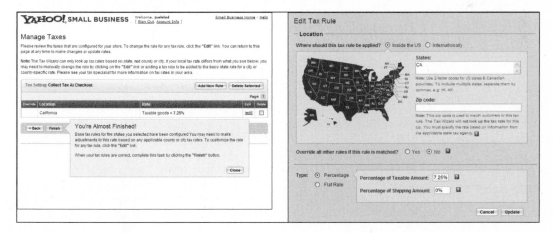

TIP

You can click the blue Do I Need to Collect Tax? info link to read more about this issue. Also, you can consult your state's secretary of state's Web site for more information on whether you need a reseller's permit and/or tax license.

9. Finally, you need to set up your shipping methods and rates. Click the Set Up Shipping link on your Open for Business checklist. Here, Yahoo! recommends that you know your ship-from location and the shipping company or companies you plan to use in order to handle your packages before you complete this step.

10. Click the Start Shipping Wizard button. You're taken to the Shipping Rates window and asked if you want to set up automatic rules with UPS or set manual rates with any carrier. Yahoo!'s software works directly with UPS and *UPS Online* — UPS's online shipping tool — so that if you pick automatic rates, Yahoo! calculates a customer's shipping total based on the weight of the customer's order and the buyer's ZIP code. The following table lists your options and the process you follow to set them up.

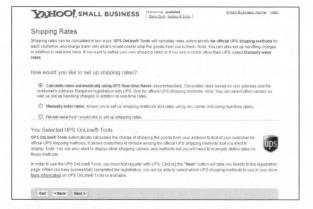

Shipping Rates	
Carrier	**Process**
UPS	If you plan on using UPS (either as your sole shipper or one of several options), make sure the Calculate Rates Automatically Using UPS Real-Time Rates option is selected and click the Next button. Yahoo! walks you through the process of registering your business with UPS Online and linking that account with your Yahoo! Web store.
Non-UPS	If you plan on using other carriers besides UPS or you don't want to create a UPS Online account, select the Manually Enter Rates option and click the Next button. You're taken to the Configure Shipping Methods screen where you can either pick specific shipping methods from companies, like UPS, FedEx, USPS, or DHL, or pick General Methods, like Ground, Express, Air, Free Shipping, and In-Store Pickup. For each General Method that you select, click the Add a Rate link next to that method to bring up the Enter a Rate table. You can specify a Flat Rate for shipping, based on a Flat Rate per order, per pound, and/or per item. You can also specify a Rate Table, where you set levels for shipping amount based on weight, number of items, or total dollar amount of the order.

If you want to assign Handling charges on top of your shipping amounts, select the Handling Charges check box on the Configure Shipping Methods screen and click the Add a Rate link next to it to finalize the handling charges. You should recognize the boxes that come up; they look like the figures in Step 10 except these will be added as Handling to the customer's order, not as Shipping.

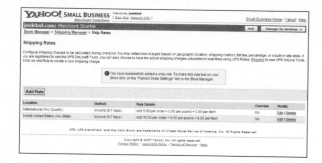

11. After you're done setting Shipping rules, click the Next button to review the rules you created. You see a screen detailing your rules. After you're satisfied, click the Finish button to save your shipping rules.

12. At this point, you've completed all the steps of the Open for Business checklist. Your checklist should have checkmarks for all the steps. After that's happened, click the View Site button to create a test order so you can truly be open for business!

Chapter 5

ProStores

Tasks performed in this chapter

- ✔ Reviewing the features and benefits of ProStores

- ✔ Creating an e-commerce account with ProStores

- ✔ Designing your store using pre-defined templates

- ✔ Defining your catalog items

- ✔ Completing the ProStores checklist to open your store

The second Web store I'm creating involves a newer vendor created and owned by eBay to appeal to their auction customers, namely *ProStores*. This company offers a variety of small, medium, and enterprise solutions based on the size and sales volume of the store you wish to create. Although they're initially designed to help augment eBay sellers with their own e-commerce sites, ProStores has built a robust platform to handle almost any e-commerce need, with or without auctions on the side.

ProStores powers thousands of small, medium, and large merchants with their easy setup, stable environment, and feature-rich Web storefronts. A quick look at their Featured Sites (as shown in Figure 5-1) shows a variety of clients, including eGizmo.com!

In this chapter, I start from the beginning: You'll sign up for a Business account, configure the account for your new store, pick a store design, add at least one inventory item, and complete their handy checklist for opening a Web store.

Because ProStores offers a lot of benefits too numerous to mention in one chapter, you can read about their different solutions at www.prostores.com/product-information.shtml.

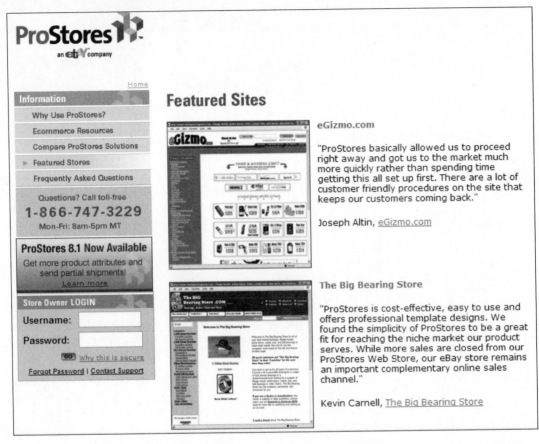

Figure 5-1: From gizmos to bearings, ProStores has a Web storefront solution.

Why ProStores?

Before I get into the step-by-step instructions, I talk about some of the benefits that a ProStores storefront can provide you. Look over the qualities of their accounts, based on the discussion in Chapter 3, and how it applies to you:

✔ **Shopping Cart technology — Check!**

- You can add at least 100,000 products to the shopping cart, including information products for digital download.

- You can manage up to 100,000 different products, and if you need more than that, you can e-mail ProStores Support about getting support for that many products.

- Customer information is stored in your system based on your ProStores ID.

- ProStores integrates with PayPal or your own Merchant account, and built-in verification tools are provided to double-check the customer's payment information.

- It's very easy to set up! Phone and online support are available.

✔ **Disk space and bandwidth — Check!**

- Each ProStores store comes with anywhere from 5 to 20 GB of disk space per store, which is enough for tens of thousands of product pictures and descriptions.

- The 50 to 400 GB data transfer limit means that thousands to tens of thousands of visitors can be browsing your Web store at the same time!

- ProStores has the capability to add extra disk space, bandwidth, or data transfer whenever needed but recommends upgrading your account if you regularly exceed your monthly limit as stated in your package description.

✔ **E-mail accounts — Check!**

- ProStores offers each store owner anywhere from 50 to 200 unique e-mail addresses.

- Each e-mail account has a generous limit, based on the level of account you ordered. Business accounts have a 1 GB limit per account.

- People can access their e-mail through a *POP (Post Office Protocol)* or *SMTP (Simple Mail Transfer Protocol)* service, or through ProStores's WebMail service at www.webmail.prostores.com.

✔ **Programming extensions — Check!**

- ProStores supports Adobe Dreamweaver and Microsoft FrontPage to help you build custom Web stores, as well as a special Dreamweaver Extension that works directly with your stored product information.

- ProStores has built-in support for features, like Flash and MP3s.

- ProStores has hundreds of templates available and a Design Services team to help you build any additional functionality that you need or want.

✔ **Application integration — Check!**

- ProStores has a built-in exporting tool to send transaction information to QuickBooks for your accountant.

- The ProStores Order Manager can integrate with UPS, FedEx, USPS, and Canada Post for easy shipments.

- ProStores works with PayPal or your merchant gateway to coordinate payments going into your credit card Merchant account.

✔ **Additional features — Check!**

- ProStores offers over a dozen reports and graphs to show everything from customer and order information to the actual path of Web pages each customer sees when they use your Web site (known as *customer navigation paths*) and the most frequently searched topics in your store.

- ProStores offers daily submission to the popular shopping search engines, including Yahoo! Shopping, Shopping.com, Shopzilla, and Froogle.

✔ **Security, reliability, and service — Check!**

- ProStores supports Secure Socket Layer (SSL) technology with 128-bit encryption to keep your customers' information private.

- ProStores also has customizable risk tools to help you identify fraud in your orders before the products are shipped out and to help keep out unwanted visitors from bringing down your Web store.

- ProStores backs up your Web store automatically every day (locally and at a remote site) and allows you to easily switch between older and newer versions of your account. If you accidentally lose data, ProStores can help you restore the most recent version quickly.

- ProStores has a 24/7 toll-free technical support hotline (1-800-422-9213), a toll-free General support hotline open Monday–Friday, 9am–10pm EST (1-800-422-9213), and initial support via telephone to help start your account (1-866-747-3229).

- ProStores has built an extensive online help section (`http://kb.prostores.com`) with a Getting Started Guide, plus built-in tutorials on basic and advanced topics.

ProStores' Plan Types

ProStores offers three basic plans plus one Express plan. The four plans offer you a wide range of options, depending on the size of the Web store you wish to create, and the features you want to take advantage of when building and running your store. Take a look through each description and see which plan is closest to your goals. Remember, you can always upgrade your package as your Web store grows!

Express

This option is perfect for the beginning merchant, as this plan allows you to sell up to 10 unique products through a customizable storefront for only $6.95 per month, plus 1.50% of any gross merchandise sales through your store every month.

Business

This option is the best all-around solution for a new Web store merchant, as it provides the powerful shopping cart that can easily handle up to 100,000 products, giving you unlimited possibilities for creating a functional Web store. It comes with ample hosting space, data transfer capabilities, as well as a core set of templates, reports, and features to help you build and grow your store. This solution costs $29.95 per month, plus 0.50% of any gross merchandise sales per month.

Advanced

This solution is designed for the small to medium retail operation that wants to grow its online arm through a variety of marketing and merchandising options. This solution contains the Business package for hosting lots of products but gives you more options for inventory management, promotion, merchandising, and payment features. This solution is for you if you plan on selling downloadable products or want to offer storewide sales and promotion codes to your customers. This solution costs $74.95 per month, plus 0.50% of any gross merchandise sales per month.

Enterprise

This solution is designed for the medium to large enterprise customer that wants to integrate a new, online solution with its existing backend infrastructure. This package allows you to add drop-shipping capabilities, create affiliate marketing tools so others can sell your products for you, and integrate your sales team more effectively. This solution costs $249.95 per month, plus 0.50% of any gross merchandise sales per month.

You can compare these options and all the features that come with each solution by going to the ProStores Feature Comparison page at www.prostores.com/ product-information.shtml#compare, as shown in Figure 5-2.

ProStores Feature Comparison

ProStores Fees	ProStores Express	ProStores Business	ProStores Advanced	ProStores Enterprise
Monthly Subscription Fee	$6.95	$29.95	$74.95	$249.95
Successful Transaction Fee	1.50%	0.50%	0.50%	0.50%
Customer Support				
Technical Support: 24/7 Toll-Free Phone Support		▼	▼	▼
Online Help and Priority Email	▼	▼	▼	▼
Website Hosting and Management				
Personalized Domain	*Add-on	▼	▼	▼
Hosted Storefront Domain	▼	▼	▼	▼
Unique Email Boxes		50	100	200
Storage Space		5GB	10GB	20GB
Data Transfer		50GB/month	200GB/month	400GB/month
E-commerce Features				
Accept instant PayPal payments.	▼	▼	▼	▼
Real-time credit card payment processing, plus store card, checks, and money orders.		▼	▼	▼
Additional payment options: purchase orders, internal department orders, and cash (COD) orders.			▼	▼
Recurring billing for products and services				

Figure 5-2: Compare the features of various ProStores packages.

Signing Up with ProStores

Stuff You Need to Know

Toolbox:
- ✔ Idea of Web store domain names
- ✔ Business credit card

Time Needed:
30–45 minutes

This section takes you step by step through signing up for a ProStores Business account:

The Get Started button

1. Go to the ProStores home page at www.prostores.com and click the Get Started button next to the Business plan.

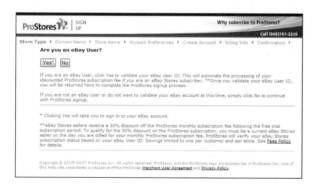

2. After 5–10 seconds, the screen refreshes and asks if you're an eBay user. Typically, eBay Store owners get 30 percent off their monthly subscription fee to ProStores while they maintain an eBay store. If you have an eBay store, follow the prompts to validate your eBay user ID. If you don't have an eBay store (even if you have an eBay account), click No to proceed with the signup process.

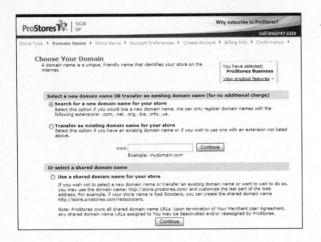

3. Next, you're asked to create your own domain name or transfer an existing domain name that you've purchased already. We are now in Phase 2 of the ProStores store creation process — Domain Name. As you can see, you simply pick the radio button to either search for a new domain name or transfer your existing name. ProStores does give you a third option of using a *shared* domain name for your store, essentially offering a URL like `http://store.prostores.com/`*yourstorename*. This strategy is *not* wise if you're trying to build your own identity because you're now dependent on ProStores and will lose this name if you ever use another storefront provider.

4. If your name is available, you see a message similar to the one in the figure on the left. If your name is not available, ProStores shows you another message similar to the one in the figure on the right. In that case, ProStores gives you other options of similar names that are available for purchase. Even if your name is available, ProStores prompts you for different extensions of your domain name, like `.net`, `.org`, `.biz`, and `.info`. If you want to completely start over, scroll down the page and click the Search Again for a New Domain Name . . . link to go back to Step 3 to enter a brand-new name. If your first choice for a domain name isn't available, go to Chapter 3 and research other methods of obtaining a good domain name for your store.

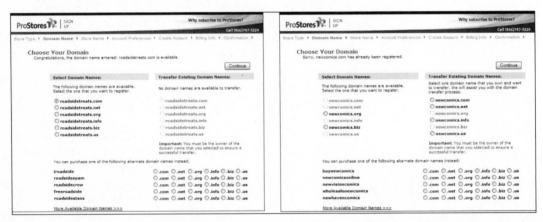

5. After you select an available domain name, click the Continue button to move to Phase 3 — Store Name. ProStores gives you up to 50 characters for your Store Name, which is used when you build your Web store. You can always change your store name after you've signed up with ProStores. The key with the Store Name is to reinforce the keywords your store represents. So, don't just think about using your domain name, like Roadside Treats, but be more descriptive: Roadside Treats — Snack Foods & Tasty Desserts.

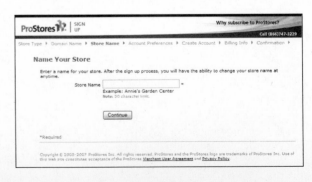

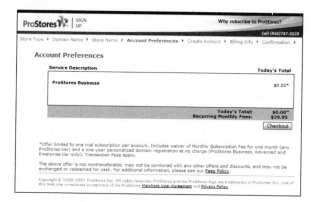

6. After you create your name, click the Continue button to review your Account Preferences and set up your account. In Phase 4 — Account Preferences — you see a screen to review the choice of accounts you made and to show your initial charges. As of the time of this writing, ProStores is offering a free one-month subscription for new users, so you pay $0 upfront and pay only your monthly fee, starting your second month.

7. Click the Checkout button to proceed to Phase 5 — Create Your Account — and enter your contact information. Every field with an * is a required field, so you can leave any optional field blank (such as Fax). If your contact information matches your credit card billing address, save yourself the hassle of retyping the same information in Phase 6 — Billing Information — by answering Yes to the question Is This Your Credit Card Billing Address?

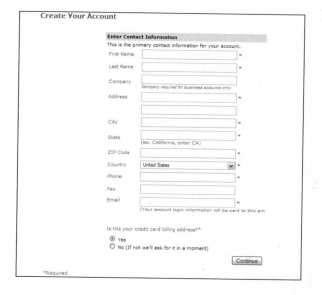

8. After entering your Contact Information, ProStores needs your Billing Information in Phase 6. In this screen, you're asked to put a major credit card on file for your ProStores account. If your billing address for your credit card is different from the contact information you gave in Step 7, adjust the address information on the right side of this screen. Be sure to review the Terms and Conditions before clicking the I Have Read and Agree to the Terms and Conditions in the User Agreement check box near the bottom of the screen and then clicking the Continue button.

9. After entering billing information, ProStores asks you to confirm and place your order in Phase 7 — Confirmation. As your final phase, ProStores presents one screen with all your options selected to this point. Review the account level you've requested, double-check the domain name you've requested, and make sure that your billing and contact information are correct. When you're ready, click the Place Order button to finalize your order.

Creating Your Store Design

Stuff You Need to Know

Toolbox:

- Your ProStores account information
- An idea of what you want for your store layout
- A store logo (optional)

Time Needed:

30–60 minutes

You did it! You've signed up for a ProStores Business account. Now, after you place your order in Step 9 of the previous task, you're shown a confirmation screen like the one in the figure here. You should definitely print a receipt and keep it in a safe place because this receipt has your initial username and password, as well as your domain information and when your credit card will be charged. When you're ready to proceed, you can either click the Getting Started Checklist link from your receipt screen or log in to your account at `http://my.prostores.com` with your new username and password.

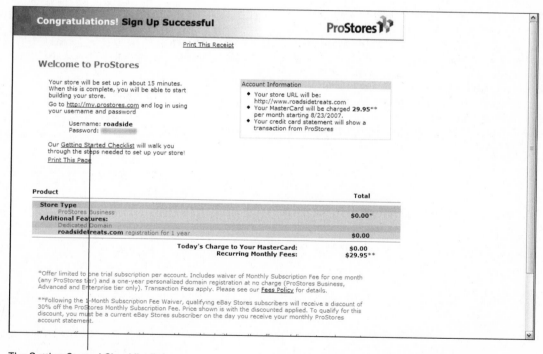

The Getting Started Checklist link

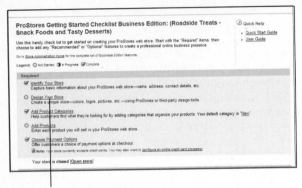

The Design Your Store link

1. When you first bring up your ProStores Getting Started Checklist, notice that ProStores has already marked a few of the items as Complete. ProStores used all the information captured when you ordered the account (completed in the previous task) to fill in as much as possible. However, just because an item has a checkmark next to it does *not* mean the item is fully completed. I review virtually every item because some items require additional information. The one exception is the Identify Your Store item, because you've set up all the basic information (which was done in the previous task) already and no further review is needed here. Let's start by designing your store. Click the Design Your Store link from the checklist.

2. When you click the Design Your Store link, ProStores loads its Store Settings Manager into your Web browser and shows you design options. When you sign up, ProStores assigns you one of its basic templates, and you can see the page design from the examples shown. You're *not* stuck with the option that was pre-selected but you're free to accept this template and move on. If you want to accept the pre-selected template, skip ahead to Step 5. To review different themes available to you, click the Change link.

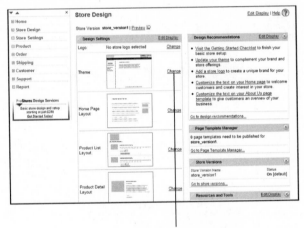

The Change link for Theme

3. The ProStores Theme page appears. Currently, over 300 themes are available for you to select, but initially, ProStores brings up its Favorites category (as shown in the figure on the left). You can look through the different themes by clicking the Theme Category drop-down box near the middle of the screen and reviewing the different categories of themes that are offered (shown in the figure on the right). Read the descriptions of each theme to understand where your pictures are placed on the screen and what resolution is optimal for that theme. Pick a theme that you feel reflects the tone and quality of the Web store you wish to offer — if you're offering fun, entertainment products, you can pick something with eye-popping colors. Plenty of options are tailored to specific niches, like children's apparel, home and garden items, and even services, like legal and accounting.

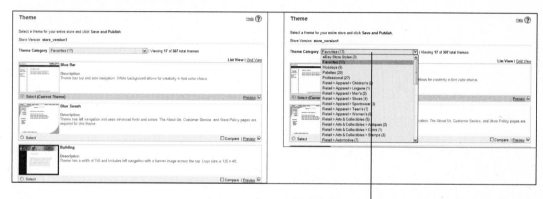

Theme Category drop-down menu

4. When you find the theme you want, click the Select button next to that theme, scroll down to the bottom of the page, and click the orange Save and Publish button. You're returned to the Store Design window with a confirmation message that your theme has been saved to your account. You should see your theme reflected in the appropriate box.

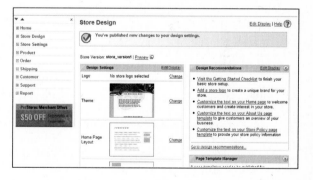

5. Next, upload a logo or create a logo for your Web store. If you already have a logo, click the Change link next to the Logo row on your Store Design screen in order to upload it onto your Web store. You'll see a page where you can click the Browse button and upload your logo file onto your account, or specify that you won't be using a logo for your store (you can always come back later to add a logo to your store, if you don't have one ready yet). If you don't have a logo, ProStores account holders can receive discounts from companies, like Logoworks or Logomaster, to have them design a logo for you. On the Store Design window, look for a promotional ad featuring savings on your logo creation. You can also get a logo for only $99 by going to LogoYes at www.logoyes.com.

6. After you decide your logo, you should decide how you want your home page layout to be set. Click the Change link next to Home Page Layout row on your Store Design screen. As of this writing, ProStores has to up to eight defined layouts for your home page. After you click the Change link, you see the eight defined layouts. The key is to read each layout description to see where the Welcome text and pictures will appear on your page, as well as the location (if any) of featured products and/or featured categories. You should have an idea of how many important categories you wish to promote in your store. It's advisable not to try and *sell* too much on the home page, but offer an avenue for people to dig deeper to find the product they want. If you know that your store has at least one hot product that makes up a lot of your sales, pick a home page layout that has at least one featured item and/or category. After you pick your Home Page Layout, click the Select button and scroll down to the bottom of the page to click the Save and Publish button. This saves your Home Page Layout to your ProStores account. You're then returned to the Store Design page.

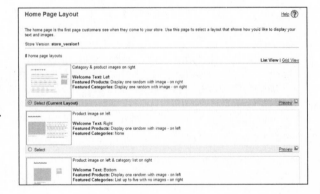

Product List Layout

Help ⑦

Product list pages appear when customers click product categories in your store navigation or use the Search feature to find a product. Use this page to select a layout that shows how you'd like to display your categories, products, or services.

Store Version: store_version1

11 product list layouts

List View | Grid View

Category image top and product images on left
Products grouped by category; category image at top
Product images on left; product names and descriptions on right
Prices at bottom; Add to Cart buttons at bottom

⊙ Select (Current Layout)   Preview ⬚

Product list with images
Products grouped by category; category image at top
Product images on left
Product names and descriptions on right
Prices underneath description; More Details and Add to Cart buttons underneath prices

○ Select   Preview ⬚

Product list with no images
Products grouped by category; category image at top
No product images
Product names and descriptions on left
Number in stock and prices on right; Add to Cart and Buy Now buttons underneath prices

7. Now look at your Product List Layout. Click the Change link next to that line item. When your customers browse through your product categories or search for something and see a resulting list of products, they see a list layout that you can specify in this step. The idea is to pick a layout that displays the right mix of product images, category images (if you have them), and product information. As of this writing, ProStores offers 11 different layout options, including 2- and 3-column approaches, a simple table, and even alternating images to fill the page appropriately. After you pick your product layout, click that Select button and scroll down to the bottom of the page to click the Save and Publish button. This saves your Product List Layout to your ProStores account and returns you to the Store Design page.

8. Finally, look at your Product Detail Layout. Click the Change link next to that line item. Now that you've decided how you want each product to look when shown as a list, it's time to pick a layout for when a customer is examining one particular product. Similar to the last step, you see a list of different product detail layouts. Currently, you have five different choices for Product Detail Layout, which offers you the ability to place the image to the left of the text, to the right of the text, above the text, or no image at all. After you pick your Product Detail Layout, click the Select button and scroll down to the bottom of the page to click the Save and Publish button.

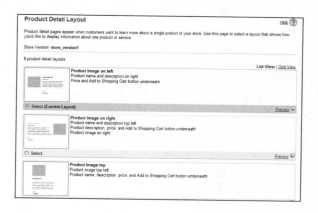

Product Detail Layout

Help ⑦

Product detail pages appear when customers want to learn more about a single product in your store. Use this page to select a layout that shows how you'd like to display information about one product or service.

Store Version: store_version1

5 product detail layouts

List View | Grid View

Product image on left
Product name and description on right
Price and Add to Shopping Cart button underneath

⊙ Select (Current Layout)   Preview ⬚

Product image on right
Product name and description top left
Product description, price, and Add to Shopping Cart button underneath
Product image on right

○ Select   Preview ⬚

Product image top
Product image top left
Product name, description, price, and Add to Shopping Cart button underneath

Product List Layout: Change

Product Detail Layout: Change

Fonts and Colors:
Page Title: "Trebuchet MS",
                 Small, black
Page Subtitle: "Trebuchet MS",   Change
                 Small, black
Paragraph: "Trebuchet MS",
                 Small, black

Page Text:
Home Page
About Us
Customer Service
Store Policy   Change
FAQ
Privacy Policy
Store Location

9. At this point, you've made decisions for all the options necessary to build your ProStores Store Design. You can always go into your Design settings by clicking the Go to Design Settings link on the Store Design window and making additional changes to your previous layout selections. Additionally, if you want to change your font selections or make text changes to your pages, click the Go to Design Settings link on the Store Design window, scroll down the page, and click the Change link for Fonts and Colors and/or Page Text.

Adding Categories to Your Store

Stuff You Need to Know

Toolbox:
- A list of product categories for your store

Time Needed:
10–15 minutes

When you create your account with ProStores, typically it assigns you one default product category, entitled New, to put your items into your store. In the Getting Started Checklist, it shows the Add Product Categories item as Complete. However, most of you will have multiple categories, and therefore, need to revisit this item before opening your Web store. Don't worry, adding multiple categories is easy!

1. Once you are done with your store design, from the left navigation bar, click the Home link. A new Getting Started sublink appears. Click the Getting Started link to bring up the store checklist. After you click the "Add Product Categories" link from the checklist, you see the Add Product Categories Wizard. From this screen, you can input your various categories and add them to your store account.

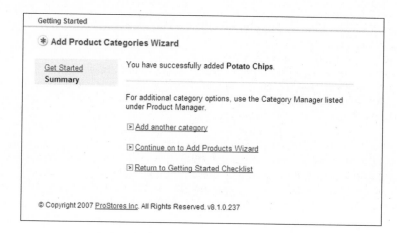

2. To add a basic category, simply type the name of the category in the Category Name box and click the Continue button. To add a major category with subcategories type the name of the category, a colon (:), the name of the subcategory in the Category Name box, and then click the Continue button. Regardless of whether you enter a category or a category with a subcategory, when you click Continue, you see a screen confirming your new category and asking you whether you want to Add Another Category, Continue On to Add Products Wizard, or Return to Getting Started Checklist. To create another category, click the Add Another Category link and repeat this step for each additional category you wish to add your store.

3. When you're finished adding the product categories for your Web store, click the Continue On to Add Products Wizard link and proceed to the next task.

TIP

When adding product categories, try to write your initial product category list before you click the Continue On to Add Products Wizard. This allows you to create an appropriate set of categories and subcategories. Although you can always go back and refine your category list later, creating a proper list first and maintaining it is easier.

Adding an Item to Your Catalog

If you've followed along so far, you've created the look and feel of your store and defined your categories. Now it's time to stock those shelves! Rather, it's time to add products to your catalog, so let's get started. You need to have your product photos and descriptions ready and available before starting this step. Otherwise, if you try to create this material while adding the item to your catalog, you'll waste a lot of time and perhaps create something incorrectly.

1. From the Getting Started Checklist, click the Add Products item to begin adding products to your store. If you clicked the Continue On to Add Products Wizard link in the last step of the previous task, you're taken to the same spot — the Add Product Wizard.

2. On the first screen of the Add Product Wizard, input the name of your product, any stock-keeping unit (SKU) number (optional), your sales price for the item, the quantity you have in stock, and whether you want this product visible to your customers and/or featured in your store. Click the Continue button when you're done. Here, you're defining the basic elements of your product for sale. Remember, don't put your cost, but rather the sales price you want to get for this product. You can use the UPC (Universal Product Code) or SKU that comes with your product, invent your own tracking system for your products, or leave the SKU field blank.

3. In the next screen, you're asked to create both a Brief Description and Long Description for your product. The Brief Description is used when customers are scanning a list of your products, whereas the Long Description is displayed when a customer is looking at the product detail page. If you only have one description to use, you can put it in both fields. However, your Brief Description should just have the basic info in a concise format. When you finish entering the descriptions, click the Continue button.

4. You now need to upload a photo (or photos) of your product for sale. ProStores asks for both a thumbnail (or small) photo and the regular photo image. In the Photo Image section, a Generate Thumbnail from Product Image check box (when checked) allows ProStores to generate a thumbnail photo for you based on the regular Photo Image that you upload. Therefore, if you don't have a thumbnail photo already, use this option to have it supplied automatically. If you do this, you're asked to create a small, medium, or large thumbnail. Any of these are fine, but take the default Medium if you're not sure. In order to upload either photo, click the Browse button to open a window that searches your computer for the photo. Navigate through your computer's directories until you find the product photo and then double-click the name, or click the name and then click the Open button. Click the Continue button after specifying your product photo locations. ProStores uses the information you specified and starts transferring the product photos from your computer to their Web site after you click Continue.

5. In the next screen (shown in the figure on the left), you need to assign a category for your product. Click the Continue button when you're done. Every time you create a new product, ProStores automatically assigns it to a New category so your customers can find the newly added merchandise to your store. However, you have the ability to assign the product to your own set of categories and even remove the item from New if you choose. Look through the list of categories you created (you did this in the previous task) and click the check box next to the category or subcategory where you wish to assign the item. Then click the Assign button to activate this designation. You see that the item is now assigned to both the New category and the subcategory you just assigned (shown in the figure on the right). Depending on how detailed your category structure is and the product you're adding, you may have several category designations for one product so your customers can find it easier.

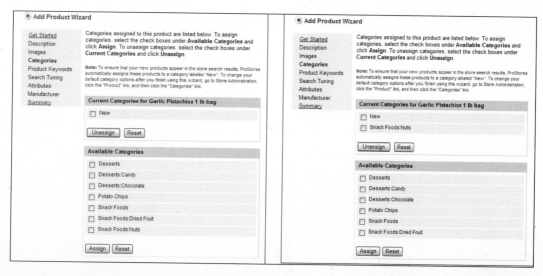

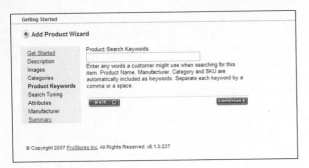

6. (Optional) Define Product Search Keywords to associate with your product. ProStores automatically defines your product name, manufacturer, category, and SKU as keywords for your product, but chances are your product for sale has additional keywords that customers use to find it, and you can define those words in this step. It's completely optional, so if there are no keywords, just click the Continue button and move on. After you define these words, simply put a space or comma between each keyword and click the Continue button when you're done.

7. In the next screen, define the keywords for your product that are sent to the search engines. In the previous step, we created keywords for your customers to find the product when they were on your Web site. Now, you're defining search terms that are used when people use the search engines to find your Web store. You can repeat the same keywords you used in the previous step or pick the keywords that most appeal to your customer market or are most desirable compared to other keywords for your product. For more information on how to optimize your products for the search engines and how to enter good values in this step, check out *Search Engine Optimization For Dummies,* 2nd Edition, by Peter Kent (Wiley Publishing, Inc.).

8. Create up to two attributes for your product. Think of *attributes* as something about your product that can be different for different users. For T-shirts, size is an attribute; so you can have small, medium, large, extra large, and so on. Instead of defining each specific item in the catalog (small T-shirt, medium T-shirt), you simply define the product and then define the attributes so customers can pick a product and the specific attributes they need. If your products don't have any attributes, meaning there is only one version of the product you defined, simply leave this entire screen blank. When you're done, click the Continue button.

9. In the last input screen (shown in the figure on the left), you can assign a manufacturer to your product. When you open your ProStores account, your Manufacturer list is empty, so you probably see only one option in the drop-down list: None. You have to add a manufacturer before you can assign it to your product. Therefore, click the Add a Manufacturer radio button and then click the Continue button. You're taken to a screen (shown in the figure on the right) where you can input your manufacturer name and, optionally, the manufacturer's Web site. After you do that, click the Continue button to save the manufacturer. You're taken back to the previous input screen, but this time the drop-down list has the manufacturer name you just created. Pick the manufacturer name and then click the Continue button to go to the Summary screen.

10. You have now successfully added your product to your catalog, and you should see a confirmation screen. You should see the Product Name and some of the summary details on this screen. From this point, you can click the Add another Product link and repeat the steps to add more products to your catalog; you can click the Continue On to Payment Preferences Wizard link to go to the next step of the store creation process; or you can click the Return to Getting Started Checklist link to go back to the Checklist and go over your steps so far.

Completing the Getting Started Checklist

You have just completed the first four of the five required items for opening your store on ProStores. The fifth item — Choose Payment Options — was partially handled when you opened your account, if you specified a PayPal account that accepts credit cards for your store. However, you should revisit this step, especially if you have a Merchant credit card account that you want to handle your online customer credit card payments.

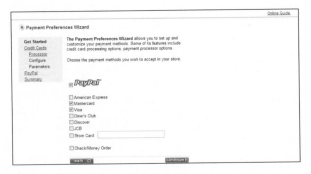

1. Click the Choose Payment Options link from the Getting Started Checklist. You're taken to the Payment Preferences Wizard. If you clicked the Continue On to Payment Preferences Wizard link in the last step of the previous task, you're taken directly to the Payment Preferences Wizard. If you specified PayPal as a payment option when you created your account, you should see the PayPal, Visa, and MasterCard check boxes marked. If you plan on taking additional credit cards, check the appropriate boxes. Additionally, if you plan on letting your customers mail in checks or money orders, be sure to check the Check/Money Order check box, so your customers will have that opportunity in the checkout process. After you make your selections, click the Continue button.

2. Decide which credit card options you want applied to your store. There are several options you can apply as rules when you accept credit cards in your store. For example, you can require the customer to provide credit card information and choose to keep that information after the order is processed. You can further specify whether the customer has to reside in the same country as your store or whether the customer must give you a phone number upon checkout. After you pick your options, click the Continue button.

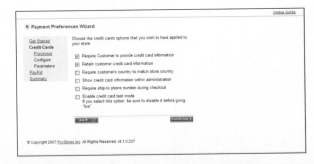

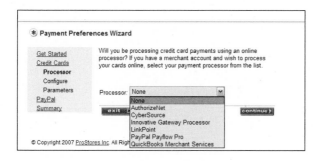

3. If you have a Merchant account, pick your Gateway processor and click the Continue button. If you plan on using your Merchant account, pick your Gateway processor from the list provided. If you have a Merchant account, you're asked to specify whether you use a Host or Terminal to process your credit cards, and whether your customers get Immediate fulfillment (like with a digital download product or a subscription) or Future Fulfillment (when you ship physical products). Finally, you're asked for the Partner Name, your Merchant ID, and Merchant password for accessing your Merchant account. If you're not planning on using a Merchant account, simply pick None from the list and click the Continue button.

4. If you're offering PayPal as your payment processor (even if you're offering others as well), specify your PayPal address. In this step, you're asked for your PayPal e-mail address, which is used to deposit money into your PayPal account when a customer uses PayPal. Make sure the e-mail address specified is the one you use (or plan to use) for PayPal. When you're finished, click the Continue button.

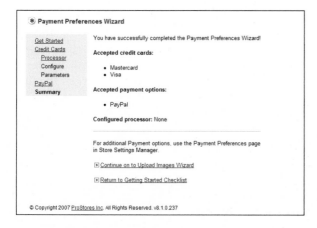

5. Review your specified Payment Preference options before moving onto the next phase. You should see a confirmation/detail screen based on your selections so far. Make sure that everything is accurate. When you're ready, you can either click the Continue On to Upload Images Wizard link or the Return to Getting Started Checklist link. For this book's purposes, click the Return to Getting Started Checklist link.

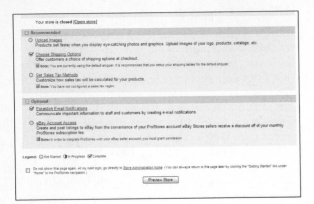

6. You have now completed the Required section of the Getting Started Checklist. Several items are still in the Recommended and Optional sections. Therefore, I go through some of these items, as most of you need to complete them.

7. When you're ready to upload pictures to your Web site, click the Upload Images item in the Recommended section. You're asked which images you want to upload to your Web store. Pick the type of image you want to upload and click the Continue button.

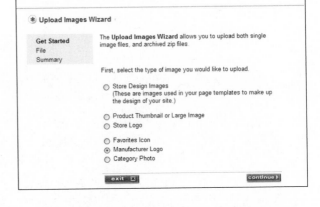

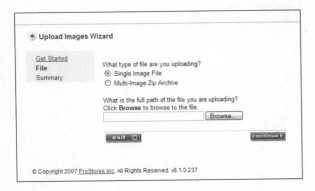

8. You need to specify whether you're uploading a Zip file that contains multiple pictures, or a single picture file. Then, you specify the image (or Zip file) location on your computer so ProStores can upload it. You see a screen where you can specify the type of file you're uploading, and by clicking the Browse button, specify the exact directory on your computer where the file is located. Click the Continue button to upload the file to your ProStores account.

9. If you have any other images you need to send to your Web site, repeat Steps 7 and 8 by clicking the Upload another Image link. You can always go back later through the Support Manager and upload more images or pictures to your Web site, but you should definitely upload any logos, product photos, or category/manufacturer logos that you already have.

When uploading pictures to your Web site, if you picked a Product List Layout that involves Category photos, be sure to upload category photos in this step.

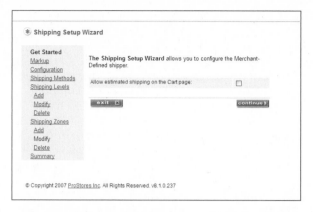

10. From the image confirmation screen (or the Getting Started Checklist), you can click the Shipping Preferences link to set your shipping preferences. You're taken to the Shipping Setup Wizard. The first question they have for you is whether you want estimated shipping to show up on your shopping cart. If you want this option, check the box indicated. After you decide, click the Continue button.

11. Define how much mark-up you want to add to your shipping price. *Mark-Up* is another word for the handling charge necessary for you to process your customer orders. Typically, this amount is meant to cover the amount of supplies (boxes, packing supplies, tape, and so on) necessary for an average customer order as well as the labor required to prepare and ship an order, whether it's by you or someone you hire. When you look at this screen, you have a few options. You can add $0.00 mark-up, assign a percentage of the order as mark-up, or create a fixed dollar amount mark-up regardless of order size. After you decide on your mark-up amount, click the Continue button.

12. Define how your shipping costs are calculated based on the order and customer address. ProStores offers you several ways to calculate the shipping charges based on a customer order. As you can see, you can set your shipping basis on either the Total Order Amount, Total Order Weight, or *Total Item Count* (number of items ordered). If you're inputting weights of each product, it's highly recommended to base your shipping charge on the actual weight of the order. If the products are light and/or uniform weight, you can probably calculate shipping based on Total Item Count. If you only want your customers to pay a percentage of their order in shipping or you wish to help subsidize their shipping based on their order size, select Total Order Amount. In addition, you're asked whether your shipping should be calculated based on the State/Province and/or Country of your customer, or the Postal Code (ZIP code) Range or Country of your customer. For more exacting numbers, it's recommended to select Postal Code Range or Country option.

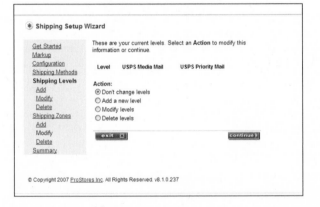

13. Define your actual shipping methods and give them a name. You're asked to define how many different shipping methods you'll offer your customers. Additionally, you're asked to give names to your shipping methods. Many stores use this opportunity to remind people of the shipping company they use. For example, a merchant may label Standard as USPS Media Mail 4–14 Days to remind their customers that if they pick Standard shipping, it can take up to 2 weeks for delivery. You have to define at least one shipping method among Standard, Two Day, and Next Day, but you don't have to offer all three. Each shipping method title can be only 25 characters or fewer. You can also offer a Will Call or Local Pickup option to your customers, if you wish. To add this as an option, select the Will Call check box and give that shipping method title a descriptive name, like Local Pickup or Local Delivery/Pickup to signify that the order isn't handled through the mail. Click the Continue button after making your selections.

14. Confirm the shipping methods you've created. You're shown a summary of the shipping method levels you just created. At this phase, under the Shipping Levels section on the left side of the screen, you can click the links to add, modify, or delete a method. After you're satisfied with the shipping levels you created, make sure the Don't Change Levels radio button is selected and click the Continue button.

15. Set up your Shipping Zones. When you set up your ProStores account, it sets up one default shipping zone as All Countries, with ZIP codes 00000 through 99999. You should see the screen, like the one in the figure on the left, where you can add zones, modify existing zones, or delete zones. In order to modify the default shipping zone, select Modify and click the Continue button. Then, you're taken to a screen like the one in the figure on the right, where you can give a name to your shipping zone, define the country of your zone, and pick the postal code range of that zone. After you fill in all the fields, click the Continue button to save your zone. After you're done with setting up your shipping zones, select the Don't Make Any Changes option and click the Continue button to finalize your shipping setup.

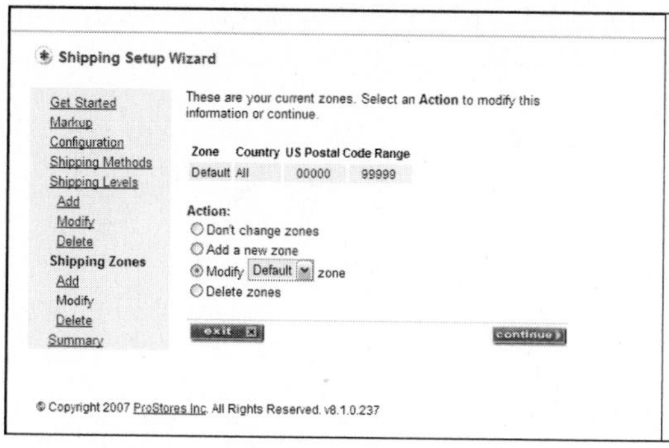

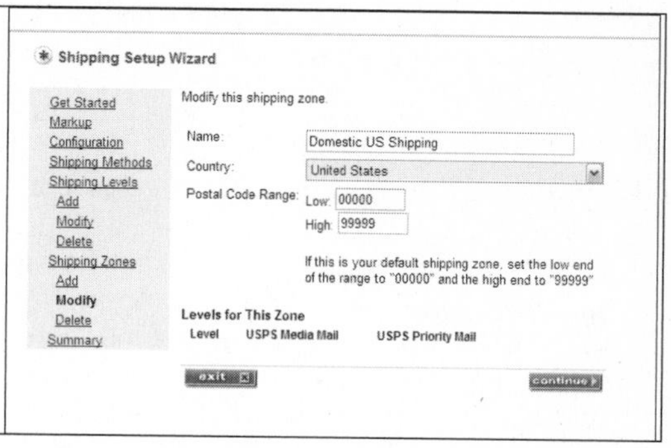

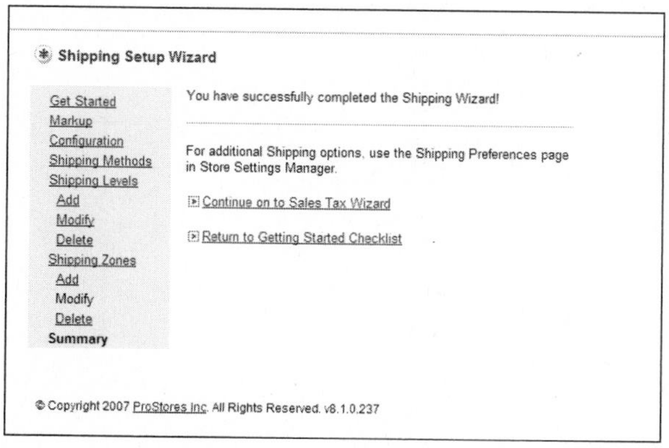

16. If you've followed along so far, you've now completed the Shipping Preferences Wizard. It's time to set up your Sales Tax Wizard. Click the Continue On to Sales Tax Wizard link to quickly set up your sales tax information. As of this writing, you currently don't have to collect sales tax from any customers who live either outside a state you do business in or outside the country where you do business. Therefore, you have to collect sales tax only from customers who live in the same state as your business, which is what I set up here.

17. Your first step in the Sales Tax Wizard is to pick a calculator. Currently, your only option is the ProStores calculator. Leave the selected one, ProStores, highlighted and click the Continue button.

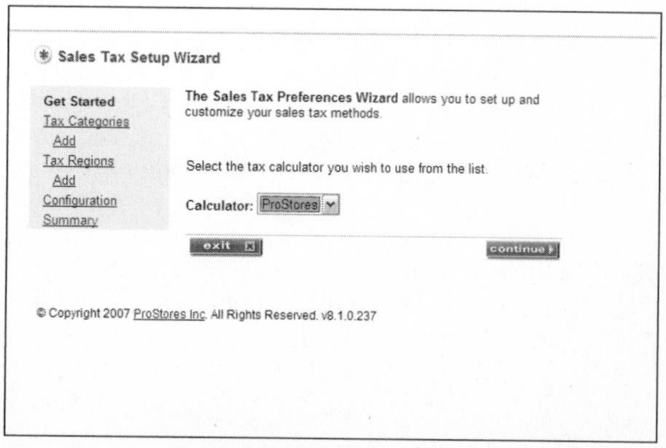

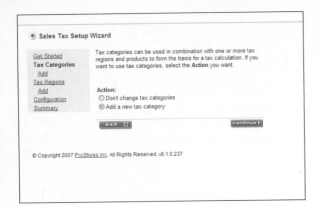

18. Establish any tax categories. Decide whether you have to set up special tax categories for your products. If you have some products that are taxable and others that are not taxable, click the Add a New Tax Category radio button and type a label on the next screen to signify the different tax categories that represent your products. If all your products fall into one category or none of your products are taxable, make sure the Don't Change Tax Categories radio button is selected. Click the Continue button to move on.

19. Next, you have to create a tax region, where you're required to collect sales tax. Go ahead and click the Add a New Tax Region radio button, as shown in the figure on the left. You're taken to a screen, like the one in the figure on the right, where you put in information about your state and fill in the tax rate for your specific state, county, district, or city in the boxes provided. If your business has locations or operations in more than one state, one county, or one city, create a unique tax zone for each location because you're required to collect sales tax for areas where you're doing business. When you're done creating tax regions, pick the Don't Change Tax Regions option and click the Continue button.

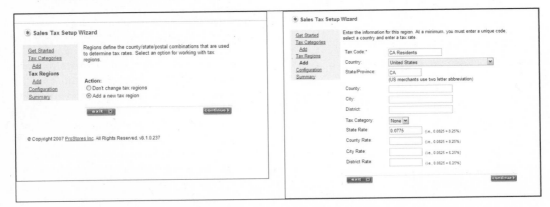

20. ProStores asks if you want to calculate tax based on where the package is going instead of the customer billing address. For most Web stores, the transaction is technically occurring between your base of operations and where your online order is going, not necessarily the billing address of your customer. Therefore, if you don't want to collect tax on any in-state customers who are shipping their order out of state, check the Use the Ship-To Address to Calculate Tax, Instead of the Billing Address check box and click the Continue button.

The Open Store link

21. You've now completed the Sales Tax Preferences Wizard — you've completed all the Required and Recommended items for opening your store. There are some Optional items about e-mail preferences and linking your store with your eBay account ID, but you can peruse those at your own pace. When you're ready to open your store for business, click the Open Store link. You're either taken back to the Getting Started Checklist, where it now says Your Store is Open: [Close Store for Maintenance], or you're taken to your ProStores home page. You did it! Of course, you still need to add more products, make sure your store is exactly the way you want it to look, and most importantly, market your store as much as possible.

Chapter 6

1&1 eShops

Tasks performed in this chapter

✔ Reviewing the features and benefits 1&1 offers

✔ Creating an e-commerce account with 1&1 eShops

✔ Designing your Web store using pre-defined templates

✔ Defining your catalog items

✔ Completing the 1&1 checklist to open your store

The final Web store I create involves a well-focused and low-cost provider of different Web hosting packages, namely 1&1. Specifically, it's 1&1 eShops (`http://order.1and1.com`, as shown in Figure 6-1) that offers different e-commerce solutions based on the size and sales volume of the store you wish to create. They've been in business for a while now and have created several levels of storefronts that have the basic elements as well as some pre-programmed templates you can use to instantly construct a solid store design and the additional functionality, reports, and e-mail marketing tools that 1&1 can offer its customers based on their size and expertise.

1&1 is an excellent example of an *à la carte* provider, where you simply pay only for the elements you need and for each additional feature that you plan on using. 1&1 offers Web hosting packages as low as a few dollars a month, represents over six million users, and has now become the world's biggest Web host. Because of the variety of packages that they offer, 1&1 can provide the right package for any skill set or budget.

They also partner with the world's leading companies as well; 1&1 is an official Microsoft Joint Development Partner as well as a partner with Google, HP/Compaq, Symantec, and Plesk.

In this chapter, I start from the beginning: You sign up for a 1&1 eShops account, configure the account for your new store, pick a store design, add at least one inventory item, and complete 1&1's handy checklist for opening a Web store.

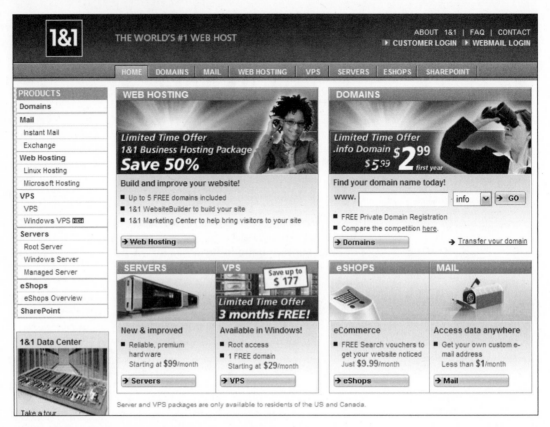

Figure 6-1: 1&1 offers a lot of Web hosting options.

Why 1&1 eShops?

Before you get into the step-by-step instructions, I talk about some of the benefits that a 1&1 eShops storefront can provide you. Look over the qualities of their accounts, based on the discussion in Chapter 3 and how they apply to you:

✔ **Shopping Cart technology — Check!**

• You can add anywhere from 50 to an almost unlimited number of products to the shopping cart, including information products for digital download.

• You can manage anywhere from 20 to an unlimited number of product categories if you have a Professional or Developer eShop (see the next section, "1&1 eShops' Plan Types").

• Customer information is stored in your system based on your Customer ID.

- 1&1 eShops integrates with PayPal or your own merchant account (via WorldPay) with no additional gateway fee, and built-in verification tools are provided to double-check the customer's payment information.

- Orders can be transmitted via e-mail, and you can import and export items via a *Comma Separated Values file (CSV)* — a regular text file where each line in the file represents an item for sale, with the item data values separated by a comma.

✔ **Disk space and bandwidth — Check!**

- Each 1&1 eShop comes with at least 50–1200 MB of disk space per store, which is enough for thousands of product pictures and descriptions.

- The 10–60 GB data transfer limit means that thousands of visitors can be browsing your Web store at the same time!

- 1&1 has the capability to add extra disk space, bandwidth, or data transfer whenever needed for an additional fee.

✔ **E-mail accounts — Check!**

- 1&1 offers each store owner anywhere from 5 to 20 unique e-mail addresses, and the ability to create up to 200 unique e-mail aliases — temporary e-mail names that forward mail into one of your established unique e-mail addresses.

- All your e-mail accounts have a limit of 1–2 GB, depending on the size of your store.

- Your employees can access their e-mail through a *POP (Post Office Protocol)* or *SMTP (Simple Mail Transfer Protocol)* service, or through 1&1's WebMail service.

✔ **Programming extensions — Check!**

- 1&1 supports Adobe Dreamweaver, Adobe GoLive, and Microsoft FrontPage to help you build custom Web stores, as well as a special Dreamweaver Extension that works directly with your stored product information.

- 1&1 has built-in support for programming languages and databases, like Perl, PHP, and MySQL.

- 1&1 has dozens of templates available and has access to third-party providers to help you build any additional functionality that you need or want.

✔ **Application integration — Check!**

- 1&1 has a built-in exporting tool to send transaction information to QuickBooks for your accountant.

- 1&1 can integrate with Fotolia to integrate Fotolia's stock photos into your Web site.

- 1&1 offers their customers access to the entire Norton Internet Security suite, including AntiVirus, Personal Firewall, AntiSpyware, AntiSpam, and Privacy Control.

- 1&1 works with PayPal and WorldPay to coordinate payments going into your credit card Merchant account.

✔ **Additional features — Check!**

- 1&1 has a Marketing Center with credit for you to use Microsoft adCenter, Google AdWords, Yahoo! Search Marketing, and CitySearch. In addition, they provide a Simple Submission tool and access to Google Webmaster tools.

- 1&1 offers a login for Registered Customers, as well as a Customer Administration feature and an E-mail Newsletter tool.

- 1&1 offers a Tax Clearing server for its Professional and Developer eShops.

✔ **Security, reliability, and service — Check!**

- 1&1 supports Proxy Secure Socket Layer (SSL) technology with 128-bit encryption to keep your customers' information private.

- 1&1 has customizable risk tools to help you identify fraud in your orders before the products are shipped and to help keep out unwanted visitors from bringing down your Web store.

- 1&1 reports that their servers have 99.99 percent uptime for their store servers — their stores are almost always on and available!

- 1&1 backs up your Web store automatically every day (locally and at a remote site) and allows you to easily switch between older and newer versions of your account. If you accidentally lose data, 1&1 can help you restore the most recent version quickly.

- 1&1 has a 24/7 toll-free phone (1-877-435-7281) and an e-mail support hotline (available through your Admin screen at `https://admin.1and1.com`).

- 1&1 has built an extensive online Help section with a Getting Started Guide, plus built-in tutorials on basic and advanced topics.

1&1 eShops' Plan Types

1&1 offers three basic plans. You can see a comparison of features among these three packages by going to their eShops overview at `http://order.1and1.com/xml/order/EshopsTariff` (as shown in Figure 6-2).

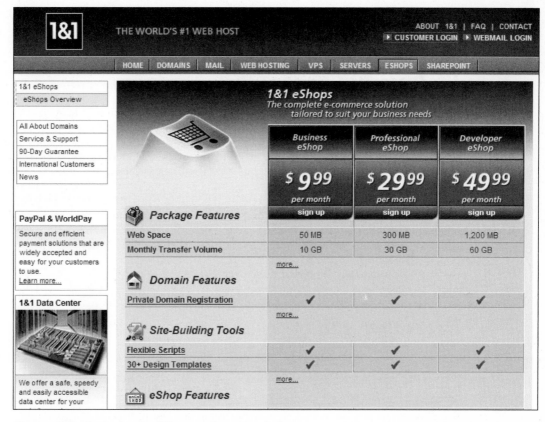

Figure 6-2: Reviewing the different options of each plan.

Business eShop

This package is designed for the beginning Web merchant and offers a solid set of features and capabilities to get anyone started, at an affordable price. You're set up with 50 MB of Web space and 10 GB monthly transfer rate, easy access to the 1&1 Control Panel to access your account, as well as a range of domain and hosting tools, design templates, scripts, stock photos through Fotolia, the ability to add to the Froogle product search, and e-mail and marketing capabilities.

This basic package runs $9.99 per month, plus the transaction cost associated with processing credit card orders, typically a percentage of the order.

Professional eShop

This package is designed for the Web store owner that is looking to add more functionality and capability beyond a traditional Web store. This package offers 300 MB of Web space and 30 GB monthly transfer rate, gives the store owner the capability to create up to 20 of his or her own product categories, offers a product search, and imports and exports his or her inventory via text files. Professional eShop owners have more payment-processing choices and access to a Tax Clearing server as well as built-in support for multiple currencies. They also get features for logging and registering their customers who visit their Web store, and a handy newsletter tool for keeping in touch regularly with their customers.

This package runs $29.99 per month, plus the transaction cost associated with processing credit card orders, typically a percentage of the order.

Developer eShop

This package is designed for the Web store owner who wants to offer some leading-edge functions to constantly stay in touch with her customers and provide a very specific experience for her store. Not only do these store owners get 1,200 MB of Web space and 60 GB monthly transfer rate, but they can create their own subdomains within their site, enjoy FTP access to their account, have full customization available when building their site, and can create automatic invoice and customer numbers. Developer eShops can offer *In2site Live Dialogue,* which monitors your customer's activities and offers instant pop-up windows to communicate with visitors while they're visiting your site as well as pre-programmed greetings. Finally, Developer eShops can offer flexible shipping calculations and group-specific discounts to their Web store customers.

This package runs $49.99 per month, plus the transaction cost associated with processing credit card orders, typically a percentage of the order.

Signing Up with 1&1 eShops

Stuff You Need to Know

Toolbox:
- An idea for your Web store domain name
- Business contact information
- Business credit card

Time Needed:
20–30 minutes

When you want to sign up for an account, click the eShops button along the Navigation bar of 1&1's home page. You're taken to their comparison of features screen (refer to Figure 6-2). For the purpose of this chapter, I sign up for a 1&1 Business eShop.

1. Click the appropriate blue Sign Up button in the column of the specific package you want (remember, for this example, I use a Business eShop package). You're taken to the first part of the Order process, appropriately dubbed *Start*. Because of their arrangement with various software companies, 1&1 can offer a premium software suite to their eShop owners for free, and the customer pays only for the shipping and handling cost. Read through the details of the Special Gift screen to see if this package interests you, but be aware that you have to sign a one year contract with 1&1 to get this package. Additionally, you can sign up for Norton Internet Security online for a reduced rate after a complimentary trial period.

2. After you decide about your special gifts, click Continue to go to the next step, Choose a Domain. Here, you're asked to pick your specific domain name, as shown in the figure on the left. This is the specific domain name that your customers use to access your Web store. If you already reserved your domain name, as I discuss in Chapter 3, you can click the Domain Names link to follow the instructions on transferring your domain name information so that it points to your 1&1 eShop. If the domain name you enter isn't available, 1&1 prompts you with similar domain names that are available. After you find a domain name that you like or you finish setting up the transfer, click the Continue button, as shown in the figure on the right, to move onto the next step.

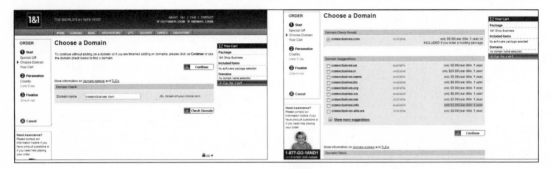

3. On the Your Cart screen, review the billing information for ordering your new eShop account. 1&1 has a six-month billing cycle for their Business eShop customers — you have to pay for six months service at a time. The Professional and Developer eShop customers pay for three months service at a time. Also review all the domain names you've signed up for and pay that appropriate amount as well. When you're satisfied that the bill is correct and you don't want to add any more domain names to your account, click the Continue button to go to the next step.

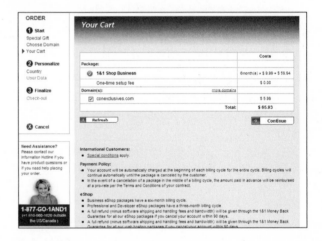

When reviewing the billing information for your new eShop account, 1&1 offers a 90-day money back guarantee. If you cancel your account during the first 90 days, they provide a full refund even if you paid for one full billing cycle.

4. In the second part of their process (dubbed *Personalize*), 1&1 needs to collect your data, starting with the country where you reside. On the Your Country screen, pick the appropriate radio button for your country of residence or, if your country isn't on the list, pick the Other Country option and choose from the drop-down list provided. When you're done, click the Continue button to go to the next step.

5. On the Enter Address screen, 1&1 needs to collect your user data. Fill in all the fields as prompted. If you're already a 1&1 customer, select the Yes radio button for the first question so they can access your account and get the information. If you're not already a 1&1 customer, complete all the fields marked with an asterisk (*) and, optionally, complete any extra fields that apply to your business. After you do that, you need to decide if you want the address you just entered to be part of the registration for your domain name. If you're paying for private registration, you don't need to worry about this step. Otherwise, 1&1 uses the address you provided when they register your domain on your behalf unless you provide new contact data that will be used to register your domain. After you've decided what contact data you want on your domain registration (if any), scroll down and click Continue to go to the next step.

6. In the Enter Password screen, create your password for your 1&1 eShop account. Your Customer ID is generated automatically by 1&1 when you complete your order, so please leave that field alone. You're asked to enter your password twice in the boxes provided. Your password must be at least 7 characters long but no longer than 18 characters. You want to create a password that you can remember but not something that other people can guess. Avoid names of people, pets, or nicknames that you or others use, and try to use a combination of letters and numbers.

7. On the next screen, Referral, 1&1 wants to know how you were referred to their organization. They provide you with a drop-down list of options where you could have heard of 1&1, based on their advertising and media coverage. Pick the appropriate option (this is a mandatory step, so you need to pick something) and click Continue to go to the next step.

8. In the last step of the Personalize part, 1&1 needs your payment information. On the Payment Method screen, enter either your credit card or PayPal information in the boxes provided. If using a debit/credit card, fill in the information in the Credit or Debit Card Details section. After you do that, in the Credit Card Billing Address section, use the drop-down list to select Other Address if your credit card billing address is different from the address you provided on the Enter Address screen. If the address you provided is valid for your credit card, leave the information as-is and click the Continue button to process the payment.

9. After your payment is processed, you're redirected to the Check Out screen to review and finalize your eShop account creation. The Check Out screen is the only step in the final part of the order process, which is appropriately dubbed *Finalize*. Look over the account information that you filled in as well as the address and payment information provided. Scroll down and review the general terms and conditions for creating your 1&1 account. Select the check box to say that you agree with the terms and conditions. After you're ready to process your order, click the Order Now button.

10. You're taken to the Thank You confirmation screen to confirm your new order. 1&1 sends you a confirmation e-mail with information on your new Customer ID and the password you created.

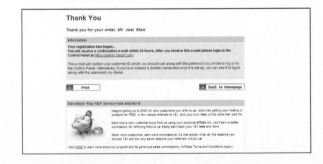

E-mail link

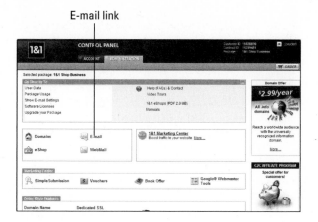

11. Go to `https://admin.1and1.com` to log in to the 1&1 Control Panel to start configuring your store. You can either wait for the confirmation e-mail to use your Customer ID to log in, or you can enter your chosen domain name and the password you created to log in to the Control Panel. When you do that, you're taken to the Control Panel. Before you start configuring your store, however, you need to create at least one valid e-mail address to associate with your store. Click the E-mail link from the Control Panel to establish your e-mail account.

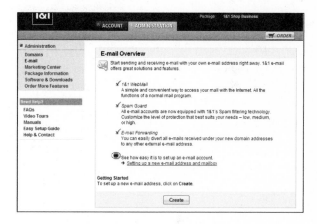

12. On the E-mail Overview screen, you can create multiple accounts and/or aliases, which can point to any e-mail address. Click the Create button at the bottom of the page to get started.

13. Use the E-mail Address screen to set up your main e-mail account for your Web store by completing the required fields. This is where you establish where all the incoming mail for your Web store goes, whether it's a regular e-mail mailbox or an existing e-mail mailbox where all your mail is forwarded. Create a name for your e-mail address in the box provided and then specify below that field whether you want a mailbox for that name or whether you want to forward all your e-mail to another account away from your 1&1 Web store account. After you're done setting this up, click OK to continue.

You need to allow up to 24 hours before trying to configure your eShop account, as 1&1 first needs to create a name server entry for your Web store to be functional.

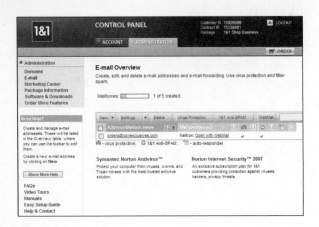

14. You have now set up your e-mail address. Click the Go to Overview button to see your requested e-mail address. On the E-mail Overview screen, you can see your newly created account and have access to add more accounts. Your limit is based on the package to which you subscribe, but you're prompted with the correct number of available accounts.

15. Click the Administration tab to go back and view your eShop Control Panel. Congratulations! You have now gone through the entire sign-up process to set up your account with 1&1 Solutions.

Creating Your Store Design

Stuff You Need to Know

Toolbox:
- An idea of your Web store design goals
- Business contact information

Time Needed:
20–30 minutes

After your account has been set up and you've gotten your confirmation e-mails, it's time to go into your eShop Administration screen to begin configuring your store design and get ready to open for business!

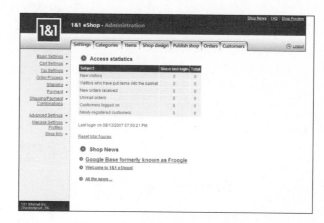

1. Log in to your 1&1 Control Panel and click the eShop button to go to the 1&1 eShop Administration screen. When you first go into your eShop administration, you may see an intermediate screen that says your eShop is ready and to click a button to launch the eShop. If you click the button to launch the eShop, you'll end up at the Administration screen. The Administration screen is organized into several tabs along the top of it and specific navigation for each tab, which is found along the left side of the screen.

2. Click the Basic Settings link on the left side of the screen to start the Basic Settings Wizard and define the general information for your Web store. In the Basic Settings window, complete the required fields to define the information you want listed with your online store. When you're done, click the Next button to continue.

3. Next, enter the contact information for customers to reach you through your Web store. 1&1 publishes the contact information you provide in this step in the form of an e-mail address, phone number, and/or fax number that you input into the various boxes. You need to complete at least one of these fields and you can choose to complete as many as you want. Click the Next button when you're done.

4. Next, you're asked to define how you want your customer and invoice numbers to be automatically generated. Using a 1&1 eShop, the software automatically creates unique customer identification numbers as well as invoice numbers, based on a scheme you create in this step. You're asked to create a prefix, a beginning number, and a suffix that combines into unique customer and invoice numbers. You can simply accept the defaults that are given or create your own system. When you're done, click the Next button to continue.

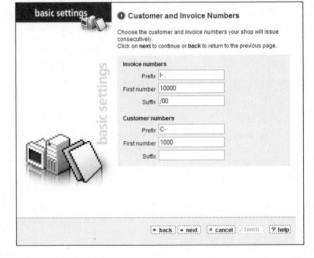

5. Next, you're asked whether you want your store products automatically sent into Google's system for comparing products online, codenamed Froogle or Google Base. You're prompted with information about Google's service for people who are searching for products online. This step is designed to get your permission to have your store products automatically fed into this engine or not. This service is getting a lot of exposure from Google and can be an excellent way to gain new customers. Please note, however, that your store will be grouped with other stores carrying the same product, and customers can sort by elements, like lowest price. You can follow the links on this screen to read more about the service. After you decide whether to participate, pick the appropriate option and click Next to continue.

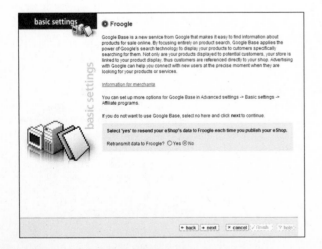

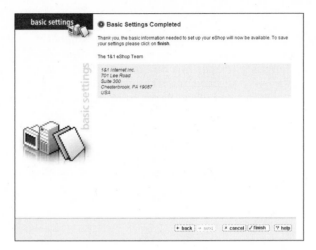

6. You've now completed the Basic Settings Wizard. Click the Finish button to store your answers. You should see a completion screen — be sure to write down 1&1's address if you want to write them about any follow-up issues.

7. Now you're ready to pick a store design. Click the Shop Design tab along the top of the Administration screen to get started. You're taken to the Shop Design window. From here, you can select and then adapt a shop design as well as create templates that will apply to the rest of your store.

8. Click the Select Shop Design link on the left side of the screen to pick your eShop design. This opens the Shop Design Wizard on your screen. You're presented with various design templates (38 at the time of this writing), and for each template, you'll see a Yes or No answer as to whether category images are shown on the screen. Use the Back or Next buttons to cycle through the list or use the drop-down list to go straight to a specific template. You can choose which design you like by clicking the Save button when you see the design of your choice. This brings up a confirmation screen that your template has been saved, and you can click the Close button to close the wizard and bring you back to the Shop Design Administration screen.

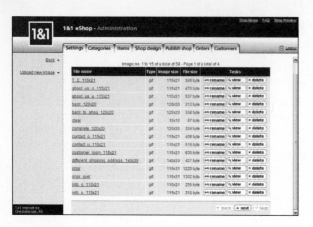

9. If you want to change any of the buttons of the predesigned template, click the Manage Template Images link on the left side of the screen to replace or add images. You're taken to a screen filled with images from the shop design you just selected. For each image, you can click the View button to see that particular graphic or click the Rename button to give that image a different name. If you don't want a specific graphic in your shop design, click the Delete button next to that image.

10. Your store design is complete. You can preview your eShop by clicking the Publish Shop tab and selecting Shop Preview.

Adding an Item to Your Catalog

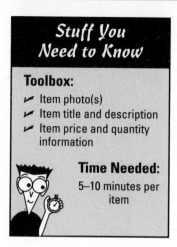
Now that you've created your store design, its time to add the products for sale to your Web store. For each item you wish to sell, gather the photo(s) for your product and a concise description for each item.

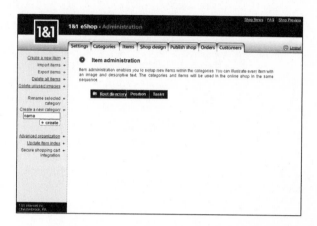

1. Click the Items tab on the main Administration window to get started. You see the Items Administration screen. From here, you can add new items to your catalog, delete old products, and organize how your items are displayed.

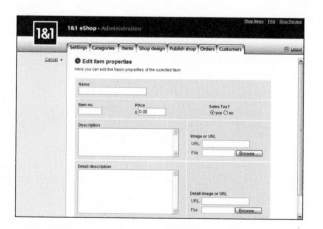

2. Click the Create a New Item link on the left side of the screen to input a product for sale. This link opens the Item Wizard. You need to input the Item Name, Item No., Price, a (short) Description, a Detailed Description, and whether the item qualifies for sales tax. For the basic and detailed descriptions, you can either provide a URL Web address where the accompanying graphic is located or use the Browse button to attach a specific file to act as the graphic. Remember, use a thumbnail picture for the description picture, and a regular- or large-sized graphic for the detailed description.

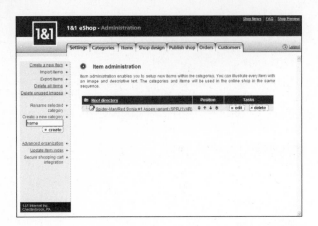

3. When all the fields are completed, scroll down and click the Finish button to save your item to your catalog. If you want to alter the templates that are used for a specific item or you want to hide the item so it isn't immediately displayed in your store, click the Next button instead of the Save button to edit these advanced settings. Otherwise, by clicking Finish, you go back to the Item Administration window where your newly created product is now sitting on the list. After you add additional items, you can use the up and down arrows next to the item description to raise or lower (respectively) an item's position on your store screen.

4. Repeat Steps 2 and 3 to add additional products to your store. If you plan on adding a lot of items at one time to your store and you have a Professional or Developer eShop package, you can click the Import Items link and send 1&1 a file of all the products you want to upload into your store. This is done by creating a *Comma Separated Values (CSV)* text file, which can be created by saving as a CSV file from a spreadsheet program, like Microsoft Excel.

When viewing your store items in the Item Administration window, the double arrow up or the double arrow down means that you'll move the specified item to either the very top or very bottom (respectively) of your directory structure.

Publishing Your 1&1 eShop

After you add your initial set of products that you plan on selling, you would click the Publish Shop tab on the main Administration window to turn on your store for business. First, however, thoroughly go through the Settings tab and make sure that everything is configured before you open your Web store to the public.

1. Click the Settings tab on the Administration page and then click the Cart Settings link on the left side of the screen, which opens the Cart Settings Wizard. The first step in this process is to format your Main Currency Settings. The default settings are based on the country you selected in the registration process, but you can change any of the fields if necessary. If you have a Professional or Developer eShop and you plan on supporting multiple currencies, click the Next button and set up your secondary currency settings. Otherwise, click the Finish button to save your settings.

2. Click the Tax Settings link on the left side of the screen to open the Tax Settings Wizard. Here, choose a service that helps you apply sales tax to any applicable customer orders. For Professional and Developer eShops, you can pick the Tax Clearing server to figure out the appropriate taxes for customer orders. Otherwise, you can pick the manual state-/province-based tax service. Pick your state or province from a list provided by 1&1 and then enter the tax rate for each state or province where you physically do business in the last screen. If your shipping and handling costs are more than the actual postage costs, the government states that you should tax the shipping fees as well. Note, however, that this does *not* apply if you live in California, Minnesota, or Ohio. If you do business in more than one state or province, repeat this step for each location where your business has a physical presence. When you're done, click the Finish button to save your work.

3. Click the Order Process link on the left side of the screen to open the Order Process Wizard. The first part of this process asks you what fields of information you want the customer to provide when he's ordering, for his invoice address. First, check the boxes of the fields you want shown on the screen. Then, check the boxes for the fields you want the customer to be required to enter. When you're done with this, decide if you want your customers to be able to give a separate shipping address from their billing address. After you decide that, click the Next button to go to the next step. If you decide that a separate shipping address is okay, in the next screen, pick the fields of information and required fields for the shipping address, not the invoice address. Click the Next button to go to the next step when you're done.

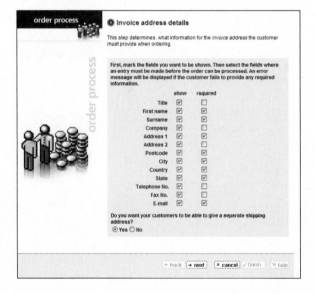

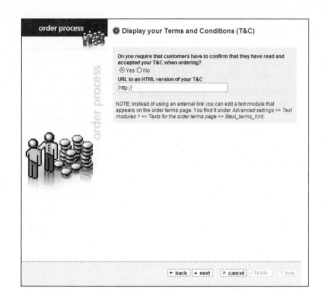

4. (Optional) Next, 1&1 asks if you want to display any Terms and Conditions to your customers when they order. You'll see a screen where you can link to a special Web page outlining your Terms and Conditions, if you want to enforce that your customers have to read those Terms and Conditions before their order gets placed with you. This is optional, but if you select this option, 1&1 will make sure your customers at least see this external page and click OK before their order gets through to you. Click the Next button to go to the next step.

5. Next, 1&1 asks you to format the e-mail your customers will receive when they place an order with you. You see a screen asking you whether to send an automatic order confirmation e-mail to your customers after they place an order in your Web store. If you select Yes, you can format the title, the first, and the last part of the e-mail, with a copy of their order automatically inserted into the middle of the e-mail. When you've finished setting up this message the way you want, click the Next button to go to the next step.

6. Next, 1&1 asks you to format the e-mail you'd receive when a customer places an order with you. This time, you're deciding whether you want the system to e-mail you, the *merchant,* when an order comes through. If you select Yes, you need to format the title, the first, and the last part of that particular e-mail as well. When you've made your decision here, click the Finish button to save your work and exit this phase of the setup process.

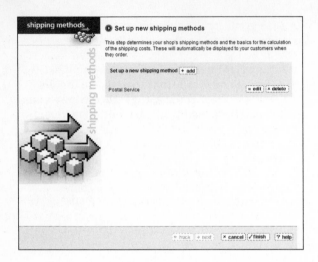

7. Click the Shipping link on the left side of the screen to open the Shipping Wizard. Here, you define the shipping methods you wish to offer your customers. You have anywhere from two options (for a Business eShop) to unlimited options (for a Developer eShop). I use three shipping options for the Business eShop — the default one, the U.S. Postal Service, and one other service.

8. First, click the Edit button next to the Postal Service line on the Shipping Wizard screen. You're taken to the Edit a Shipping Method screen. You need to have a clear title for your service and a minimum shipping amount you'll charge for orders using this shipping method; you can also set appropriate thresholds and corresponding shipping amounts. For example, you can establish that orders up to $50 have a $5 shipping fee, orders between $50 and $100 have a $10 shipping fee, and so on. In order to add a threshold, click the Add button next to Choose New Threshold Order Value. You're taken to another screen to enter your upper order amount and corresponding shipping fee for that order amount. After you pick your threshold amount, click Finish to save your work, and go back to the Edit a Shipping Method screen. Click the Add button again to add more thresholds until every order amount is covered. When all your thresholds are created, click the Next button to finish editing this method.

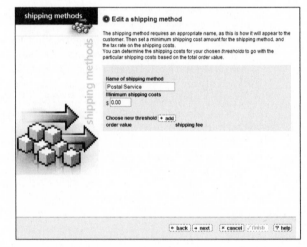

Can't come up with a good shipping amount? Figure out what an average order weighs at given amounts, like $50, $100, and so on and then use the U.S. Postal Service rate calculators at www.usps.com to come up with a figure that covers shipping that average weight order to a U.S. ZIP code thousands of miles away from your business.

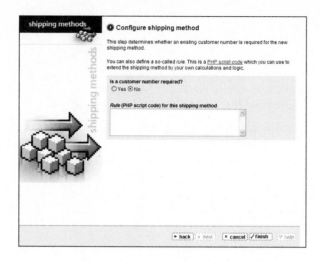

9. At this point, you're asked whether a customer number is required to use this shipping method. Additionally, if you want to create additional shipping rules using the PHP programming language, you're given a spot to input those rules. After you're done customizing this method, click the Finish button to save your work.

10. To add another shipping method, click the Add button next to Set Up a New Shipping Method on the Shipping Method screen. You use the same process to add an additional method as you did editing the Postal Service method earlier.

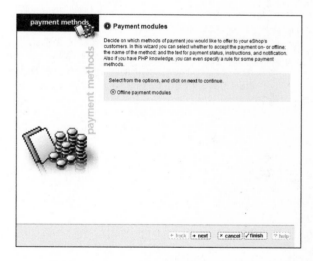

11. Click the Payments link on the left side of the screen to open the Payment Methods Wizard. This is where you set up your online and offline payment methods so customers can pay you for their orders. For a Business eShop, you only have offline payment methods whereas Professional and Developer eShops can integrate PayPal and WorldPay to accept credit cards online. After you pick a method to update, click the Next button to proceed.

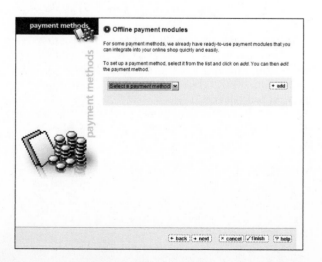

12. Let's say that you have a Business eShop and want to accept credit cards manually, which you process yourself using a merchant account or PayPal. You select Credit Cards (Manual) from the drop-down list of options and click the Add button.

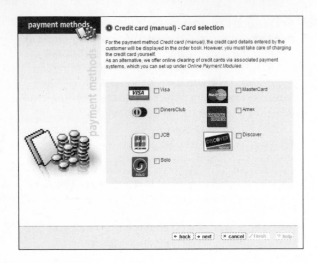

13. On the resulting screen, pick which credit cards you accept manually.

14. After you pick your credit cards and click Next, give this method a title for your customers to see as well as a message to reflect their order status when using this method and some rules to enforce. Leave the defaults in place or customize as you wish and then click Next to continue.

15. On the next screen, you can type a message that your customers will see when they have to enter their information. The plain message Please Enter Your Credit Card Details . . . is a default, but you can customize it to give more specific information. When you're done, click Next to proceed.

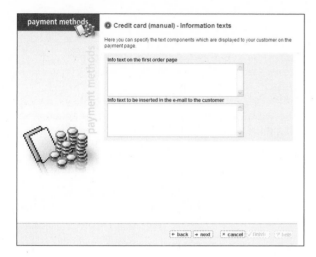

16. (Optional) On the next screen, add any text messages that your customers will see, both on the first order page and in the order confirmation e-mail that the customer gets. These are optional, but it's best to give information about when the customer can expect to be charged, under what business name the order amount appears on their credit card, and so on.

17. Finally, if you know the PHP programming language, you can set up a specific payment rule for your customers. This method is optional and should only be used for stores with sophisticated pricing and order rules. Click Finish to save your work for this payment method. After you define one payment method, you can repeat Steps 11–17 to add another payment method or click Finish again to save your work and exit the Payment Methods Wizard.

18. To make any advanced changes to your store setup, click the Advanced Settings link on the left side of the screen. If you want to make specific changes or rule updates to how your shopping cart is displayed or set up additional security measures, for example, you can do so under the Advanced Settings screen. This screen is recommended only if you know what specific settings you want to change. It is *not* recommended for you to poke around and try out things here.

Publish Shop link

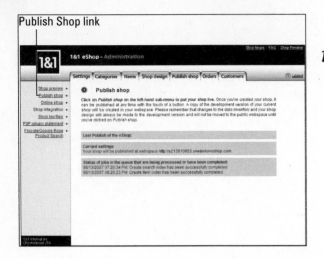

19. When you're done altering your settings and you've uploaded your initial product list, it's time to publish your store! Click the Publish Shop tab and then click the Publish Shop link on the left side of the screen. At any time when you bring up the Publish Shop link, you see the last time your shop changes were published to the Web. When you move forward with your 1&1 Web store, make sure that you always click the Publish Shop link after making any changes to your store design or item list.

Chapter 7

Establishing Your Payment Options

One of the most important aspects of running your own Web store is being able to collect payments from your customers. In the physical world, that amounts to having a functional cash register with an attached credit card processing terminal. Imagine trying to run your store if you couldn't take payments automatically! How would your customers take their purchases home if you couldn't collect a payment when they're ready to check out and go home? In the online world, this is even *more* important, as it is much less likely that they'll go back to your Web store and pay later than it is for them to drive back to a physical store.

When it comes to shopping on the Web, the essential currency to accept is credit cards. Although there are other options to pay without a credit card (some of which I explore in this chapter), the main option that almost everyone wants to use is a credit card, primarily Visa and MasterCard. Therefore, I spend this chapter talking about how your Web store can process credit card payments.

There are two main avenues for accepting credit cards for your Web store. The more traditional route is the Merchant credit card account, which is available through your bank and many other outlets. The other rapidly growing option for Web merchants is PayPal. I cover both methods as well as other payment collection options, like Bill Me Later.

I start this chapter by looking at the features and fees of a Merchant account and PayPal as well as how to evaluate them in relation to your store. I then discuss the steps you need to take to apply for a Merchant account or a PayPal Business account. Finally, I look at alternative payment methods and how to sign up for them online.

Features, Fees, and Required Information for a Merchant Account

In essence, a *Merchant account* is simply a special type of account that allows a business to accept credit cards as a form of payment. A business owner has to apply for a Merchant account and then the issuing bank or Merchant Service Provider checks the credit status as well as certain business factors to see if the business qualifies to have a Merchant account.

Although you can choose from a variety of credit and charge cards, the main two companies that any Web store owner needs to be aware of are Visa and MasterCard. Although American Express has grown in popularity among business users — some of their accounts are *charge cards* — the customer must pay the bill in full every month. Because of this, American Express has a different arrangement than Visa or MasterCard with merchants. If you're interested in offering American Express as a payment option, I recommend discussing their arrangement with your local bank to see if they offer American Express as an option and to have that bank go over the specific arrangement.

Many fees are involved with a Merchant account that a business owner needs to be aware of, which is due to the relationship between the bank and credit card issuing company and how the credit card payments are processed. Some of the charges are monthly in nature, independent of how many payments are received. Most charges, however, are based on the individual charges your customers make with you, and those fees are based on a percentage or rate of each charge amount you receive from your customers. Therefore, here's a quick summary of the different charges you can expect to pay:

- **Interchange Rate:** This is also known as the *Interchange Fee,* or the *credit card rate*. In essence, this is the percentage you pay every time you accept a credit card from a customer. When you see a Merchant Service Provider advertise a special rate for their credit card processing, like 1.87 percent or 2.3 percent, typically they're referring to the lowest or average Interchange Rate that they charge.

  The Interchange Rate depends on the type of credit card used in the transaction and how that credit card was processed by the merchant. Because hundreds of different combinations apply here, banks normally group their rates into a few categories and quote rates for only those categories. Typically, a lower rate applies when there's less work (or less fraud potential) on the bank's part. Any credit card swiped into a terminal is easier than keying in the number manually, so swiped credit card transactions typically have a lower Interchange Rate than cards processed manually. However, keying in a credit card number to a credit card terminal is seen as easier, or less risky, than keying in a credit card over the Internet, so the former has a lower Interchange Rate than the latter.

- **Qualified Rate:** This is also known as the *Discount Rate.* Depending on a merchant's typical way of interacting with their customers and getting the credit card information, the bank establishes a Qualified Rate for transactions that are considered standard for the merchant. For example, retail customers usually have a Qualified Rate for credit cards swiped into a special credit card terminal whereas Internet-based customers have their Qualified Rate based on accepting credit cards electronically through a Payment Gateway over the Internet.

  When you set up your Merchant account, make sure your Qualified Rate is based on the actual way you plan to take credit cards. If you're only going to do business over the Internet, your Qualified Rate should be based on an Internet merchant, not a retail merchant.

- **Non-Qualified Rate:** This rate applies to the merchant when a credit card is processed differently from a merchant's normal mode of business. This rate is always higher than a Qualified Rate, and occurs when, for example, a retail merchant keys in the credit card number into a terminal instead of swiping the card or an Internet merchant settles the batch order after an unusual amount of time. Therefore, to avoid getting hit with this rate, make sure you process as many of your orders as possible within the set guidelines of your issuing bank or Merchant Service Provider.

✔ **Authorization Fee:** This is a small fee that is assessed each time you send a credit card number to be processed to the issuing bank. Typically, this fee is an average of 10–30 cents and is charged regardless of whether the transaction is successful.

✔ **Statement Fee:** This is a monthly fee assessed by your issuing bank or Merchant Service Provider, and it's supposed to cover the cost of your account provider, providing a detailed monthly statement of the credit card charges you collected and the different fees you have to pay. Although some issuers don't have a Statement Fee, most do charge anywhere from $5–$30 per month.

✔ **Batch Fee:** Every time you, as the merchant, send a batch of credit card orders to be processed by the bank, you may be charged a specific Batch Fee. Some accounts come with a standard amount of batch requests included, and this fee would be charged only when you exceed your standard allotment of batch requests.

✔ **Chargeback Fee:** When one of your customers tries to dispute a charge, the issuing bank may issue a chargeback in an attempt to retrieve the customer's funds. When that occurs, you may experience a Chargeback Fee to cover the bank's efforts of resolving this conflict. Unfortunately, you pay this fee regardless of whether the chargeback is successful.

✔ **Minimum Monthly Fee:** This isn't necessarily its own fee, but many Merchant account issuers require that you have a minimum amount of fees charged against your account every month. Therefore, they put a Minimum Monthly Fee into place, so if you have a month where you charge very little, the issuing bank or provider can assess a minimum volume of fees regardless of activity. This minimum can be anywhere from $10 or $15 to $30, $50, or higher.

✔ **Setup Fee:** This is a one-time fee charged by many Merchant Service Providers to create your Merchant account, and the amount varies by provider. Be aware that some providers make more of their income through a higher Setup Fee, which allows them to charge a smaller Interchange Rate. I've seen Setup Fees range from $25 or $50, all the way to $250 or $500.

Shop around for a competitive package, especially when the Setup Fee is involved. Many Merchant account providers have special promotions where they waive the Setup Fee during a specific time period or to price-match a competitive provider.

So, you're ready to apply and open your own Merchant account. Before you run to your local bank and ask for an application, make sure that you have the following information, documents, and estimates before you get started:

✔ **Startup documentation:** Most of the time, you're doing business under a name that has nothing to do with your last name. Therefore, the bank wants to see that you have the appropriate documentation, licenses, and permits that allow you to do business under your assumed business name. Therefore, you should have copies of some (or all) of these different documents to help establish your business identity:

- **Reseller's Permit (or Sales Tax Permit):** Issued by your state government, typically the Board of Equalization or a division of the Secretary of State.

- **Fictitious Business Statement (also known as Doing Business As [DBA]):** issued by your county government.

- **Proof of Publication of Fictitious Business Statement:** Typically, you're required to publish your Doing Business As statement in a local newspaper for several weeks, and the bank wants to see proof that your ad was published. The newspaper that runs your ad prepares a standardized receipt for you.

- **Business License (or Tax License):** issued by your city government or town hall where your business is occurring (such as your home, your physical office space, or your warehouse location).

- **Incorporation, LLC (Limited Liability Corporation), or Partnership agreement:** If you're setting up a special type of business that isn't a Sole Proprietorship, you'll have a document on file stating the ownership nature of your business that, usually, is prepared by an attorney and filed with the state and federal governments.

✔ **Business statistics:** In order to estimate what type of Merchant account to give your business and what Interchange Rates you qualify for as a merchant, the bank or provider wants to know certain statistics (or estimates, if you're a brand-new merchant) regarding your business and expected credit card volume. Specifically, some of that information is

- *Type of goods sold:* This isn't necessarily a moral or ethical question for the bank (although there are some cases, like online gambling, that banks can't support in the U.S. anymore), but rather a question of how stable and sustainable your business is, whether you may experience a high level of returns and/or chargebacks, and if the goods are customized to the point that they can't be returned.

- *Average order amount:* If you're a new merchant, obviously you have to estimate this amount, but if you've done business before, simply calculate the average order size you've experienced so far. Providers want to know how big each average transaction will be, and your rate will typically be lower as your average order amount goes up.

- *Average monthly amount:* This is the average amount you'll be receiving in credit card charges per month. Typically, the banks have a rate for different ranges (say, fewer than $5,000 per month, $5,000–$10,000 per month, and so on) and calculate your average every three or six months to see if you continue to qualify for your designated rate. If you're a new merchant, estimate as best as possible and use any research, business plans, or financial information to help solidify your estimate. Similar to the average order amount, the more you charge every month, the lower your Interchange Rate should be. However, if you state a high average monthly amount and fall dramatically short, the penalties and fees involved could more than erase any cost savings from claiming a high monthly amount.

- *Length of time in business:* Once again, questions like these are asked to gauge the reliability and trustworthiness of your business. Because of the many fraud issues facing Visa and MasterCard are occurring with Internet-based transactions (like with a Web store), they're giving extra scrutiny to new applications for Internet-based Merchant accounts.

Therefore, the longer you've been in business, the better chance your application has of being approved. Even if you're just starting your Internet phase of doing business, be sure to put the length of time for your business in any form — Internet, retail, or otherwise.

✔ **Type of credit card transaction:** There are different ways for merchants to process a customer's credit card, and based on the merchant's interaction with the customer, the banks can set different Interchange Rates for your account. Therefore, the way you process cards influences your account. Here are the most common options:

- *Payment Gateway:* Virtually every e-commerce store has to process their credit card orders through a Payment Gateway, which allows the merchant to send their credit card orders through a special, security-enhanced page over the Internet to be processed by the issuing bank or Merchant Service Provider. Typically, the bank contracts with a third-party Payment Gateway to handle the transmission of data although some organizations now have their own gateway.

- *Credit Card Terminal:* If you plan on having any physical interaction with your customers, you may consider getting a Credit Card Terminal with your account. This allows you to swipe a physical credit card and qualify for lower rates than using a Payment Gateway because these terminals are less risky and require less effort on the bank's behalf. This is beneficial only if you have a retail operation alongside your Web store or plan on setting up at any conventions, trade shows, markets, or any other venue where your customers come directly to you.

- *Automated Response Unit:* These are special phone numbers that merchants call to process credit cards over the phone and receive an automated response code that they would handwrite on a credit card receipt for their client. If you plan on doing sales at remote locations where terminals have bad or no reception (like swap meets or trade fairs), this could be a viable option for your business, but only for those sales you generate at these venues. Your Internet sales should still be handled through a Payment Gateway.

Features and Fees of a PayPal Account

In the late 1990s, interest in eBay exploded as people started using the auction site to buy and sell goods from each other around the globe. One of the hardest parts of that process became the payment phase — buyers had to mail checks or money orders to their sellers, the seller would wait for the payment to clear, and the seller couldn't mail the item until the payment had cleared. Therefore, new companies arose to handle electronic payments for goods using the Internet and credit cards. One of those companies was PayPal, which quickly rose as a favorite service among eBay users. The site grew in such popularity that eBay abandoned their own internal payment service, known as BillPoint, and acquired PayPal in 2002.

Today, PayPal is focused on reaching every Internet merchant, not just eBay users, which means they offer a very competitive and easy-to-use package for Web store owners. They offer several levels of Merchant Solutions to accommodate the smallest or largest Web store owner, all without any setup or statement fee and without any minimum monthly fee. You can see an overview of PayPal's merchant services on their Web site, www.paypal.com, as shown in Figure 7-1.

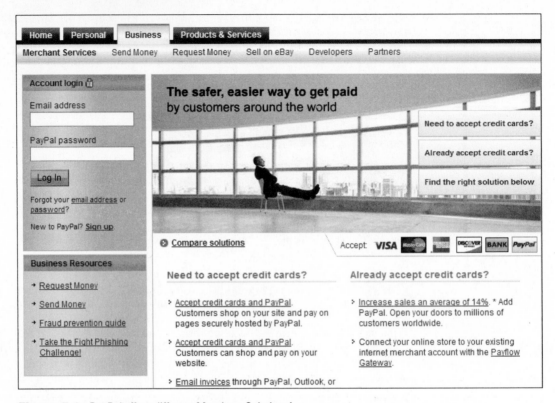

Figure 7-1: PayPal offers different Merchant Solutions!

Currently, three types of PayPal accounts apply to Internet merchants and their ability to take credit cards from their customers:

✔ **Website Payments Standard:** This package allows you to place a button on your Web site that interfaces with PayPal. After your customer places his order, he's taken to PayPal's server to handle the authentication and payment information part of his order. After his credit card has been processed, PayPal returns the user to your Web site to show complete confirmation on your order. Then, the funds from that order are deposited into your PayPal account.

✔ **Website Payments Pro:** This package allows your PayPal account to directly interface with one of hundreds of shopping cart providers and e-commerce systems. After your customer places her order, she inputs her credit card or PayPal information on your Web site. The information is transmitted electronically to PayPal for authorization, and your customer never leaves your Web site, seeing confirmation of her order as soon as PayPal returns the successful authorization message to your Web site. The funds from her order are deposited automatically into your PayPal account.

Currently, the Website Payments Pro package is available only to PayPal business customers from the United States.

✔ **E-mail Payments:** This package allows you to use PayPal as an invoicing tool, where you can create invoices from PayPal, QuickBooks, or Microsoft Outlook. You send your customer a specific invoice for a bill that's due and then that customer follows the instructions on the invoice she receives and enters her payment information into PayPal. PayPal then processes that invoice and deposits the funds into your PayPal account.

You can review the different features of these three plans by going to `www.paypal.com/cgi-bin/webscr?cmd=_profile-comparison`, as in Figure 7-2.

When it comes to fees for these packages, basically worry about one fee — the cost per transaction for accepting credit card orders. Currently, the basic rate for PayPal transactions is 2.9% plus $0.30 per order. If you plan on receiving more than $10,000 per month in transactions, you can apply to PayPal for a lower rate, which goes as low as 1.9% plus $0.30 per transaction. If you're receiving money from someone outside the U.S., there's an additional currency conversion fee that is 1 percent of the order amount.

Furthermore, if you use Website Payments Pro or the Virtual Terminal product with Website Payments Standard, an additional $20 per month flat fee is added regardless of transaction level. There's no Setup Fee, no Minimum Monthly Fee, no Statement Fee, and no Batch Fee for any of these packages.

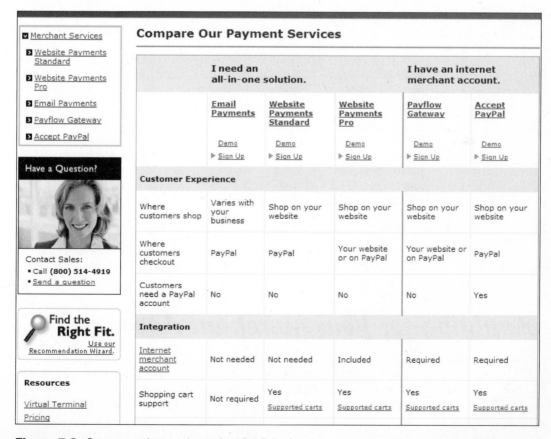

Figure 7-2: Compare various packages from PayPal.

When it comes to deciding whether to get a PayPal account for your Web store, it helps to weigh the pros and cons of this account. Here's a brief list of a few of the pros:

✔ **Very low startup cost:** No Startup or Statement Fees, and you pay only when you receive money. This solution has become ideal for many small merchants, where the various Merchant account fees translate into a sizable percentage of sales.

✔ **Easy application process:** In many cases, you're approved automatically for most of their packages without paying money to find out you don't qualify.

✔ **Shopping cart technology built-in:** You can use PayPal's pre-programmed buttons to build your own shopping cart or use their API (Application Programming Interface) technology to interface with one of hundreds of different shopping cart technologies so you don't need an extra payment gateway to handle your credit cards.

✔ **Your buyers don't need PayPal accounts:** Nowadays, your customers don't need to join PayPal to use these services. They can simply enter their credit card numbers, and the money is deposited into your account.

✔ **You don't have to store or see credit card numbers:** With PayPal, the customer enters his number, and all you see as the merchant is the deposit of money. You don't have to worry about storing, encrypting, or protecting the customer's credit card information, as you never see it or need it to get paid.

Here's a brief list of a few of the cons:

✔ **Extra step to receive money:** Your PayPal account doesn't automatically withdraw the funds or *scrape funds* automatically into a checking or savings account. You have to log in to PayPal and manually transfer the funds into your bank account. Typically, the transfer can take as long as three to four business days.

✔ **Less chargeback protection:** With a Merchant account, the issuing bank defends you against a chargeback by getting the documentation for a dispute first and not withdrawing the funds until a judgment has been found against you. With PayPal, the money is frozen upon a dispute being filed, and there are limited tools for a seller to provide proof and defend her case against a customer chargeback.

✔ **Possible higher cost:** If you'll process a high volume of credit card orders, you may save money with a competitive discount rate from a Merchant account because the other fees barely factor into a percentage calculation if you're processing a lot of volume each month.

Applying for Your Merchant Account

There is no definitive way to apply for a Merchant account nowadays, as any new Web store owner will find out. Many companies are fighting for your business in this area, so you have plenty of options for applying for and receiving a Merchant account. Here are some of the most common ways to get a Merchant account:

✔ **Contact your local business bank:** If you have a bank account established for your Web store already, you should ask that bank if you can create a Merchant account as well. If you're still setting up your Web store, you may want to create your own business checking account to separate your finances. When doing that, ask the bank you're considering if they offer Merchant accounts or Merchant Credit Card accounts. This way, you have one operation to handle all your banking needs, instead of dealing with multiple organizations.

✔ **Pick a low-cost provider of Merchant accounts:** When you sign up for your Fictitious Business Statement, you'll be amazed at the volume of offers that start showing up in your mailbox. Many of these companies buy lists of the names of newly formed businesses and send out offers of setting up your own Merchant account. As I state earlier, read the fine print when it comes to each offer, as some companies waive Startup Fees for higher Interchange Rates down the road, for example.

✔ **Use a membership or group association to get your account:** Based on your membership with various organizations, you may have a great link to a company that will handle your Merchant account. Some examples of groups that offer their members credit card processing accounts include Costco, the National Federation of Independent Business (NFIB), and more. Check with your local trade organization, chamber of commerce, and even your school alumni organization.

✔ **Pursue an alternative, such as PayPal:** In the next section, I discuss opening an account with PayPal, which is an alternative to the Merchant account. In any case, have as much information and paperwork as possible when you apply and allow some time for your application to be processed before you can begin accepting payments. Typically, you should get an answer within one to two weeks, at most, and you can get more specific timelines from your issuing bank or provider.

Signing Up for a PayPal Account

Stuff You Need to Know

Toolbox:
- ✔ Business bank account and credit card information
- ✔ Business tax ID or your Social Security number
- ✔ Business name and contact information

Time Needed:
15–20 minutes

When you're ready to sign up for a PayPal account, be sure to have a credit card and a bank account in the U.S. as well as your tax identification number and business information ready to go for your application. For this example, I sign up for a PayPal Business account.

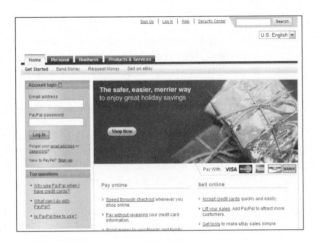

1. Go to the PayPal home page at `www.paypal.com` and click the blue Sign Up link at the top of the screen. You can always click the Business tab (along the top half of the page) to read more about the different options, which I discuss in the section "Features and Fees of a PayPal Account," earlier in this chapter or read some of the Questions or Learn More articles and guides available on the home page.

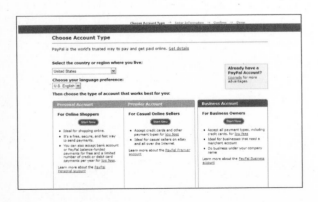

2. PayPal has three levels of accounts: the Personal account, designed to trade money among you and your friends; the Premier account, designed for individual eBay sellers to accept credit card payments from eBay buyers; and the Business account, designed for businesses to accept credit cards on and off eBay. After clicking the Sign Up link, pick the PayPal Business account as your account type and then click the Start Now button. The Merchant Services packages are designed exclusively for Business account holders. Therefore, I recommend you establish a Business account.

3. Pick your specific Payment Solution and click the Continue button. At this step in the process, you can pick from a drop-down list of PayPal's different Merchant Solutions offerings, including Website Payments Standard, Website Payments Pro, and E-mail Payments. Based on our discussion in the section "Features and Fees of a PayPal Account," earlier in this chapter, pick the one that best fits your situation and click the Continue button. You can always change package levels later on, and an I Don't Know option is on the list. Be aware of the monthly fee with Website Payments Pro, as you should only pick that option if you're certain it will fit with your storefront provider.

4. You're asked to provide your business information (which PayPal verifies) and then you set up your payment solution. Click the Go button to start entering your information. At this point, PayPal walks you through their 3-step process for opening an account. First, they ask you to fill out an application with all the pertinent business information. Alongside that, you need to provide a valid U.S. bank account for your business. PayPal verifies your information, and after you're confirmed and verified, you're given tools, links, and other necessary information to start setting up your payment account.

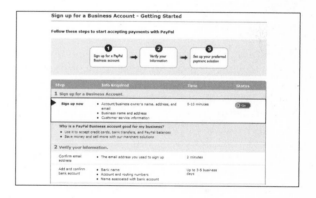

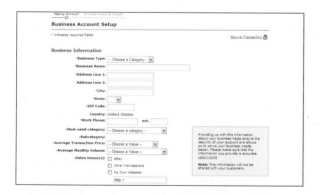

5. Fill out your pertinent business information on the screen provided. You're taken to the Business Account Setup page. Complete all the required fields (anything with a red *) and click the Continue button at the bottom of the page to go to the next step.

TIP

If you still can't decide, click the Need Some Help Finding a Payment Solution link and follow the screens presented to you for more advice.

6. Fill out your Business Owner Contact Information and create an account. In the first part of the page, input the information for the business owner of this account. You can use the same address as your business or a separate mailing address if you wish, but make sure the owner's contact information matches the billing information for the bank account. After you complete this section, scroll down to create your PayPal account. Instead of a user ID, your PayPal account is based on the e-mail address you use to define your account. Enter the e-mail address where you want all PayPal-related information to go and then enter a password for your account. I recommend that you create a separate e-mail account and/or e-mail alias for your PayPal account so it isn't tied to one specific employee or user who may leave your business down the road.

7. Set up your password recovery questions and review the Terms and Conditions. When you scroll down the page, you see the Password Recovery questions. When you pick a question and set up an answer, you can recover your password in the future if you forget or lose your password. Secondly, you can review the PayPal Terms and Conditions and check the boxes when you agree to those terms so you can create your account. You're asked to enter some letters into a designated Security Measure box as a security measure to ensure that a person, and not a computer, is creating this account. After you do that, click the Continue button.

8. Enter your bank account information (and optionally, your business credit card information). In this step, you're asked to enter your bank account information. You can use one of your blank checks as a guide to get the important information needed, primarily your 9-digit *ABA(American Banking Association) number* (or a *routing number*), which identifies your particular bank and your 10-digit checking account number. Both numbers can be found along the bottom of a blank check. After you enter your bank account information, you can add additional security to your account by defining a credit card tied to your business. This is optional, and if you check the box, you're asked on the next screen to input your credit card information. When you're ready, click the Continue button to complete the process.

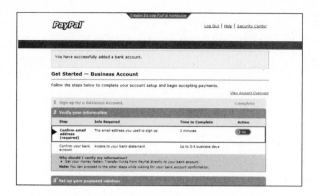

9. You've successfully added your bank account information! Now you need to wait for information to verify your account. You should see a confirmation screen.

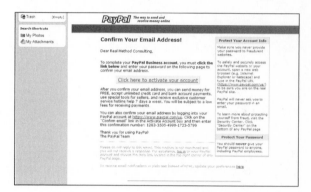

10. Now you need to confirm your e-mail address. When you created your account, PayPal sends an e-mail to your designated e-mail address with a Confirmation link that you can click to confirm the address. Check your e-mail account and look for an e-mail from PayPal. Click the highlighted link to confirm your account.

11. When you click the link, you're taken back to PayPal and asked to put in your password. After you do that, you've confirmed your e-mail address and should see a confirmation screen. Click the Continue button to go back to the PayPal main screen.

Many fraudulent people are sending fake e-mails pretending to be from PayPal, eBay, or your local bank, asking you to click a link that secretly takes you to their Web site, not the real site, in hopes of getting valuable account information. When you click the link from the e-mail, make sure the address starts with *xxx*.paypal.com, where *xxx* is the name of one of PayPal's servers.

12. After you confirm your e-mail address, you have to confirm your bank account. At this point, PayPal deposits two small amounts into your bank account in the next 24 to 48 hours. You need to access your bank account and find out what those deposits are. After you know the amounts, you can log in to PayPal again and enter that information to verify your account. This means that you can transfer funds between your PayPal account and your bank account.

This information takes several days to show up on your banking statements, so you need to allow up to three to five business days to finalize this step.

Adding PayPal to Your Web Store

After you create your account, you can start to implement your account while you're waiting on verification from your bank account (and/or credit card). Depending on the package you select and the storefront provider that's powering your Web store, you'll be implementing PayPal in different ways.

In this section, I cover the most common uses that people do when adding PayPal capability to their Web store. For this exercise, I use a Yahoo! Merchant Solutions Web store. Although these steps are meant for Yahoo!, they should work on the other storefront providers (such as ProStores and 1&1 eShops).

1. Log in to your Yahoo! Merchant Solutions account at `http://smallbusiness.yahoo.com` by clicking on the button marked "Small Business" and entering your Yahoo! Merchant Solutions user ID and password. You will be taken to your Merchant Starter page. After you look at your Merchant page, you need to go to the Order Settings column and click the Payment Center link.

Payment Center link

YAHOO! SMALL BUSINESS — Merchant Solutions

Welcome, joelelad [Sign Out, Account Info]   Small Business Home - Yahoo! - Help

joelelad.com: Merchant Starter   Mail | Manage My Services ▾

Small Business Home   Domain | Web Hosting | Store

Drive More Customers to Your Store   Do not show
$ Sell to customers searching on Yahoo!. Sign up now and get a $100 credit towards your new Yahoo! Sponsored Search account. Find out more

Get included in Yahoo! Shopping with 20% off in Product Submit   Do not show
ⓘ Reach millions of motivated buyers in Yahoo! Shopping and in highly relevant areas across Yahoo! by signing up for Product Submit. As a Yahoo! Store merchant, you are eligible for an exclusive **20% discount**. Sign up today and start driving traffic to your store. Learn More

Product Tips   Do not show
ⓘ Submit your site for free traffic.
Make sure your store and products show up in the Yahoo! and Google search results. Visit the Search Engines section today and authenticate your store with Yahoo! Site Explorer and create a sitemap.xml for Google. Learn more

Edit	Process	Statistics	Order Settings	Site Settings
Store Editor	[View Site] Orders	Page Views	Checkout Manager	Store Account Info
Design Wizard	Requests	Sales	Order Emails	Access
Catalog Manager		References	Shipment & Order Status	Preferences
Add Product Wizard		Graphs	Configure Inventory	Domain Names
Store Tag Hub		Reports	Payment Center	Customer Access
		Repeats	Shipping Manager	Ratings
			Tax Rates	
			Foreign Orders	
			Risk Tools	
			Shipping & Tax Test	
			Published	

Click this button

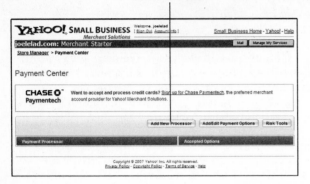

2. After you log in using your Yahoo! Security Key (which you created when you signed up for a Yahoo! account), you're taken to the Payment Center. Click the Add New Processor button to add your new PayPal account. Your Payment Center contains records of all the payment gateways that you use to process credit cards for your store.

Select this option

3. Select the Sign Up for PayPal Express Checkout option and then click the orange Next button. At this point, you could select the Sign Up for a Merchant Account option and walk through the process of applying for an account through Chase Paymentech, you could sign up using an existing Merchant account, or you could assign your PayPal account to your Web store, which is what I select.

4. You now begin the PayPal Express Checkout sign up process. Click the orange Sign Up for PayPal Express Checkout button to proceed. At this point, you're prompted with a summary of what you need to complete this process. Be sure to have the necessary information available before you click the Sign Up for PayPal Express Checkout button to be taken to PayPal.

5. Log in to your PayPal account. At this point, you're logging in to your PayPal account so you can grant access for your storefront provider (Yahoo! in this example) to access your PayPal account.

6. Grant permission for Yahoo! to access your PayPal account by clicking the I Agree button. This step is for you to give specific permission for Yahoo! Merchant Solutions to access your PayPal account using special computer language — *API,* or *Application Programming Interface.* By clicking the I Agree button, your Yahoo! store can access your PayPal account so that funds from new orders can be deposited into that account.

7. You've now linked the two accounts (PayPal and Yahoo! Merchant Solutions). On your main PayPal screen, Express Checkout is defined as your payment option. You should be taken automatically to your main PayPal screen. Now, you will see Express Checkout defined as your payment solution, which means you added your PayPal account successfully to your Yahoo! Merchant Solutions account. If, for some reason, this does not show up automatically, click the link "Getting Started Steps" from the left hand navigation bar under the header Set Up Your Account.

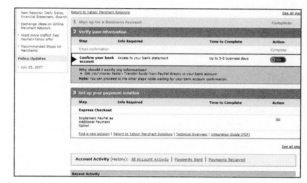

Of course, PayPal is integrated with lots of other shopping carts besides Yahoo! Merchant Solutions. You can peruse the PayPal Solutions Directory to find instructions on integrating your own shopping cart at www.paypal.com/en_US/html/SolutionsDirectory/sd_ec-compatible.html.

Adding PayPal Buttons to Your Web Site

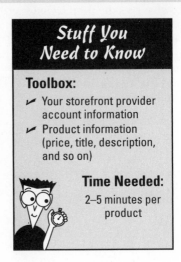

Stuff You Need to Know

Toolbox:

- ✔ Your storefront provider account information
- ✔ Product information (price, title, description, and so on)

Time Needed:

2–5 minutes per product

If you don't have a shopping cart to use and are selling only a few select items, you can use PayPal's system to have a *virtual shopping cart* in which you can place pre-programmed PayPal buttons on your Web site that act as a shopping cart for your customers.

Click this link

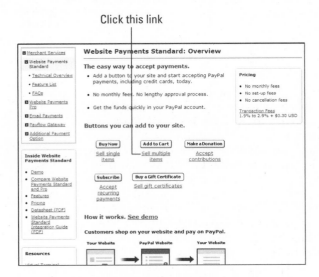

1. Log in to your PayPal account and click the Merchant Services tab. Then click the Website Payments Standard link. On the page describing the Website Payments Standard package, you see the various buttons you can create with PayPal. These are examples of the buttons you can create with the PayPal system. Let's say that you want to sell multiple items; click the Sell Multiple Items link to start using the PayPal shopping cart.

Get Started! link

2. When you click this link, you go to the PayPal Shopping Cart page. This page explains that you can add buttons to your Web site and process payments with PayPal as easy as their other methods. After you read the page, click the Get Started! link.

PayPal Shopping Cart   See Demo

Add a PayPal Shopping Cart to your website so your buyers can browse your entire site, then make their purchases quickly and securely on PayPal-hosted payment pages.

More Resources
Techniques, examples, demos & more.

Enter the details of the item you wish to sell

Item Name/Service:

Item ID/Number:
(optional)

Price of Item/Service you want to sell: ($2,000.00 USD limit for new buyers) ?

Currency: U.S. Dollars ?

If you want your buyer's payment form to default to a specific country, select a country below. Otherwise, do nothing and your buyers can choose for themselves.

Buyer's Country: United States ?
(Optional)

Select an Add to Cart button

The image you select below will be used by your customers to add items to their shopping cart.

Add to Cart   Choose a different button

Customize your button by entering the URL of an image on your website.

Yes, use my custom image

Button Image URL: http:// ?

3. Start adding buttons to your Web store by entering all the details for the button you wish to create. At this point, you're on the PayPal Shopping Cart button creation screen. Here, you first enter all the details about one of the products you want to sell on your Web store, including the Item Name/Service, Item ID/Number, Price of Item/Service You Want to Sell, Currency, and Buyer's Country. Next, you can choose to keep the predesigned button or upload your own button graphic to use instead. When you scroll down, you see two options: You can click the Add More Options button to add more information into your button (like sales tax and shipping amounts) or you can click the Create Button Now to create the programming code necessary to put a real, clickable button on your Web store.

4. Click the Create Button Now button to generate your button programming code. When you click this button, you see the necessary programming code on the next page. Simply copy and paste the text in the corresponding box to draw either the Add to Cart button for a specific product or the View Cart button, so customers can see what is currently in their shopping cart. When you want to create more buttons, simply scroll to the bottom of the page, click the Create Another Button button, and repeat Steps 3 and 4.

Chapter 8

Laying Out Your Design from the Ground Up

Tasks performed in this chapter

- Putting your basic store design on paper
- Deciding on your category structure
- Creating your Web store home page
- Making your Navigation bar
- Designing your featured products section

When people think of store design, they typically think about what kind of shelving units are needed to hold their products, how wide to make their aisles, what display will be visible from the front window, and other concerns of the retail world. When you translate that into online store design, most people assume that a shopping cart, some buttons, and graphics are enough to qualify as "design." Given the growing competition for reaching online customers, however, store design is quickly becoming an important and differentiating factor as customers are looking for quality, uniqueness, and a good value for their money.

Today, the design of your store speaks as loudly as your slogan, brand image, and value proposition. This does not mean you have to use the latest and greatest technologies, since most of those rise and fall in popularity. The core values of a good store design apply on the Internet just as they do in the brick-and-mortar "offline" community. Those values include a clean and intuitive design that makes it easy for customers to shop and gives your store a professional appearance.

In this chapter, we present the basic steps to consider for your Web store. We start with good old fashioned pen and paper, as you map out the page and category structure for your store. From there, you will use your road map to construct the most important page on your Web store — the home page. One of the essentials of your home page, which will also exist on every other page within your Web site, is the navigation bar, so we go through creating a navigation bar and the basics that will help you decide the contents of that area. Finally, we talk about the items that typically take up the middle of the home page — the "featured" products or specials for your Web store, and add them to the home page.

Creating Your Store Design . . . on Paper

Even though you are building an electronic commerce store, and you are using the Internet and all this computer automation, it does not mean you should abandon a good old piece of paper and a pencil as your starting point. The best store owners are those that plan out in advance how they want their stores to look, and then use those plans when constructing their store, whether it's a physical retail store or an e-commerce Web store. Therefore, we are going to discuss some common things to consider when laying out your Web store design.

First and foremost, you should decide up front on your purpose — what kind of a Web store you wish to implement. Yes, we know, you want a Web store that is profitable and makes money, right? What we mean is whether your main goal is just selling products, or whether you want to provide functions, tools, and other mechanisms on your Web store that draw people back regardless of whether they want to purchase something.

In Web terms, building functions that keep customers on your site longer or keep customers returning to your site is called "making your site sticky" because these functions mean your customers "stick around" longer. Typically, this leads to more loyal customers, or more revenue opportunities through increased advertising revenue, more frequent sales per customers, and so on.

Once you decide on your purpose, you can begin thinking about your design, because the number one question you should always consider when mapping out your store design is "Does this fit my store's purpose?" If it doesn't directly (or indirectly) serve your purpose, then it should be considered as an extra step, to be done only if you have finished everything else and have extra time and money to implement it.

As you turn your purpose into a full store design, you can break down your goal into actual sections of your store by answering these questions:

- ✓ **Are you going to focus solely on selling products?** The number of different categories and product pages will make up the bulk of your Web store, and the navigation to your main product category home pages should be only one click away from your home page.

- ✓ **What are your main product categories?** There is a fine line between having too many categories available from the home page and having very general categories that require extra clicking on the customer's behalf. *Your goal is to make any product no more than 3 clicks away from the home page,* as anything that requires more than 3 clicks will not capture the interest of your customers (or the search engines, for that matter) and be a waste of virtual space.

- ✓ **Are customers going to have an account on your system?** If so, you need to create a unique section where customers can log into their account, view past orders, make changes to their profile, and access special "customer-only" Web pages, like discussion forums or sales pages.

- ✓ **What extra functions (if any) do you want to provide on your site?** If you plan on adding extra functionality to your Web store, do you want those functions available (and visible) to anyone who comes by your Web store? If so, they should be readily available from the home page and a part of your navigation bar.

- ✓ **How much communication do you plan to have with your store visitors?** For some companies, a simple page explaining their history, mission, and contact information is sufficient. Other companies have an entire section dedicated to press releases, the company blog, feedback forms, and other ways to connect with their customers.

- ✓ **How much help are you going to provide on your web store?** For some companies, a simple page with Frequently Asked Questions is sufficient. Other companies have an entire section where you can look up questions from a database, send in a problem report, and interact on discussion boards with company employees and even other customers.

Once you have defined your list of core functions or categories, it is time to draw out your Web site "map" on a piece of paper. At the top of your map is the home page (the starting point, or launch pad, for all your customers), and you create a box for each Web page that is required, drawing links in between the boxes to indicate the relationship between pages. Don't worry about the actual look of each web page yet, just identify how many different Web pages are required and how they are inter-linked. When you are done, you should have something that resembles a flowchart, as shown in Figure 8-1.

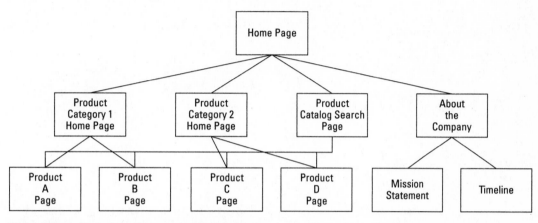

Figure 8-1: You map out your entire Web site first.

Determining Your Category Structure

Once you have mapped out your Web store as a whole, you probably need to be more specific in the products section of your store, which means you need to devise a good category structure. Depending on the products you plan to sell, your category structure may already be devised for you. In other cases, however, you may want to create your own unique categories that speak to your customers very specifically. You may want to create a "Bargain" or "Under $10" category, or dedicate a category to a specific person or cause. Remember, it all goes back to your purpose and what best serves that purpose.

To that end, here are some guidelines to keep in mind as you design your category structure:

- ✓ **Use terms and headers that your customers are familiar with hearing.**
- ✓ **Don't make one product an entire category.**
- ✓ **Individual products should be within three clicks of the home page.** This was mentioned in the section above but bears repeating. Create a mix of categories and main subcategory headers so that the third click, if necessary, goes from a subcategory directly to a product detail page.
- ✓ **Look at your competition for ideas.**
- ✓ **Your categories should be independent of your promotions.**

Designing Your Web Store Home Page

After you lay out your store design on paper, your next step is to translate that map into your online store. Therefore, the most important page to create is your home page, since that will serve as the entry point for your customers and visitors. For this exercise, we are creating a home page for a Yahoo! Merchant Solutions Web store. Your template will automatically create the basic elements of your home page, so this exercise is designed to refine that first draft.

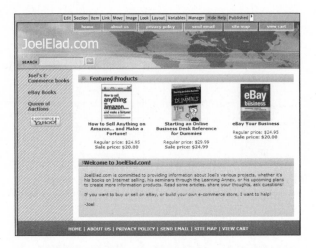

1. Log into your Yahoo! Merchant Solutions account by going to `http://smallbusiness.yahoo.com` and clicking on the Small Business button next to the header Manage My Services. Once you're on your Merchant Starter page, click on the Store Editor link to view your initial home page.

2. Click the Edit button from the top toolbar to load the Properties screen for your home page. This screen is where you can update the elements of your home page. Review the text in the Message field to make sure that is the introductory text you want your customers to see on your home page. Give your home page a title in the Page-title field (be sure to use keywords that apply to the products you sell) and if you have a logo, click the Upload button next to the Image header to put that logo on your home page.

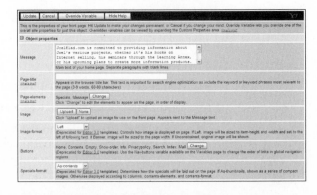

Home Page Guidelines

There are definite guidelines to consider when you are constructing your home page:

✔ **Do not overload your home page.** While your Web store may offer a lot of Web pages, you don't want to overwhelm your customers when they first visit you. Provide a general roadmap on your home page for customers to get started, and give them more specific information and links as they explore further.

✔ **White space is your friend.** Don't feel like you have to cover every square inch of the screen with a graphic or text header. You will emphasize the information you have on your Web store by surrounding it with lots of white space, so customers eyes will zero in on the important sections.

✔ **Use either a two-column or three-column approach on your page.** The two most prominent designs for a Web site home page today are the two-column approach, with a navigation bar along the left and a main section for promotions and ads in the middle, and a three-column approach, with a navigation bar, middle section, and right-hand column reserved for promotions.

✔ **Put your most important information at the top.** Newspapers use the terminology "above the fold" to indicate the top half of their page that is visible without turning over the paper. For Web sites, above the fold means the top part of the Web page that does not require the user to scroll down the page. If your customer has to scroll down to see something important, there is an excellent chance they won't take the time and instead go to a competitor's Web site.

Edit List Position (page-elements)

Element Position

Element	Position
Address	
Buttons	
Contents	
Final-text	
Image	
Intro-text	
Message	2
Name	
Search	
Specials	1

[Update] [Cancel]

3. In order to arrange the position of content on your home page, click the Change button in the line marked Page-elements. You'll see a table of items labeled Edit List Position. Basically, on this screen, you assign the order of elements that will appear on your home page. For example, the default home page that was created in my example puts the Specials (or Featured items) first, and then my introductory message second. Pick which elements you want to appear on your home page, and put a number (1, 2, 3, and so on) next to each element in the order you wish them to appear on your home page. When you are done, click the Update button.

4. Scroll down the page to finish updating your home page. The last four fields on this screen determine how your Featured products are displayed on the home page. Most importantly, the Contents-elements field decides which aspects of a product are displayed on the page. The default is normally Image, Screen-text title, and Price. I would highly advise you to add the Order aspect (by holding down the CTRL button while clicking on Order from the list), it will put an Add to Cart button next to each item, so your customers can order a Featured product directly from the home page. Finally, the Columns field is designed to arrange your Featured products in the designated number of columns. Make sure you stick to two or three so you avoid having a crowded home page.

5. Click the Update button when you are done making changes to your home page. You'll see your new home page with the changes you specified. (In my example, I changed the order of the Specials and Message, compared with the first figure.) Click the Publish button on the top toolbar to send all of your changes to your live Web store.

Creating Your Navigation Bar

Stuff You Need to Know

Toolbox:
- An idea of which sections you want on your navigation bar
- An idea of what label names you will use on the navigation bar

Time Needed:
10–15 minutes

If you equate your home page with the clean company lobby with the helpful receptionist, then think of your navigation bar as that helpful building directory that hangs by every elevator. After all, if your customers or visitors can't easily find their away around your store, how can they be expected to build an order, checkout, and help you make money with your venture? Therefore, you should spend some time in planning exactly how you want your navigation bar, or "nav bar" for short, since this will be an important tool for customers to use throughout their shopping experience with you. Again, for this exercise we are using a Yahoo! Merchant Solutions Web store to edit or revise the navigation bar that was automatically created when you started creating your store.

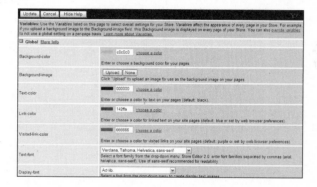

1. Log into your Yahoo! Merchant Solutions account and click on the Store Editor link from your Merchant Starter page. (If you just completed the last task, click the Return to Editor link from your Publish Changes confirmation page.) Click the Variables button from the top toolbar.

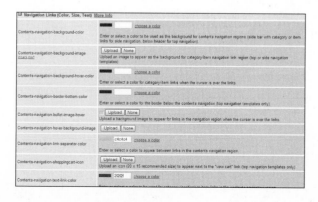

2. Scroll down the page until you see the Navigation Links section. The first set of variables shown controls how your navigation bar will look in terms of colors, links, and presentation. If you want to include a background image or change the color scheme of your navigation bar, you can do so in the fields provided. Otherwise, you can leave the values as Yahoo! assigned them when your store was first created.

Navigation Bar Guidelines

Here are some helpful guidelines for you to use when designing your navigation bar:

- **Pick the 3-6 most important sections of your website to appear in the navigation bar.** Any less than 3 sections means that you don't have a lot of sections for your site, and more than 7 options turns your navigation bar into more of a "site map" where you try and detail everything at once.

- **Each section on your navigation bar can have its own "sub-navigation bar" with more specific categories.** If your Web store has lots of different product categories, you don't have to limit your navigation to only the biggest category headers without additional assistance. You can "expand" your navigation selections once someone picks a specific category or item on your navigation bar, and show a whole sub-list of more specific pages or subcategories that are available only from the main section header.

- **Always include a link back to the home page in your navigation bar.** The first constant to any good navigation bar is that, somewhere in the navigation, a user can click a link and be taken back to the home page. This way, regardless of which section your customer is browsing, if they get lost, confused, or bored, they can easily go back to your home page.

- **Your shopping cart should have a fixed location on your navigation bar or screen.** At any time while a customer is visiting your Web store, they need to have access to see what items are currently in their shopping cart. Therefore, it is encouraged to create a special place on the page, preferably in the navigation bar or along the top of the screen, where the customer can easily go into their shopping cart to review their order or go ahead and purchase their items.

- **Certain pages don't need a fixed location on your navigation bar.** While it's very important to have a clearly defined privacy policy on your Web site, that page does not need to be accessible throughout the entire Web site. Your navigation bar is meant for sections of your Web site that need to be easily accessible regardless of where your customers are in the shopping or ordering process.

- **Make sure your navigation bar is in the same place on every page of your Web site.** There is very little that is worse than having to hunt around a Web page every time to locate the navigation bar. The key is consistency, as your customers expect to see the navigation bar as their fixed constant when they browse and click around your Web store.

- **Have a text-only version of your navigation bar appear at the bottom of the page.** Whether you have buttons or text for your nav bar, including a text-only copy at the bottom of your page is good for customers, in case the buttons don't load correctly. It is great for search engines as well, which ignore any graphical navigation bars and go straight for the text links to find and index the rest of your Web site.

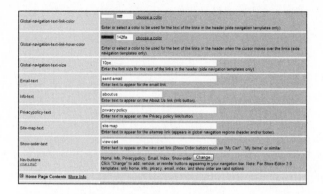

3. Scroll down the page past the Contents-Navigation fields until you see the last variables (for Navigation) before the Home Page Contents section begins. If you want your navigation bar to be bigger, change the Global-navigation-text-size field to 12px or 14px to increase the size. You can update the text in the next five fields to indicate what will appear on the referenced button; you don't have to accept the default that Yahoo! put in that field. Give those navigation bar elements an appropriate name based on the style of Web store you wish to create.

4. Click on the Change button in the Nav-buttons variable line to update the order of buttons that appear on your navigation bar. Decide on the order of elements you wish to include in your navigation bar, put a 1 next to the 1st/top element, a 2 next to the second element, and so on. When you're done, click the Update button to save your choices.

5. Scroll down to the bottom of this page and click the Update button to save all of your choices. This will take you back to the Store Editor screen, showing your home page with your newly updated navigation bar. Review how your choices have affected your navigation bar and click the Publish button to update your Web store with your newly updated navigation bar.

You should almost always select Home as your first element so customers can return to your home page easily, and you should consider assigning Index (your Site Map), Privacypolicy (your Privacy Policy page), and Info (your About Us information) as parts of your navigation bar.

Adding Your Featured Products or Sale Items

Stuff You Need to Know

Toolbox:

✔ An idea of which products in your catalog will be featured

✔ An idea of which products in your catalog you wish to put on sale

Time Needed:

5 minutes per product

Sometimes, having to pick your favorite product among your catalog of inventory is like having to pick a favorite child or pet. You want every piece of inventory to sell well, otherwise you wouldn't be carrying it, right? Well, there are some products that are going to sell more often than others, whether it's a "fad" item (like Tickle Me Elmo for the holiday shoppers), a seasonal item (coats and jackets at the beginning of winter), or a new product that's entering the marketplace (the release of a new video game system, like the Sony Playstation 3 or the Nintendo Wii) that require a special placement and more emphasis. Hence, we have the "featured" product, which typically gets a prime placement on a Web store home page — usually the very middle of it. For this exercise we are using a Yahoo! Merchant Solutions Web store to create a Featured Products section by selecting products you created in your catalog to become Featured or put on sale.

1. Log into your Yahoo! Merchant Solutions account by going to `http://smallbusiness.yahoo.com` and clicking on the Small Business button next to Manage my Services. When you get to your Merchant Starter page, click on the Catalog Manager link to access that function. When you get to your Catalog Manager page, click on the Manage My Items link to view the table with your product catalog.

2. Click on the ID name of the product you want to feature or discount, and this will load the Edit Item page for that product. To put the item on sale, simply fill in the Sale-Price field with your new sale price, then click Save to update your account. Buyers will see the original price and the sale price when viewing that product, and will have to pay only the sale price.

Featured Products Guidelines

Since you are using important space on your store home page to emphasize a particular product (or two or three), there needs to be some consideration as to which product(s) to use as "featured" and for how long. Let's take a look at the questions you need to ask yourself to help figure out this dilemma:

✔ **What are your customers asking for?** One of the goals of a featured item is to satisfy a burning demand from their customers. If you are consistently fielding questions, online or offline, for a particular product, feature it on your home page. Even if the product is not out yet, or you are out of stock currently, don't hesitate to promote the product, even if all you can do is take down their name and number so you can contact them when the item is available.

✔ **What products are you currently overloaded or carrying too much inventory for?** Retail stores hold sales all the time, specifically to clear out older or "dead" merchandise to make way for newer or fresh merchandise, and the same can be said for online stores. If you are sitting on too much of a specific product, create some action and excitement by featuring that product for sale, perhaps reducing the price for a limited time to match the promotion.

✔ **Is the product an introductory item for a entire category of products you will carry?** There are several products that are designed with a razor and blades strategy, meaning you sell them the razor, or introductory product, cheap, and make your profit selling the blades,

or accessory products. Similarly, if you are selling a product that will encourage additional sales of accessories or extra products, feature the introductory product and hook them in from the beginning. Make sure that there are links from your featured product page that are cross-selling or up-selling any of the hot accessories.

✔ **What products are generating the most margin/profit?** Let's face it, if you are trying to decide between two products to promote, one of which gets you $5 in profit, the other gets you $50 in profit, if all else is equal, pick the product with the better profit or margin. Even if the higher profit means it is a tougher product to sell, the added exposure of a featured product should help justify the "real estate" of giving space from your home page to promote it.

✔ **How long have you been promoting the same product?** If you promote the same product, over and over, for months on end, your customers will ignore that promotion, and quite possibly, ignore any future promotions as well, seeing your site as stale or static. Featured items get attention online because, typically, they are not featured for a long period of time. Now, if your featured product is experiencing high, steady sales, leave it alone until sales start to drop or you can't obtain any more inventory to satisfy orders. Otherwise, plan to change out your featured items at regular intervals, whether it's every week, every month, every quarter, and so on.

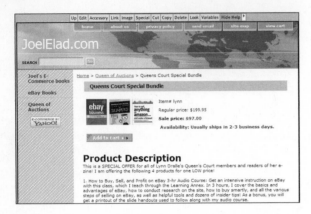

3. To designate an item as Featured, click on the Store Editor link from the Merchant Starter page to bring up your Web store. Click on the product you wish to promote as Featured. In the toolbar at the top of the page, you should see a button marked Special. Click that button to mark the product as Featured. Then, click Publish from that toolbar to update your changes to your store.

4. Repeat either Step 2 or Step 3 to mark other products as Featured or on sale. Be sure to Publish your changes before you log out of your account, in order to save your work.

Part III
Filling In the Blanks (and Shelves)

The 5th Wave   By Rich Tennant

"So far our web presence has been pretty good.
We've gotten some orders, a few inquiries,
and nine guys who want to date our logo."

In this part . . .

*I*n this part, I cover the process of filling in all the necessary details to make your Web store a reality. I start by
discussing how to build your catalog of products for sale,
and then move into the process of gathering (or creating)
the pictures and descriptions necessary for this product
catalog.

I then expand the discussion by talking about different
functions you could add to your Web store to make the
site more appealing and useful to your customers.

Finally, I discuss how to tie your new Web store into your
existing, or brand new, operations that will handle these
new sales.

Chapter 9

Setting Up Your Catalog of Goods

We're now going to move the discussion from building your Web store in general to the core pieces that will make up the store. In other words, you've built the outer walls of your store, created shelves, hung your sign above the door, and painted the walls. Now it's time to fill the shelves with products, add any special functions to your store, and get everybody ready to handle the orders.

The first step in this process is setting up your catalog of products for sale. Your catalog is your store's essence, after all. Without something to sell, your store is simply a collection of empty shelves. Therefore, you want to organize the information that makes up your product catalog so you can easily make updates when needed and be able to track your orders to figure out which product lines to expand and which to eliminate.

Furthermore, if you set up your catalog correctly, you can take advantage of newer Internet technologies like *RSS (Really Simple Syndication)* to allow your customers (and other Web sites) to get automatic updates every time you update your catalog so they are seeing only the newest items for sale and not just everything you are selling. We will discuss how to set up something called an RSS feed and some of the tools available to distribute your RSS feed automatically.

Defining the Data for Your Catalog

In Chapter 1, we talked about different types of products that you can carry in your Web store. In this chapter, we are going to talk about different types of information you need to store about each product for sale. There are a lot of pieces of data that can make up an item listing, and the more information you keep track of in your catalog the more analysis you can do with your incoming orders about what products to keep or liquidate.

Now, there are some basic pieces of information you should have for every item in your catalog:

- ✔ **Title:** Every product needs to have a title to represent the item in one clear, concise phrase or sentence. Typically, this title can contain the manufacturer name, model number, and type of item — for example Sony XJ-3000 CD Player. In some cases, like for a book, DVD, or music CD, it will contain the artist or writer involved.

- ✔ **Description:** Every product needs to have at least a few sentences or one paragraph to explain exactly what the product can do, what benefits the product offers, and/or a summary of the contents of the product.

  In some cases, you may need to have two different descriptions available. You may need a summary, or brief description, as well as a detailed description. Many times, you can simply use the first sentence or two of your detailed description as your summary.

- ✔ **Photo:** Since you are constructing a Web store, odds are your customers will never be able to hold the product in their hands, turn it over, or even "kick the tires." Therefore, in an Internet environment, a photo is *crucial* to successful sales. This is a visual marketplace, as customers want to see what they are purchasing, even if it is a stock or manufacturer's photo of the item.

- ✔ **Price:** Every item you sell needs to have an associated price with it, otherwise, you're just giving away the store . . . literally! This field should have the regular retail price you plan on charging your customers for any given item.

- ✔ **SKU or UPC:** In terms of retail products, *SKU* stands for Stock-Keeping Unit, while *UPC* is Universal Product Code. In other words, you should have some sort of unique label or number that identifies your item. In some cases, this piece of information may be standard and already created. For example, every new book published in the US has an ISBN number that identifies that particular book. You could simply track the ISBN number as your item SKU or record-keeping number.

- ✔ **Quantity:** Before you start selling anything, you need to know how many of that item you have available to sell. It's helpful to have your quantity stored in advance, so you don't end up selling 10 of something if you have only three available.

While some e-commerce programs will require additional fields as mandatory or required, the above fields should be universally required for any Web store to maintain. You will know what fields are mandatory for your particular storefront solution when you try to add a new product because the fields are usually marked with an asterisk (*), as seen in Figure 9-1. A good piece of advice is to fill in every field presented, not just the ones marked as mandatory.

Add New Product

This page allows you to enter information and attributes for a new product.

Current Category: Home

| Add New Product | Page Help Video Tutorial | Save | Save and Add another | Cancel |

Key Product Details   ⊟ Show/Hide

Product Type*   --- SELECT PRODUCT TYPE --- ▾

Product Name*

Sale Price (per unit) $

List Price (per unit) $

Quantity in Stock   Item(s)

SKU

Available   YES ▾

Product Tax Class   Non-Taxable ▾   Add Product Tax Class

     * = Required Field

Main Product Image   ⊞ Show/Hide

Product Descriptions   ⊞ Show/Hide

Shipping Information   ⊞ Show/Hide

Search Engine Information   ⊞ Show/Hide

| Save | Save and Add another | Cancel |

Figure 9-1: E-commerce providers indicate what fields are required for your catalog.

In addition to the fields in your catalog that you must have, there are some other fields in your catalog that you should consider having:

- ✔ **Cost:** You won't know if your e-commerce store is truly profitable until you can calculate the profit per item sold, and for that you need the item cost as well as the item price so you can compute gross profit.

  If your per item cost is questionable (perhaps it was purchased as part of a large, one-time-payment collection), you can either calculate and put in a rough average for each unit, or figure out a more appropriate cost based on the percentage value for that one item in the collection, multiplied by the cost of the collection. For example, if you paid $1,000 for 20 units, but one unit was rare enough that it was probably worth 15–20% of the collection price, your cost could either be $50 (1000/20) or $150–200 (1000 * 15–20%). Discuss this further with your CPA or accountant.

- ✔ **Attributes:** Many of the e-commerce platforms out there allow you to create an item in your catalog and then assign attributes, rather than creating individual items for every attribute you carry. For example, you can define a 2007 T-Shirt item with three color attributes of blue, black, and white, rather than having to create three different items — 2007 blue T-Shirt, 2007 black T-shirt, and 2007 white T-shirt.

Different attributes to keep track of can include:

- Color

- Size

- Weight

- Model/Make number

- Signed/Unsigned

- Edition/Version/Printing (1st print, 2nd print, special printing, and so on)

If different attributes will affect the price of the item, you will need to store that price difference as well. For example, if you charge $2 extra for XXL shirts compared to S-XL, when you store XXL as an attribute you should store a +$2 to indicate that the price of an XXL shirt is $2 more.

✔ **Manufacturer/Designer:** In some cases, this information may not be in your item Title, so you would want to track it in its own field. In other cases, you want this field so you can run reports or comparisons based on different manufacturers, independent of the individual items you sell. Many times, this field is used to define a category.

✔ **Category Assignments:** If you have multiple items, then you should create categories that group together similar items. Every item in your catalog should belong to at least one category (and maybe more), so you need to identify the category assignment somewhere in your catalog entry for your item.

✔ **Keywords:** Given all the importance placed on search engine results and placement, it would be helpful to store the specific keyword phrases that apply to each item in your catalog. This way, they could be included in each product detail page using techniques like the META tag so the search engines know which keywords to associate with each product.

✔ **Thumbnail Photo:** In some cases, you may have to create an additional version of your item photo that is resized down to create a thumbnail (preview) photo. Some e-commerce software packages will do this automatically (like Yahoo! Merchant Solutions), while others (like 1&1 eShops) ask for a thumbnail and detail photo separately.

✔ **Weight:** Depending on how you calculate your shipping, it would help you tremendously to automatically have the weight of the item, so shipping could be calculated properly instead of being based on averages.

✔ **Dimensions:** Many of the shipping companies, including the US Postal Service, now look at the physical dimensions of an item to compute the shipping cost. Therefore, having the dimensions of your product may become necessary to figure out an accurate shipping amount.

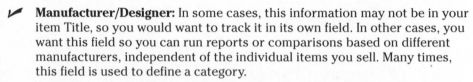

Understanding RSS Feeds for Your Catalog

In the past, when you wanted to let your customers know that there was a new version of your catalog, it typically involved creating a print announcement, mailing out thousands of glossy catalogs or flyers, and making a big deal to announce any new changes. Thankfully today, in the "Internet age," sending out updates is handled in an automatic fashion using a technology known as RSS.

RSS has different meanings, depending on which version you are discussing, but it is typically referred to as *Really Simple Syndication*. RSS is a group of formats used to publish content that changes frequently. RSS feeds are documents that contain the most recently changed content from a website, or the full text with specific notes.

The most typical use of RSS has been for blogs, since that content usually changes on a daily basis. RSS aggregators receive the different RSS feeds and show their users the newest content from multiple locations so the user doesn't have to track down the changes themselves. Besides blogs, however, there are product search engines that can be set up to receive RSS feeds from merchants, just like you, so they can know your product catalog at any given time to give their users a sense of what products (and prices) you are offering.

Therefore, it's handy for you to understand the basics of this technology so you can choose to implement it, especially if you have to update and re-price your catalog often to keep up with your competitors. Some e-commerce packages have some of these tools built-in, while other packages rely on you to create and distribute these files yourself.

Anatomy of an RSS feed

When it comes to products, the RSS feed can be pretty simple. After declaring the basics of your Web store at the top, the contents of the RSS feed file are simply the new items in your catalog. You have to declare a title, link, and description for each item, and you have some choices for additional fields after those three.

For more information on different e-commerce fields you could add to your RSS feed, check out an example of the Discovery Store's RSS feed at `http://shopping.discovery.com/erss/`.

Here is a sample version of what an RSS feed would look like, including some specific e-commerce RSS 2.0 specifications:

```
<xml version="1.0">
<rss version="2.0"
  xmlns:ecommerce="http://www.yourstorename.com/erss">

  <channel>
    <title>Your E-Commerce Store Name</title>
    <link>http://www.yourstorename.com/</link>
    <description>The best place to buy and sell.</description>
    <language>en-us</language>
    <pubDate>Tue, 01 Jan 2008 00:00:00 GMT</pubDate>
    <docs>http://www.yourstorename.com/rss</docs>
    <item>
      <title>Hot Product #1</title>
      <link>http://www.yourstorename.com/product1.html</link>
      <description>This hot product is burning up the shelves, as customers are
            fighting each other to get it. Here's your chance to add this to your
            collection.</description>
      <ecommerce:listprice>29.99</ecommerce:listprice>
      <ecommerce:SKU>HOTPROD001</ecommerce:SKU>
      <category>New Products</category>
```

```
       <pubDate>Tues, 01 Jan 2008 00:00:00 GMT</pubDate>
     </item>

     <item>
       <title>Hot Product #2</title>
       <link>http://www.yourstorename.com/product2.html</link>
       <description>If you have already picked up our Hot Product #1, then you
              definitely had to add this Product #2 for even BETTER
              results!</description>
       <ecommerce:listprice>19.99</ecommerce:listprice>
       <ecommerce:SKU>HOTPROD002</ecommerce:SKU>
       <category>New Products</category>
       <pubDate>Tues, 01 Jan 2008 00:00:00 GMT</pubDate>
     </item>
   </channel>
</rss>
```

If you manually create your catalog, like with Microsoft Excel, you could use a basic text editor and follow the commands given in the sample RSS feed file above. However, if you use your e-commerce software package to maintain and update your catalog, you should first look in that package to see if they can automatically create and send your RSS feed for you. If neither of those options are viable, you can consider using a third-party source for RSS feed creation, such as FeedforAll (www.feed forall.com). They provide software and tools through their Web site to allow you to create, edit, and publish your RSS feeds to various search engines.

Using Microsoft Excel to Create Your Catalog File

Stuff You Need to Know

Toolbox:
- Your product data (UPC/SKU numbers, product titles, prices, and so on)
- A list of your product data headers

Time Needed:
15–60 minutes

Once you've come up with the different data fields you plan on tracking in your catalog, it's time to create a catalog file to store all this information. If you have a copy of Microsoft Excel (or any spreadsheet program, for that manner), you can create your own catalog file.

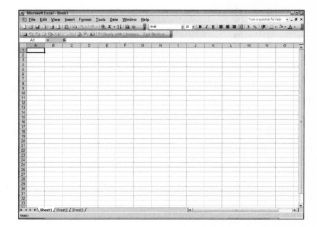

1. Start the Microsoft Excel application. When the program loads, you should see an empty spreadsheet in front of you. In some cases, you may be prompted whether you want to create a new file or open an existing file. If you see that screen, pick the Create a New File option.

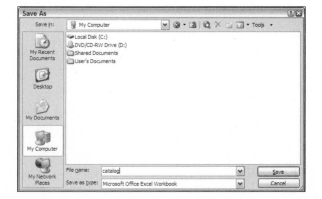

2. Select File⇨Save As and save your new file as `catalog.xls`. Later on, you will probably save your catalog file under a different format, but in the beginning, have a copy saved as an Excel spreadsheet so it will retain all the features of a spreadsheet file and load quicker into Excel for easy access to you.

Options for Creating Your Catalog File

Thankfully, you have several options to choose from when it comes to creating your catalog file, depending on your e-commerce software platform and what software is already on your computer.

Many full-featured software platforms, like Yahoo! Merchant Solutions, ProStores, and similar vendors will create the catalog file for you, and allow you to enter information for each item through guided screens known as wizards (see Chapters 4 and 5, where each screen prompts you for certain item data fields like Name, Quantity, Price, and other fields).

However, you may want to create your catalog before you start working on your e-commerce store, which means you need to create this independent of your storefront provider or package, and have a copy on your local computer. In this case, the most popular program for small businesses to use to store their inventory seems to be Microsoft Excel, which was designed for financial spreadsheets.

One big reason that many small business owners use Excel is that they can create special versions of a text file, known as *Comma Separated Values files* (or *.CSV*), that can be easily imported into and exported from many of the e-commerce software packages available. Many small business owners already own a copy of Excel by having Microsoft Office on their computer, or they use Excel for their financial needs already, so they can add a benefit by keeping their catalog information on Excel as well. Also, many people enjoy the ease of use and simplicity of storing their catalog information as a table that they can update without the need for a sophisticated program.

Microsoft Excel is not your only option for a locally created catalog file, however. There are many programs that will help you design and maintain your own catalog. While many large corporations use software like SAP, you can use Microsoft Access or FileMaker software to create your own catalog as a database.

3. Along the first row of the spreadsheet, enter names for the different fields you want in your catalog. The first row of your catalog file is known as the *header row* because it contains the headings of all the columns you wish to create in your catalog. Give a meaningful name to each header you wish to create.

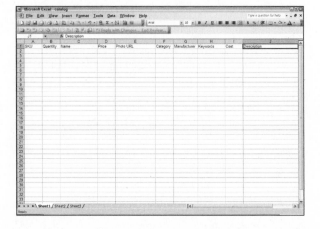

The first column should be reserved for your ID or SKU field, whatever will be the unique identifier for your different products. This way, you can easily sort based on your identifier, and see the different values easily.

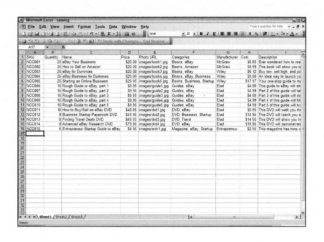

4. Underneath the header row, start entering your different products, row by row, based on the SKU or ID number. Make sure that each product has at least the SKU or ID number, and as much information as you know to complete the file. If you have to leave a field blank, that is okay, as long as it is not the SKU or ID field. Before you open your store to the public, however, you should have every essential field completed. After a while, you should start to have a catalog file like the one in Figure 5 below. The great thing about creating your catalog file in Excel is that, if you ever want to add additional catalog fields, you just create a new column header in Excel and fill in the appropriate fields as they apply to each item. You don't want to re-order, re-program, or massively change an already defined system, or lose your previous data, when you want to add something new or extra.

5. To create a CSV (or Comma Separated Values) file of your catalog data, select File⇨Save As and pick CSV as the file type in the window prompt. Where it says Save As Type, click on the down arrow to bring up a list of options of different file types. Scroll down about 10-15 options until you see CSV (Comma delimited), and click that option. Then click the Save button to save the file as a CSV file.

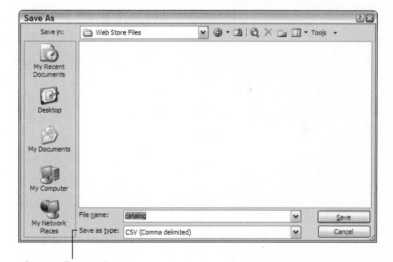

Save as Type option.

TIP

While Microsoft Excel has the capability to store images in their fields, it is better to store the pathname to your image files in this catalog file rather than storing the actual images in this file. Even if you haven't created your images yet, create an image location in this file then use the same naming scheme when you actually create your catalog photos later.

6. Excel will prompt you about whether you want to save this file as a CSV file. Click the Yes button in both windows as they appear on your screen. Microsoft Excel can store a lot of different information in their workbook files, but a Comma Separated Value file can store only one screen's (or sheet, in Excel terminology) worth of basic text. Therefore, when you save the file as CSV, Excel warns you that you may lose information when you save as a CSV file. Typically, you will not lose any critical catalog data by doing this step, so click Yes to both.

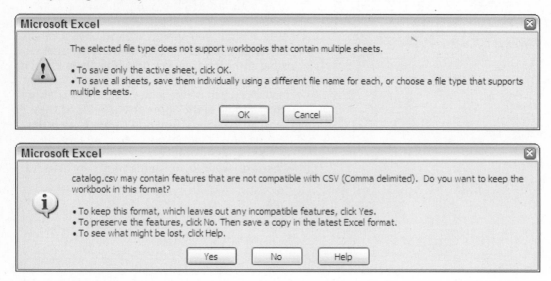

7. If you want to keep working on your catalog file, it is recommended to go back and do a Save As and save your document as an Excel workbook again. Any changes you make to this document after saving it as a CSV file will attempt to update the CSV file, and not the Excel workbook file. Therefore, we have to save the document again as an Excel workbook so any future updates get saved properly. When you are done updating your document, you can re-save it as a CSV file to get all the new updates.

Creating Your RSS Feed Using WebReference RSS Creator

Once you've created your catalog file, it's time to create an RSS feed. For this task, we're using WebReference RSS Creator to create our RSS feed.

1. You can access the RSS creator tool by typing in `http://www.webreference.com/cgi-bin/perl/makerss.pl` into your Web browser. When you do that, you'll see the RSS Creator form on your screen.

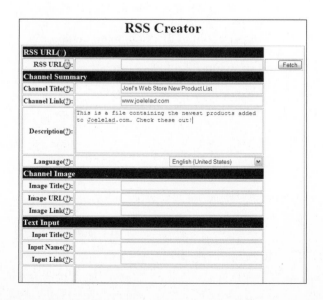

2. For the box labeled Channel Title, enter the name of your Web store and a description for your RSS file. An example would be "Joel's Web Store New Product List." You can't leave this field blank. For the box labeled Channel Link, enter the URL of your Web store. An example would be `http://www.joelsstore.com`. For the box labeled Channel Description, enter a description of what your RSS file will contain.

Item1			
Title(?):		Joel's Store First New Product	Build RSS
Link(?):		www.joelelad.com/product-id1.html	
Item2			
Title(?):		Joel's Store Second New Product	Build RSS
Link(?):		www.joelelad.com/product-id2.html	
Item3			
Title(?):		Joel's Store Third New Product	Build RSS
Link(?):		www.joelelad.com/product-id3.html	
Item4			
Title(?):		Joel's Store Fourth New Product	Build RSS
Link(?):		www.joelelad.com/product-id4.html	
Item5			
Title(?):		Joel's Store Fifth New Product	Build RSS
Link(?):		www.joelelad.com/product-id5.html	
Item6			
Title(?):		Joel's Store Sixth New Product	Build RSS
Link(?):		www.joelelad.com/product-id6.html	
Item7			
Title(?):			Build RSS
Link(?):			

3. Scroll down to the Item section of the form. For each new product you just added to the catalog, enter the name of that product in the Title box next to an Item header. Then, enter the URL for that new product in the Link box. For example, if you created a product in Yahoo! Merchant Solutions, and Yahoo! created a Catalog ID of *product_id1*, then the URL would be: www.*yourstorename.*com/*product-id1.*html.

```
- <rss version="0.91">
  - <channel>
      <title>Joel's Web Store New Product List</title>
      <link>www.joelelad.com</link>
    - <description>
        This is a file containing the newest products added to Joelelad.com. Check these out!
      </description>
      <language>en-us</language>
    - <item>
        <title>Joel's Store First New Product</title>
        <link>www.joelelad.com/product-id1.html</link>
      </item>
    - <item>
        <title>Joel's Store Second New Product</title>
        <link>www.joelelad.com/product-id2.html</link>
      </item>
    - <item>
        <title>Joel's Store Third New Product</title>
        <link>www.joelelad.com/product-id3.html</link>
      </item>
    - <item>
        <title>Joel's Store Fourth New Product</title>
        <link>www.joelelad.com/product-id4.html</link>
      </item>
    - <item>
        <title>Joel's Store Fifth New Product</title>
        <link>www.joelelad.com/product-id5.html</link>
      </item>
    - <item>
```

4. Once you have entered all the new products into the form, click the Build RSS button next to the last Item Title you filled in. You'll see your RSS file generated in the Web browser window. Copy and paste the text into a word processing or text program (Windows Notepad is sufficient) and save the file as feed.rss.

Submitting Your RSS Feed to Google Base

Stuff You Need to Know

Toolbox:

- RSS feed file
- Location of your RSS feed file
- Google account information

Time Needed:
5–10 minutes

Once your RSS Feed is created, it's time to distribute it! You can find dozens of RSS Feed submission tools online by going to Google and typing in "submit RSS feed" or going to `http://www.rss-specifications.com` and clicking on Submit RSS Feeds from the Navigation bar. Of course, your interest mainly lies with sites that catalog and compare different products for sale online, and as of this writing one of the up-and-coming premier sites is Google Base, previously known as Froogle.

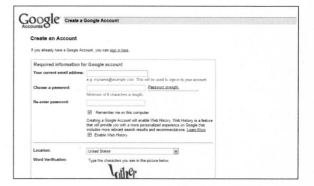

1. Create a Google account by going to `www.google.com/accounts/newaccount`. You'll be taken to the Google account creation screen. You will need to give them your e-mail address, create a password, and define your location. Scroll down, review their Terms of Service, and click the I Accept. Create My Account button.

2. Check your e-mail and click the verification link in the e-mail from Google to confirm your account. Once you click the link, you should be taken back to Google and your account should be ready to use.

Click this link.

3. Go to Google Base at `http://base.google.com` and click on the Bulk Upload link.

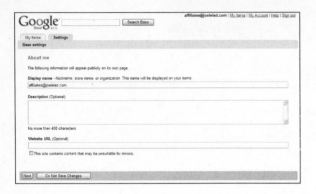

4. Once you log into Google Base and accept the Google Base Terms of Service, you will be taken to your Google Base Settings page. Fill in the fields as best as you can. Before Google will take your RSS feed, they need to know about your Web store. Therefore, complete the different fields in the Basic Settings page.

5. Once you are done, click the Next button. You will be taken to the Specify a Bulk Upload page. Pick the Products option from the list of Item Type, and enter the File Name of your RSS feed in the box specified.

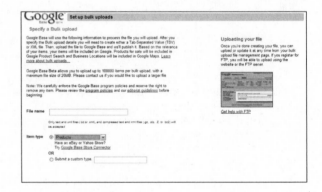

6. Click the Register the Bulk Upload File button and follow the remaining instructions. Depending on the upload, Google may prompt you for more information. Otherwise, your submission is successful and your products will be entered into their database!

Chapter 10

Adding Pictures and Copy to Your Catalog

Tasks performed in this chapter

- ✔ Finding sources for pictures and copy
- ✔ Using the right format for your pictures
- ✔ Enhancing descriptions to enhance sales
- ✔ Improving your search engine placement

Once you have picked out the products to fill your Web store catalog, it's time to make those products *pop* in the eyes, minds, and wallets of your consumers. The two most sure-fire ways to capture the shopper's attention are through clear, crisp pictures and dynamic, compelling titles and descriptions. Once you have gotten the visitor to your Web store, your pictures and descriptions need to convince the visitor to become a customer.

In this chapter, we walk you through the process of gathering the necessary pictures and copy for your catalog. My goal isn't to turn you into a professional photographer, but rather to understand what customers are looking for (and what you should look for) in order to make the customers' experience as clean and easy as possible. We then take your regular product descriptions and turn them into action-oriented descriptions that customers and search engines will enjoy scanning.

Identifying Sources of Pictures and Copy

In many cases, the bulk of this process will already be provided for you. If you are reselling goods for a manufacturer or distributor, typically there are "stock" or catalog photos that you are allowed to use on your Web site, along with the standard product description, set of features, and additional information. For example, if you look at Figures 10-1 and 10-2, you can see that Circuit City is re-using Sony's photos and description to re-sell the Sony Cyber-Shot DSC S650 Digital Camera.

Just because you are re-selling goods from a major manufacturer, that doesn't mean you can automatically go to their Web site and copy all their photos and descriptions to use in your catalog. Check with your wholesaler or distributor to see if there are any terms or conditions attached to re-using this information. If necessary, contact the manufacturer directly to get permission.

Figure 10-1: Sony has pictures and descriptions for their items . . .

Even when you get permission to re-use a manufacturer's information, you may choose to add or enhance the information to fit your Web store. For example, you may choose to create bullet points of the different features for your initial description, like Circuit City did for the Sony S650 Digital Camera (refer to Figure 10-2), and then make the full description available by clicking a link to read more.

Never add any information to a standard description unless you know the information is 100 percent accurate. Make sure you have the right to truncate or slightly alter descriptions as well, since some manufacturers want to ensure the customer gets a full idea of their product and not just "the highlights" you present.

Going one step further, if you are unable to gain full permission to re-use a description, you should be able to provide a link from your Web store to the manufacturer's Web site so customers can read up on technical specifications and features. It's recommended that, if you do this, the link opens a new browser window so your customer still has a window on your Web site and a pop-up window displaying the technical specifications, which they can close to see your Web site again and order the product.

Figure 10-2: ... which retailers like Circuit City can use for their Web sites as well.

Picking the Right Format for Your Pictures

There are lots of options nowadays for taking your own digital photos of your products, as every major camera manufacturer and many computer and electronics manufacturers have created digital cameras ranging from the sub-$100 entry model to the high-resolution, professional feature-laden models. You should pick a digital camera that fits your budget and needs, whether you need a camera that has a lot of automatic setup features or a camera that lets you zoom and take a crisp shot.

Chances are, however, that you may need professional assistance in turning your pictures into the high quality images you want to portray with your Web store. In that case, you may want to hire a professional photographer to take your photos and prepare them for your Web site.

It's useful to understand, however, the different file formats that your digital photos can be stored as, because different formats are suited for different situations. Specifically, these are the most common file formats:

✓ **JPEG format (.jpg):** This format, short for *Joint Photographic Experts Group,* is considered the standard for the Internet as many images online are saved using this format. It stores 8 bits of information per color (red, green, and blue) and does not take up as much disk space as other photo file formats, which means it typically loads quicker on a customer's screen. Every Internet Web browser knows to load and display a JPEG image in the window, so there are very few display problems. One of the downsides to the JPEG format is the loss of quality in the photo, especially if you are going to re-edit and save the file again. Typically, you would save your photo as a JPEG file when the picture is ready to be displayed on your Web site and requires no additional editing.

✔ **GIF format (.gif):** This format, short for *Graphic Interchange Format,* was the older standard for how pictures were displayed on the Internet. This format can store only the most basic 256 colors because it has only a total of 8 bits to store color information. While most Web browsers can display GIF files easily, it is typically reserved for the simpler graphics or buttons that don't require any complex or animated GIFs (which are a combination of different GIF files that display in succession providing an animation effect for the viewer).

✔ **TIFF format (.tif):** This format, short for *Tagged Image File Format,* is mainly used for an image when you want to print it instead of posting it on the Internet. It does store up to 16 bits per color (red, green, and blue) so it can handle detailed images, and some digital cameras can save the picture directly as a TIFF with very little loss in quality due to how it compresses the picture. TIFF files are best suited when you want to use the picture in a physical print environment (like a flyer, catalog, or brochure) and then you can convert the file from TIFF to JPEG when you need the photo to be used on your Web site. (Most Web browsers *don't* know how to display TIFF files properly.) If you think you would ever need to physically print this picture for any reason, keep a version of the photo in TIFF format.

✔ **PSD format (.psd):** This format is known as the *Photoshop Document format,* named for Adobe's Photoshop digital software editing tool. Images are stored in this format when you are using Photoshop to create or edit the picture. This format stores a lot of additional information that is used by Photoshop when the image is loaded into the software. In order to view a PSD file, you need to either have Photoshop installed on your computer or a special file to view this image. If you plan on using a graphic designer or professional photographer, it is highly encouraged to keep a version of each image in PSD format, in case they need to go back and re-use or edit the image again.

Other file formats include:

✔ **PSP format (.psp):** This format is like the PSD format, but is geared for the Paint Shop Pro software tool.

✔ **PNG format (.png):** This is the *Portable Network Graphics format,* seen as the successor to the GIF format. Web browsers can display this graphic, but it isn't used often.

✔ **Raw format (extensions vary depending on camera manufacturer):** Some digital cameras store pictures in this format, which keeps virtually every bit of data that the camera stores when taking the picture. Unfortunately, not every image editing software tool knows how to handle this format, and these files are very large.

✔ **BMP format (.bmp):** This *BitMaP format* is exclusively used by Microsoft Windows to store images within Windows. Some Web sites use an image like this to control their navigation bar or menu, but it isn't recommended for product photos on the Internet.

Taking Quality Digital Photos

If you are going to take your own digital photos of your products for sale, keep the following points in mind:

✔ **Don't overload your pictures.** Your goal when taking product photos is to make the product stand out on its own. For example, you do not want to crowd too many objects into one photo to show a complete collection.

✔ **Beware the Flash.** When it comes to lighting, outdoor (natural) light is the best. Realistically, you are not going to photograph your laser printer that is resting on a cliff overlooking the ocean, so you will need sufficient indoor lighting. Because of this, many people rely on the flash to provide that light. The downside is that the flash can wash out the colors and, when there is anything reflective or shiny, provide jarring flash spots that can be seen as covering up damage or imperfections.

✔ **A blank background is better, except for light-colored items.** In most cases, you want a white background, so the object itself is more emphasized to the viewer. The only exception to this rule is lightly colored items, like diamonds and gemstones. Make sure the background highlights the product you are shooting, and add a special background prop, like a shade, covering, or blank paper to isolate the product from everything else.

Depending on your digital camera, you can also set the white balance to Cloudy (from Auto) to add more warm and brilliant colors to your picture.

✔ **Steady your shot.** Remember, you are taking shots of products, not people running in a marathon. Therefore, you want your "still" pictures to be focused and clear. The best investment in this case is buying a tripod, which stabilizes the camera on a 3-leg platform.

Another trick is to lower the ISO Shutter Speed of your digital camera, so the lens is only "open" for a fraction of a second to capture the picture.

✔ **Use the highest resolution possible when shooting.** Your digital camera will have different settings to capture a varying level of quality for each picture. It is recommended to take pictures at the highest resolution your camera offers, because you can always resize your photos later to compress them for the Internet. It is better to resize from a high quality picture than try to adapt a lower quality picture.

✔ **Sometimes, one is not enough.** Remember, you may not capture everything about your product in one photograph. Your first photo, often used as the thumbnail photo, should have a front-on view of the product, but if this is a complex item, you should take multiple photos of different angles, showing off different features of the item. The optimal number of photos for a complex item is typically 2-4 for an e-commerce setting.

✔ **Macro Mode is a must.** Most digital cameras have a special setting known as *Macro,* which allows them to focus the camera when the camera is approximately one inch away from the surface of the item they wish to photograph. This allows for excellent close-up shots, where you want to highlight any special functions, the product logo, or any other details about the product.

✔ **Put it in the middle . . . the product, that is.** When taking a still photo of a product, you want to position the camera viewfinder so the item sits in the dead middle of the picture. You can turn the item (or the photo) slightly to the side, so you're examining the product from an angle, but make sure the product fills most of the picture.

✔ **Focus on getting the right focus.** If you rely on the digital camera to automatically focus the item before you take the

(continued)

(continued)

picture, hold the shutter button down about half-way, wait for the camera to find the right focus, and then, when the camera beeps or indicates through the LCD screen that the focus is there, continue to press down on the shutter button until the picture is taken and stored in the camera.

✔ **Resize to the right size.** Since some of your customers will still be using dial-up services to access your Web store, you don't want to host large versions of your pictures on your site. Customers who have to wait for highly detailed pictures to download, one line at a time, will feel like they are being "put on hold" and will most likely leave your store to find another store whose pictures load quickly. Therefore, one of your last photo editing steps should be to resize your photos to take up less pixels or inches so it will load quicker.

✔ **Find balance in your photos.** Since your photos are designed to highlight your products, make sure that there is some symmetry in your photos. If there is something large in one half of your picture, make sure there is something equally large or important in the other half.

For more tips and tricks on using good Digital Photography techniques to capture your product photos, you can check out *Digital Photography For Dummies, 5th Edition*, by Julie Adair King (Wiley Publishing, Inc.).

Using Action Words to Enhance Your Sales

While a picture can speak a thousand words, it is important to consider the words you are going to use to describe the products in your catalog as well. When it comes to writing for the Internet audience, the rules are slightly different than other mediums. On the Web, the focus is on clarity, brevity, grabbing attention, and using the right keywords. In addition, you're not just appealing to human visitors. You are also hoping to use the words in your product titles and descriptions to convince the search engines, such as Google and Yahoo!, to consider your Web store a reputable source for your store products. That way, they will help recommend your Web site to potential visitors searching for your store products.

In short, your descriptions have to pass a "3-part process" to be truly effective. They have to:

1. **Convince the search engines to index your product descriptions, so the descriptions get stored in their database.**

2. **Convince a user who finds that product description (by using a search engine) to check out your store.**

3. **Convince that same user, now a store visitor, to want to buy a product from your store.**

When you begin to think about writing your product titles and descriptions, try to make sure that your writing is:

✔ **Clear:** Don't beat around the bush when it comes to describing a product. Just state in plain English what it can do, what benefits it can provide, and why it's a good product to buy.

✔ **Concise:** Use bullet points, numbered lists, and short sentences whenever possible. White space is your friend. Don't feel like you have to fill the screen with text. Use **bold** and *italic* words to add emphasis.

✔ **To the point:** When writing your product description, the first paragraph should have all the key details of the product. After that, you can list out the product benefits, features, and/or testimonials. Your goal is that the customer completely understands what the product is after reading that first paragraph.

Once you have written your descriptions to cater to the needs of your human customers, it doesn't hurt to go back and look at everything to make sure your catalog appeals to that "secondary" customer, the one that relies on the keywords and hypertext links — the search engines.

In Chapter 17, we discuss how to get your Web store pages and overall site ready and able to be interpreted by the search engines. Here, we focus on your product titles and descriptions, with some basic rules to consider:

✔ **Make sure every title and description are consistent.** Your goal with enhancing search engine placement is to associate your product with a specific keyword phrase that applies to your product. If you use one phrase in your title, but a slightly different phrase in your description (hoping to "cover your bases" with two different phrases), the search engines don't know which phrase is more relevant, and in the process, neither becomes relevant, and you lose your placement. You are allowed very little repetition, so use your keyword phrase once in the title, and one or two times in the description to make a point.

✔ **Don't overload your descriptions.** *Keyword stuffing* is the act of putting the same exact keyword phrase too many times in a product description (or Web page) in hopes of telling the search engine that the phrase is *really* representative of the product. Today, the search engines will actually penalize Web sites that practice keyword stuffing, so make sure that your main keywords are mentioned throughout the description, but not necessarily on every line or page.

✔ **Use the terms your customers are searching for.** You may have the greatest products known to humanity, but if your customers are typing in different words, acronyms, phrases, or slang to find the product, and you don't use those words to describe your product, you are missing out on sales. In other words, learn the language of your buyers. If they use special acronyms, make sure those acronyms are part of your product titles and descriptions.

Use sites like www.wordtracker.com and Yahoo!'s Search Marketing tool (http://searchmarketing.yahoo.com/?mkt=us) to find the most popular keyword searches and phrases, and incorporate the top ones into appropriate product descriptions.

Adding Product Pictures to Your Web Store

Stuff You Need to Know

Toolbox:
- Name or ID of each product
- Digital picture(s) of each product

Time Needed:
3–5 minutes per product

If you took quality digital photos of your products and want to replace the stock images you initially uploaded to your site, or if you created your product list first and didn't previously upload any pictures for your product, then this section is for you. For this example, we're going to use a Yahoo! Merchant Solutions Web store to illustrate this process.

1. Log into your Yahoo! Merchant Solutions account at `http://small business.yahoo.com` by clicking on the button marked "Small Business" and entering your Yahoo! Merchant Solutions user ID and password. You'll be taken to your Merchant Starter page. After you look at your Merchant page, you need to click on the Catalog Manager link and then click on the Manage Your Items link from the Catalog Manager.

2. Once you have clicked on the Manage Your Items link, you'll see the Items default-table. Click the hyperlinked Product ID of the item whose picture you want to upload.

3. Once you've clicked the Product ID, you'll see the Edit Item screen for your product. Scroll down to the Store Fields section, under Image, and click the Upload button.

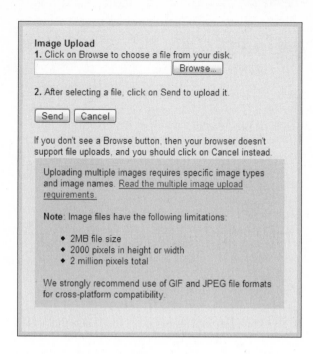

4. At this point, you'll be on the Image Upload screen. Click the Browse button to find the directory on your computer where the digital photo is stored, and select the digital photo you wish to upload to your store. After you select the photo, click the Send button to upload the photo.

5. At this point, you'll be on the Image Upload screen. Click the Browse button to find the directory on your computer where the digital photo is stored, and select the digital photo you wish to upload to your store. After you select the photo, click the Send button to upload the photo.

6. Once the photo has been uploaded, you'll be returned to the Edit Item screen for your product, but now, a thumbnail representation of your photo should be visible in the Image section. Click the Save button at the top of this screen to save your new photo with the Item information.

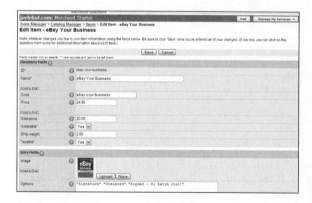

7. You'll now see your Items default table again. Repeat Steps 2–6 for any additional product where you want to upload a new or initial product digital photograph.

Enhancing Product Descriptions on Your Web Store

If you want to replace the stock or placeholder product descriptions you initially uploaded to your site, or if you created your product list first and didn't fully write out descriptions for your product, then this section is for you. For this example, we're going to use a Yahoo! Merchant Solutions Web store to illustrate this process.

1. Log into your Yahoo! Merchant Solutions account at `http://small business.yahoo.com` by clicking on the button marked Small Business and entering your Yahoo! Merchant Solutions user ID and password. You'll be taken to your Merchant Starter page. After you look at your Merchant page, you need to click on the Catalog Manager link and then click on the Manage Your Items link from the Catalog Manager.

2. Once you've clicked on the Manage Your Items link, you'll see the Items default-table. Click the hyperlinked Product ID of the item whose description you want to enhance. When you see the Edit Item page on your screen, scroll down to the Store Fields section.

3. In the field marked Headline, you can add an eye-catching Headline to describe your product that has a designated keyword phrase that represents your item. This headline will appear instead of your product item title. (This field is optional.)

4. In the field marked Caption, you need to make sure your full product description is typed in here. Follow the guidelines described earlier in the chapter in the "Using Action Words to Enhance Your Sales" section and make sure that you separate every paragraph by hitting the Enter key. Additionally, you can put a shorter version of your product description in the Abstract field, which is below the Caption field.

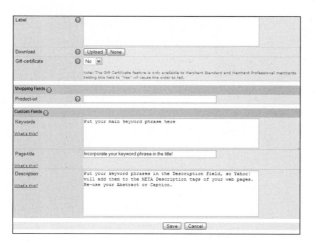

5. Scroll down the page until you see the Custom Fields section. In the Keywords field, put in the main keywords associated with this item. In the Page-title field, be sure to incorporate one keyword phrase into the title of the item. Finally, in the Description field, type in a paragraph (perhaps your Abstract or first paragraph of your Caption) that has your main keyword phrases incorporated. The information you enter here will be incorporated into commands called META tags which are read by search engines and help determine your placement in the search engines.

6. When you are done, click the Save button at the bottom of the page. You'll be taken back to the Items default-table. Simply repeat Steps 2–5 for each product in your catalog, and you'll make sure your product descriptions are optimized!

Chapter 11

Building Your Store Features and Functions

When you build an e-commerce Web store you should always make sure the core of your site (your catalog and products) are set up correctly, which is what we spent the last two chapters discussing. If you want to move your store to the next level, however, you need to provide more than just commerce — you need to provide some functionality that engages your customer, gets them more involved in the process, and gives them something extra beyond the item in the box. As more and more e-commerce sites compete for the customer's business, it's usually those companies that provide something extra that win out or sustain their revenue.

There are a lot of different ways you can enhance your Web store to add this functionality. The basic level of functionality should already be present, where customers can pick multiple items from you, add them to a shopping cart, and checkout and pay without interaction or communication from you, the store owner. Additional functions increase the "interactive" nature of business, where customers get to interact with you, your employees, and your other customers more easily and naturally.

In this chapter, we look at the most common (or usual) functions that Web store owners like to add to their site — customer accounts, search engines, and discussion boards. We then give some hands-on instructions on how to implement these functions on your Web site. *Please understand that these functions are by no means the only functions available to your Web store.* For all the functions available to your Web store, we encourage you to consult with your e-commerce storefront provider and see what functions are standard with your package, as well as what functions cost extra but can be plugged into your store setup.

Understanding Customer Accounts

There're several reasons why you may want your customers to have the ability to log into a special account, created just for them, on your Website. Offering customer accounts means you can store each customer's personal information in a protected way so other customers can't view it. This allows a customer to store their financial information, like their credit card info, so it's very easy for them to place future orders and pay for them. The best example of this is Amazon.com, which allows "1-click" ordering for their products because every Amazon customer has to store a credit card in their account and pay for every order with that credit card. They offer lots of functionality in their customer accounts, as you can see in Figure 11-1.

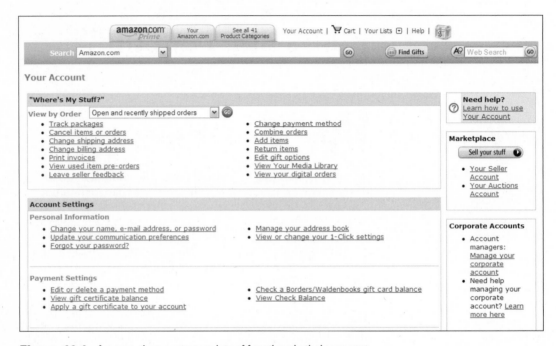

Figure 11-1: Amazon gives customers lots of functions in their account.

Quick payment isn't the only reason to have customer accounts, however. Sometimes, you may want to add exclusive content that is meant for only your paying customers and/or registered users, and the only way to ensure this exclusivity is to hide the content on a Web page that requires your customers to log in and view it. As long as you provide something with value, like extra articles, product previews, exclusive announcements on upcoming merchandise, or even the first chance to order a new product, customers should be willing to file their personal contact information with you.

Some companies earn extra revenue by taking this concept one step further and offering "subscriptions" to their Web site. That is where customers pay a monthly fee for exclusive access to special sections of that Web site. One good example is The Wall Street Journal, who even charges their print subscribers an extra fee to read articles posted only on their subscriber Web site.

Customer accounts give you, the store owner, several benefits that can be worth the time and cost of creating this functionality. First and foremost, you get detailed access to your customer's information, from their personal demographics to order and purchase history. This can be very helpful when planning future product lines or predicting upcoming sales.

Secondly, you begin to develop brand loyalty with your customers. If they went to the trouble of creating their account and get used to accessing it, now there is a "cost" if they leave your store and go to someone else's Web site. You make it easier for them to shop with you and you give those customers benefits or perks to encourage repeat buying. This ongoing relationship between you and your customers is what truly builds a business.

Lastly, customer accounts give you an excellent field for testing or trying out new promotions. You can offer limited sales to your registered customers, or roll out a new promotion to your customers first, without alerting your casual Web store visitor. You can study the effects of that sale or promotion and decide whether to roll it out on a larger scale, without a lot of upfront investment.

Putting a Search Engine on Your Store

When it comes to doing business on the Internet, people are trained to search. Many Internet users have Google or Yahoo! bookmarked as their starting page, and start every Web session by searching for what they need.

This need to search has invaded the e-commerce arena as well, where some customers will ignore the featured items and navigation bar, and simply perform one search to see if the product they need is available on your Web store.

Therefore, more and more Web stores are adding a search box capability to their Web site, and placing it either on the home page near or inside their navigation bar, or they are placing it on every single Web page within their site, so search is always readily available for their customers. While some e-commerce software packages already offer a built-in search box, others don't. Later in this chapter we look at how to add a simple search box using one of the biggest names in searching . . . Google.

Bringing Discussion Boards to Your Store

Sometimes, the key thing your customer is searching for is not a physical product, but some advice, recommendations, or information provided by another human being, whether it's you (the store owner), a store employee, or simply another customer. On the Internet, there are several mechanisms that can provide customers this interaction on a virtual level, and the main way is called a *discussion board.*

Also known as *message boards* or *bulletin boards,* discussion boards allow anyone to start a conversation (known on the board as a *thread*) and then have replies to that conversation appended to the initial reply. Users can search the discussion board for previous conversations that they're interested in, and get involved with current discussions that could range from technical support to their favorite products to asking the staff for their recommendation or advice.

Discussion boards have evolved into the "next level" of technical support for many Web sites because not only can members search past threads for an explanation on how to fix a common problem, but if you really get your customers actively using your discussion boards, these customers will start answering other customer's questions about your Web store before you or your employees can respond. A perfect example of this in action is on the eBay Community page (shown in Figure 11-2), where hundreds of discussion boards are monitored and filled with eBay buyers and sellers helping other buyers and sellers with their questions without eBay customer service getting involved.

While it can be simple to add this technology to your web store, you shouldn't add this function unless you're prepared to spend some time in the beginning to use the boards, respond to customer questions, and post new information on a regular basis. It can reflect negatively on your Web store if your discussion boards are empty or not used for long periods of time, or even worse, initial discussions go unanswered . . . by anyone! Given some time and encouragement, however, your customers should start to use it more regularly.

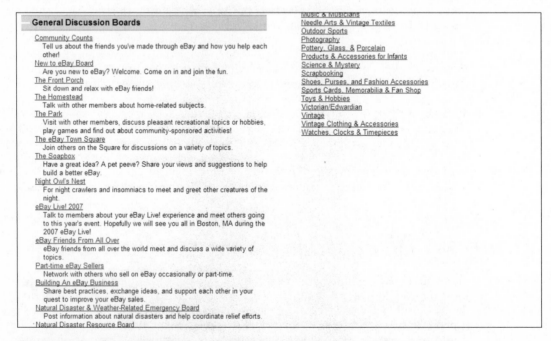

Figure 11-2: eBay provides discussion boards for new sellers, part-time sellers, and more.

Adding Customer Accounts to Your Web Store

Stuff You Need to Know

Toolbox:

✔ A name of a members-only subdirectory of your store

✔ A members-only user ID and password that you'll give out to members

Time Needed:
10–15 minutes

You have several options when it comes to adding customer accounts. You can simply require a user ID and password to access part of your Web store, which you would give to any customer who wants an account. You could implement software to allow any customer to create their own unique account name and password, and have functionality tied to that specific customer ID. If you just want to set up a "members-only" area of your Web site, you need to create a password-protected section of your Web site. Some e-commerce packages, like Yahoo! Merchant Solutions, have this capability built into the package.

Click this link.

1. Go to your Web Hosting Control Panel and click the Manage tab to create a members account and password. Your first job is to create a new user, which is basically your member account. Therefore, in your Web Hosting control panel, you click on the Manage tab and then click the Password Manager link.

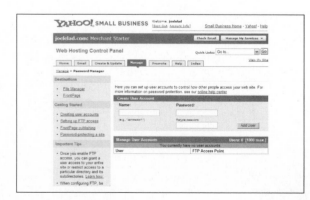

2. Once you click the Password Manager link you should see the Add User screen. Create your own user ID to represent your members, and then come up with a password for that account. Click the Add User button to save this information in your account. If you want to create different levels of user accounts, or special accounts for your first few users, repeat this step and create multiple accounts.

Adding Dynamic Customer Accounts

If you want to add the ability for customers to create their own accounts, monitor and update their account information, and have advanced functionality, then you need to install a custom software package to help facilitate this. Consult your storefront provider to see what programming languages are supported on your Web site, and whether they have any special promotions with companies that provide these functions.

Many times it's the shopping cart software that will have the ability to add customer accounts. After all, your customer has to enter their information the first time they order something from you, so your shopping cart software may have a module where the customer places their order and creates an account on your system, simply by adding a password in the order form and agreeing to store their information for future use.

Click this link.

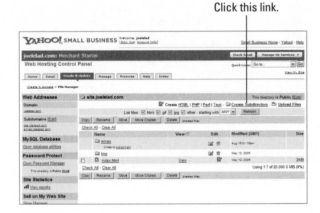

3. Click on the Manage tab or link to go back to your Web Hosting Control Panel and then click the File Manager link to create your member directory. When you click the File Manager link, you should see the directory structure of your Web site. First, you should create a subdirectory where your member content will reside. Click the Create Subdirectory link near the top right of the screen.

4. Once you are prompted for the name of your new subdirectory you can enter whatever name you'd like. (I chose members since it is easy to remember and represents what the directory will contain, which is information for members.) Then click the Create Subdirectory button to create it.

Click your newly-created directory.

5. After you have created your new subdirectory, you will be taken back to the File Manager. Click on the members directory (or whatever you named it in Step 4) link.

Click this link.

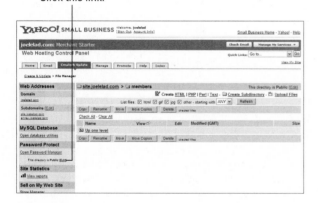

6. Once you are in the members directory, go to Password Manager by clicking the Edit link underneath the Password Manager header.

7. When you get to the Password Manager, you will see your new members' ID. Select the Has Access? checkbox to grant access to that ID to view items in the members directory. When you click the Change Access button, you will see the same screen, but with the message "Access has been successfully changed" on the top.

8. When you're done, click the Finished button to exit this process. Now, when you offer a link to any content in your members subdirectory, your users will have to enter the user ID and password you created. You can distribute this information via e-mail, a membership card, or flyer in the box you send them with their order, or whatever method you would like.

Adding a Google Search Box to Your Store

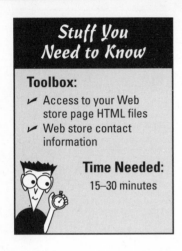

Stuff You Need to Know

Toolbox:
- Access to your Web store page HTML files
- Web store contact information

Time Needed:
15–30 minutes

When it comes to search engines Google is currently the king of search, so who better to provide a free search box you can use on your Web site? In this task we are adding a Google search box to a regular web page. For e-commerce providers like Yahoo! Merchant Solutions, ProStores, or 1&1, a search box is built in to the templates these providers offer you to build your store, so this task is unnecessary if you use one of those providers.

Click this link.

1. Go to the Google Web Search page at www. google.com/services/websearch.html to get started. As of this writing, Google offers a few different applications to help Web site owners with search-related issues. The function we are interested in is Google Free WebSearch, since that provides the Site Search capability we wish to install. Click on the Google Free WebSearch link to get started.

2. You are now on the Google Custom Search Engine start page. From this page, you can learn more about the different custom search engines that are available for your Web site, non-profit organization, and business.

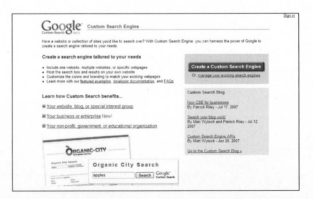

3. Click the blue Create a Custom Search Engine button to start the process. Most likely, you will be asked to log into your Google account. If you don't have a Google account yet, click the Create an Account Now link in the bottom right corner of the page, and follow the instructions to create your own Google account. Once your new account is ready, repeat Steps 1 and 2 to get back to this login screen. If your account is ready, enter the details and log into your account in order to continue.

4. Provide more detailed information about yourself in the boxes provided. Click Continue when you are ready. You may be prompted to enter more information about your new Google account. Complete the fields that are asked of you and click the Continue button when you are done.

5. Provide the basic information that will power your search box in the fields provided. You'll be asked to give Google some basic information about your Web store. You'll need to create a name for your search box, a description, and keywords. I would gear this information to your Web store and use your basic store description and keywords to answer the fields provided. When you scroll down this page, you'll be asked to enter Web sites that you want to be searched by customers when they use this new search box. Simply provide your own Web store URL as the only Web site on the list, and this box will serve as your own Site Search box. Once you have added your Web store URL, scroll down to the bottom of the page and click Continue.

If you are in an alliance with other Web stores that complement your area, but don't directly compete with you, it might be ok to include those stores in the search engine list, but this is purely optional.

6. Google will show you a sample of what your new search box will look like, based on the selections you just made. You can test out this search box by typing some sample queries and seeing the resulting page that will pop up. When you're done testing this search box, scroll to the bottom of the page and click the Finish button to save this search box to your Google account, so you can retrieve the code and add it to your Web store.

Click this link.

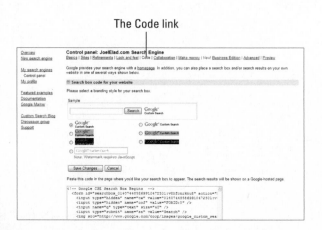

7. Once you have clicked the Finish button, you should be taken to a page displaying your newly created search engine. Pay attention to the links in the row displaying your new search engine, as you need to click the Control Panel link to retrieve the code to insert into your own Web store pages.

8. Click on the Code link from the Control Panel navigation bar along the top of the screen to get to the Code page for your search engine. First, you are asked to pick the look and feel of your search box, meaning you decide how the Google Custom Search graphic appears next to the search box. Once you make your selection and click the Save Changes button, the text box underneath that button will be updated with the HTML code required to display the search box on your Web store. Once you copy that text, go to your e-commerce storefront provider, and paste the text into each Web page of your store, or simply the home page, if you want only to provide search capabilities from your home page. That's it! Every time someone brings up one of your Web pages, the code will automatically call Google and display the search box and accompanying graphic.

The Code link

Control panel: JoelElad.com Search Engine

Overview
New search engine

Basics | Sites | Refinements | Look and feel | Code | Collaboration | Make money | New! Business Edition | Advanced | Preview

My search engines
  Control panel
My profile

Business Edition status

JoelElad.com Search Engine is not a Business Edition search engine. Compare the benefits of the available versions.

Featured examples
Documentation
Google Market

Convert to Business Edition

Business Edition overview

Custom Search Blog
Discussion group
Support

With Custom Search Business Edition you'll enjoy these additional features and support to help you integrate Google search into your website.

- **Ads-free results pages**
  Ads do not appear alongside search results, so you can keep traffic on your website.

- **XML feed of search results**
  Use this raw XML feed of search results to integrate search results with your website's look and feel.

- **Customizable search results**
  Through the XML feed, you can reorder search results as you see fit.

- **Google branding optional**
  You have the option of whether to brand your search engine as being powered by Google.

- **Email support**
  Google will provide access to help center and e-mail support for paying customers on a 24 x 7 basis. Standard Support requests are responded to with a target initial response time of one business day during Business Hours only. Service Unusable Requests are responded to 24 x 7 with a target initial response time of one hour. Phone support is also available for an additional fee.

- **Easy payment with Google Checkout**
  Custom Search Business Edition costs $100 per year for websites with less than 5,000 web pages, and $500 per year for websites between 5,000 and 50,000 web pages. Payments are made through Google Checkout, and payments do not automatically bill each year. If your website has more than 50,000 web pages, contact us for pricing.

9. (Optional) If you want an ads-free version of this search box, then click the Business Edition link from the navigation bar of the Control Panel and convert your search engine. The search engine box you have just created with Google in the above steps will accept any user's search for your Web store but display the results on a page that Google creates, with advertisements that Google (and only Google) makes money from when clicked. If you want to provide a search box that is free of advertisements and stays on your Web site, then you can convert to Google's Business Edition. As of this writing, the cost for Google's Business Edition search box is $100 per year for small to medium Web sites (less than 5,000 Web pages) and $500 per year for medium to large Web sites (less than 50,000 web pages). You can customize and automatically sort the search results displayed and are able to integrate the search engine results with your Web site's look and feel for a truly integrated experience.

Adding a BoardHost Discussion Board to Your Site

Stuff You Need to Know

Toolbox:
- The name you want to give your discussion board
- Business credit card information (if you choose a paid account)

Time Needed:
10—15 minutes

For this task, we're setting up a discussion board with BoardHost for a Yahoo! Merchant Solutions Web store. The discussion board will reside on BoardHost's server.

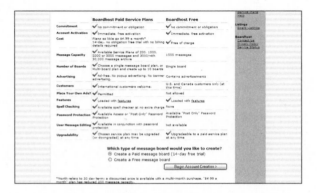

1. Go to BoardHost's Web site at `www.board host.com` and click the Join Now link. When you click the Join Now link, you'll be taken to a comparison chart where you can look at their Paid options (and get a 14-day free trial) or their Free options. Pick the option you would like and click the Begin Account Creation button.

2. Review the terms and conditions and create your own username for use on their system. Go through the terms and conditions they present on the next page, then scroll down and enter your requested username in the box provided. BoardHost will ask you to certify that you are at least 13 years old, agree not to use spam to advertise the boards, and that you agree to their terms and conditions. Once you have checked all the boxes, click the Begin Account Creation button.

Adding a Discussion Board to Your Web Site

There are two main ways to add a discussion board to your Web store. The first way is to install the software so the discussion board resides on your Web site. You should consult your e-commerce storefront provider to see what programming languages and software are supported on your Web store. Your provider may have a partner agreement to install this functionality on your Web site or know a good software package that their other customers have used.

Many storefront providers support programming languages like PHP and Perl, and therefore you can take advantage of software from companies such as:

- **vBulletin** (www.vbulletin.com): Paid software

- **PHPbb** (www.phpbb.com): Free open source software

- **IP.Board** (www.invisionpower.com): Paid software

- **Ikonboard** (www.ikonboard.com): Free software

- **Discus** (www.discusware.com): Paid and free software

The second way to add discussion board to your Web store is to use a provider that hosts the forums on their Web site, not yours. This method is much easier to add, since you simply provide a link from your Web store to the specially created forum section of their Web site, geared for your users. There is nothing to install, and you don't have to worry about Web space or bandwidth concerns affecting your main Web store.

There are several vendors to choose from, including:

- **Atomic Boards** (www.atomicboards.com)

- **Board Nation** (www.boardnation.com)

- **BoardHost** (www.boardhost.com)

- **eZBoard** (www.ezboard.com)

- **Hostboard** (www.hostboard.com)

3. You'll need to finish creating your account, and the amount of information you provide depends on whether you choose a Paid or Free account. If you choose a Free account, you should see a screen similar to the one in the figure on the left, where you have to enter your name and provide a phone number where you are available at that moment. Once you enter the information, you will get a phone call (or text message) with a verification code needed to complete the process. If you choose a paid account and are signing up for the 14-day free trial, then you'll see a screen similar to the one in the figure on the right. You simply provide your name and click the Continue button to finalize the process.

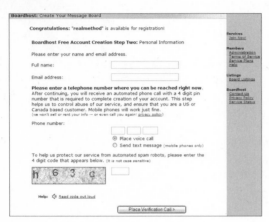

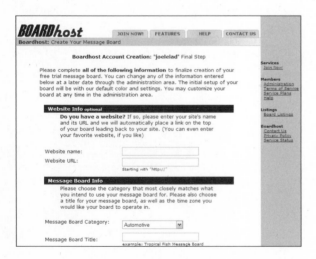

4. In the final step, you need to answer some questions about your Web site, what category your board will fall into, and a name for your discussion board. Simply fill out the prompts. You can create any name you want, but I highly suggest putting your Web store name in the title so people know what is associated with the discussion board. When you have finished entering the information, click the Submit button at the bottom of the page.

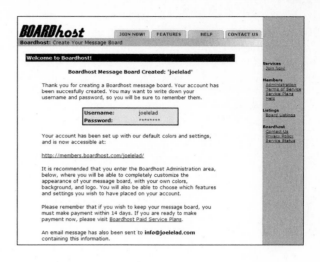

5. You are taken to an account completion screen. This screen contains the Web address of your new discussion board, so start updating your Web pages with the appropriate link. You'll also get an e-mail with instructions on how to start setting up your board categories and maintaining the board.

Joel Elad Online Selling Message Board
[Post a Message | JoelElad.com]

• **Welcome to your new message board, and welcome to Boardhost.com!**

We've started your board out with a few settings and features we think you'll enjoy, however, please be sure to bookmark and log in to the administration area to begin customizing your board, and choosing the features that are right for you. If you have any questions, be sure to let us know at **support@boardhost.com**.

This will disappear after your first posting.

Search Messages: [   ] (Submit)

Post a Message Post a Poll

Your Name: [   ]   Your Email: [   ]

Subject:
[   ]

6. Click the link for your new discussion board and examine it. Of course, your discussion board is empty to begin with, so you may want to kick off the festivities by posting an introductory message, explaining the purpose and ground rules of the discussion board, so your customers have a good starting point.

REMEMBER

When you link to this discussion board, you should open this function in a new window, so your users still have a web browser window pointed to your store, in case they want to go back and place another order or use your store immediately after participating in the discussion.

Chapter 12

Setting Up Your Back Office

Tasks performed in this chapter

✔ Knowing your shipping company options

✔ Creating your online shipping accounts

✔ Signing up with FedEx, UPS, and the US Postal Service

✔ Printing out sample labels

In the frenzy, or excitement, of setting up all your Web store operations, it's important not to lose sight of the final piece of the puzzle — the real world back office (the everyday pieces that keep your Web store operational) component of your store. This includes everything from your accounting to your inventory management to shipping and handling your products. While a lot of steps have translated onto the Internet, when you are reselling physical products, there are some steps that have to be handled offline, which is where your back office comes into play.

In this chapter, we focus mainly on your shipping and handling operations, since many of you probably won't need a sophisticated inventory management system, and many of you will set up your own accounting mechanisms through a local CPA, accountant, or using your computer with a program like QuickBooks. We start by looking at the various shipping companies (for companies in the U.S.) and comparing benefits as well as online options. We walk through, step-by-step, how to create accounts with several of these companies and how to order supplies and print your first sample label. We also talk about shipping international orders, and the customs forms that come into play there.

Understanding Your Shipping Company Options

After your customer places their order on your Web store and the thrill of immediate gratification kicks in, an invisible clock starts ticking. That clock is tied to your customer, who wishes that their order had already arrived in their mailbox, and waits (patiently, we hope) for that order to come. Over time, that clock ticks louder, and so does that customer, as they begin to inquire about their package status. Therefore, it's important to pick a shipping company that is responsive, quick, and offers their customers tracking capabilities at all steps of the shipment process.

Thankfully, all of the main shipping companies in the U.S. offer rich online tools for you to manage your shipping needs. Some of them go one step further and are able to integrate with your e-commerce shopping cart programs, sales programs, and storefront providers to instantly feed orders into their systems to create shipping labels.

In order to take advantage of any of these shipping company options, you should consider investing in a high quality scale that can accurately weigh your packages. If you mail light items, anywhere from a 5 to 100 pound scale should be sufficient. If you sell bulkier items, like electronics, you should get a 150 or 300 pound industrial scale.

When it comes to picking a shipping company to handle your needs, consider the features you'll most likely use:

- ✔ **Online label creation:** Waiting in line at the post office (or a shipping counter) is no longer a day-to-day requirement for an e-commerce store owner. Every major shipping company now offers their customers the ability to print out shipping labels that you can stick to your packages and hand off to the shipping company. These labels are generated online, your credit card is billed for the total, and usually your customers get an e-mail with their tracking information automatically, which is one less step for you to worry about in your day-to-day operations.

- ✔ **Tracking capabilities:** The first step is getting a tracking number generated when you are going to send a customer order. With companies such as UPS, FedEx, or DHL, that is automatically done. With the US Postal Service, you can request *Delivery Confirmation,* which tracks acceptance and delivery of a package, or *Signature Confirmation,* which requires the customer (or someone at that address) to sign for the package. When the package is being sent, your customers can input their tracking or Delivery Confirmation number online and see the status of their order.

- ✔ **Address book:** When you start seeing repeat customers placing orders (or you sell products on a weekly, monthly, or yearly basis) you will want the capability to store and retrieve customer's addresses and information in an address book so you do not have to re-type that information when it is time to ship out another package. In addition, if you plan to send out catalogs, promotional mailers, or other information to past customers, you want an easy way to retrieve that mailing list.

- ✔ **Reports and shipping history:** In case you ever need to go back and review a shipment that has been made, it's helpful to have all your shipping information retrievable through a reporting or history function instead of digging through a pile of receipts from manually sending off packages at the post office. In addition, if you want to review your costs, identify patterns in shipping, and try to optimize that part of your business, it will be helpful to have your past history available at your fingertips.

- ✔ **Order pick-up:** Once you've generated your labels and prepared your packages, the last step is getting the boxes to the shipping company. Some companies, like UPS, FedEx, and DHL, offer automatic daily or weekly pickup based on your order volume and allow you to order a pick-up when labels are generated. The US Postal Service offers a service called *Carrier Pick-up,* where you specify a 2-hour window for the postman to come and retrieve your packages. If you set up an account with UPS or FedEx, work with your account representative to get a daily or weekly pick-up included with your account for free. Typically, they're looking for a steady stream of packages, and may offer that on a trial basis until you can establish a suitable monthly average of packages to justify a continued free daily or weekly pickup option for your account.

The main shipping companies in the U.S.

When it comes to the main shipping companies available to small businesses in the United States, there are four that deserve mention:

✔ **Federal Express (FedEx):** When it absolutely, positively has to get there, FedEx is the company that will make it happen. They're well known for their high levels of customer service, and reach hundreds of countries around the world. They offer many levels of service, from their Next Day Air (with Early Morning Drop-off available in some cases) to Ground Residential and Business services. They have a robust online site and a Shipping Manager tool to help you organize your shipments.

   FedEx is now available in thousands of locations in the U.S. due to their purchase of Kinko's Copy and Print shops a while back. This means you can drop off your packages at a nearby Kinko's (in some cases, 24-hours a day) or have your packages processed at a Kinko's and billed to your FedEx account.

   On average, FedEx Express costs more than other companies, but their newer Ground service is competitive with UPS Ground and offers coast-to-coast ground shipping in an average of 4 business days. When you sign up to get an account with FedEx, you can save up to 15 percent off the normal rates.

✔ **UPS:** The King of Shipping, Brown can do a lot for you. UPS claims to ship more packages for e-commerce related purposes, like eBay purchases, than any other shipping company around. Like Federal Express, UPS has an extensive reach to hundreds of countries around the world and offers a wide array of shipping options, from Next Day air to the very popular UPS Ground service. When it comes to online operations, UPS has invested heavily in their software, which means their UPS WorldShip software has the most integration options with lots of leading software and e-commerce storefront providers. Their online services with My UPS allow you to generate labels and inform your customers as to their tracking numbers.

   UPS is available in over 3,000 locations in the U.S. due to their purchase of Mail Boxes Etc. (now the UPS Store) back in 2003. You can drop-off your already-prepared packages at a UPS Store, but if you plan to have them pack and ship your items for you, be prepared to pay a mark-up over your online UPS rates. In addition, you can drop off your already-prepared packages at office supply stores like Office Depot or Staples and enjoy UPS counter rates when they process your packages for you.

   When it comes to a major shipping company, UPS rates are competitive with similar companies like FedEx and DHL. UPS Ground is typically cheaper than some US Postal Service rates (like Parcel Post), and unlike the US Postal Service offers a guaranteed delivery date and better tracking capabilities. When you sign up for a UPS account, you can qualify for some business discounts based on your shipping volume and current promotions.

✔ **US Postal Service (USPS):** Through rain, sleet, snow, or damaged packages, the Post Office is there to deliver your packages. They're a big supporter of e-commerce, especially eBay, where the post office has co-branded certain boxes with the online auction giant and offers integration with eBay and

PayPal for their users to ship packages. The Post Office has recently stream-lined their systems, offering four main shipping options, from Express Mail to Priority Mail to First-Class and Parcel services, depending on your speed. Their reach can't be beat, as they will ship your package to any known country in the world. Their online operations allow you to print out your own shipping labels, and they work with companies like Stamps.com and Endicia that also print out specialty shipping labels for the Post Office.

There are thousands of post offices across the U.S. where you can drop off your packages or have them process your packages, at retail counter rates. In addition, if you prepare your labels online, you can drop some of your packages at the tens of thousands of blue drop boxes. Due to security concerns, any International package over one pound must be handed to a postman or retail agent, for example.

Typically, the US Postal Service offers the cheapest rates of the main providers, depending on service. Their tracking capabilities are improving, but are nowhere in detail like UPS or FedEx, and typically you pay extra for tracking or signature capabilities. While UPS or FedEx will promise ship-ments in a number of days, USPS relies on "averages" of 2–3 days for Priority Mail, and 1–3 weeks for Parcel Post or Media Mail. While the Postal Service will go to any country in the world, as of May 14, 2007, they will only ship that package via air mail, putting the cost on the same magnitude as UPS or FedEx, and additional services, such as Insurance or Proof of Delivery, vary by country.

✔ **DHL:** You have probably seen their yellow vans zipping around town, but perhaps wondered who they are or what they represent. They are DHL, one of the largest shipping companies in the U.S., with extensive operations out-side the U.S. as well. Unlike the other "big 3" shipping companies mentioned above, DHL focuses primarily on the business customer. You can't walk into a DHL office and process a shipment; you have to establish a DHL account first. They also offer an array of Air and Ground options for their customers, and offer an online site and software for your computer to process orders and create shipping labels.

While there are no retail locations to use DHL, they have offices in every city and maintain delivery routes to many locations, relying on the US Postal Service for rural deliveries. You need to consult their Web site (www.dhl.com) to set up an account and get assigned to a delivery route.

DHL can be very competitive with the other shipping companies, and they are hungry for your business. Your rates will depend on distance and volume, but check your bills and watch out for additional fees and sur-charges, like a Residential Delivery Charge. Their account representatives are pretty responsive, and insurance claims are sometimes much smoother to process with DHL than with other companies.

Picking your shipping company

In some cases, the question of which company to pick is moot, as you'll probably want to establish accounts with multiple companies based on different needs. As mentioned in the previous section, there are some countries in the world where UPS and FedEx don't go, which requires using the US Postal Service. In addition, companies like FedEx won't deliver packages to P.O. Boxes, which some customers may give you as their only shipping address. In those cases, you'd have to rely on the US Postal Service as well.

There is the question, however, of which shipping company deserves the majority of your business. Using a different shipping company every day would be counter productive to your business and save you nothing, as the best discounts come from being loyal to one shipping company. Given the choices out there, here are some questions to consider when making that decision:

✔ **Which company works best with my Web store infrastructure?** Depending on the storefront provider and the software you are using to build your Web store, this question alone may help you make your final decision. Companies like UPS have invested heavily to make sure their software works directly with your storefront provider, and as your company grows, you'll want to automate as much as possible, especially this step. Pick a company that will link with your operations and require as little intervention from you as possible.

✔ **How much do I expect to ship, and to where?** When you set up a business account with any of these shipping companies, they're going to ask you for an estimate of the volume you expect to generate, and the percentage of your shipments that go out Air/Express, Ground, and International. When you are starting-up, advise the company that you are providing estimates and not actual numbers, as you can always re-evaluate your account in 6-12 months and see if you qualify for a better rate. Based on your volume and mix of destinations, companies can offer you specific rates which you can compare based on the weight of an average order and the zones of the U.S.

✔ **How many options do I want to offer my customers?** As mentioned before, customers want their order quick, and because of this, some customers are willing to pay extra to get their order faster than other customers. Therefore, you are highly advised to offer different shipping methods, such as Next Day Air, 2 Day Air, and Ground service, for example, and charge appropriate rates for each service. When offering Next Day Air service, be sure to establish a cut-off time when orders must be received, as most companies require a Next Day package to be at their offices by mid- to late-afternoon in order to guarantee delivery the next day. Build in a window of time to receive the order, package it, and get it to your shipping company.

As long as we are talking about choice, the other reason you probably want to establish accounts with multiple companies is that some customers want a choice of shipping carrier, not just the shipping method and speed of delivery. Typically, offering two companies to choose from is enough variety for most e-commerce store owners, and usually, one of those choices is the US Postal Service (due to their exclusive delivery to P.O. Boxes and certain International destinations). Most shipping accounts are free to establish and maintain, unless you pay for daily pickup or other advanced options.

Shipping international orders

Thanks to the power of the Internet, your next order could come from Boston or Bangalore. Web stores are enjoying access to a global marketplace, which can mean increased interest and a bigger audience to support your business. When it comes to order fulfillment, however, it can also mean knowing a little something about the customs forms and requirements for shipping orders outside your country.

Thankfully, the shipping companies have responded to this increased demand in international shipments by augmenting the services they offer and integrating the necessary information into the documents and labels they create that you print out and attach to your packages.

When dealing with your international orders, here are some things to keep in mind:

✔ **Country-specific restrictions:** In many countries, the postal service there is controlled by the government, which means that certain countries have specific restrictions on weight, size, and types of items that can be sent to citizens of that country. In addition, the tracking capabilities vary by country, as some of them inspect packages before final delivery to the customer, which can affect delivery time. Consult the shipping company's Web site for specific information regarding country-specific limits and restrictions.

✔ **Customs forms:** Today, all the major shipping companies will print out the customs documentation to go with your shipping label. They'll ask you to provide additional information, so have this information ready when you prepare an international shipping label:

   • Quantity and description of each item in the package.

   • Value of each item in the package.

   • Country of origin of each item in the package.

   • Type of package (Gift, Documents, Commercial Sample, or Other).

For even more detailed information on how to complete the advanced paperwork to ship packages overseas, consult the U.S. government's Export Web site at www.export.gov.

Creating Your Online Shipping Accounts

When you have decided on the shipping company (or companies) where you want to set up your business shipping accounts, the next step is to sit down in front of a computer, log in, and create your accounts.

For several of these companies, like FedEx and UPS, the registration is actually two parts: signing up for an account with the shipping company, and signing up for an online account with their Web site.

Before you actually log on, however, you should have some information ready to be entered:

- ✔ **Average number of packages:** Almost every carrier will ask you what your average shipments are, either per week or per month. If you are starting out, then think of an estimate of what you plan or hope to achieve within one to two months' time. This number can always be changed or updated later, but it'll be used when your account is created to determine features like daily pickup fees (if any).

- ✔ **Form of payment:** For many of these companies, putting a credit card on file is sufficient. In some cases, you may set up a billing invoice system where your accounting department will receive and pay invoices sent by the shipping company.

- ✔ **Business address:** If you plan to process your shipments in a warehouse, remember to give that address as the pick-up location and business address whenever possible. The last thing you want is your delivery driver coming to get 100 boxes from your apartment or house when they are sitting at your warehouse.

Signing Up with Federal Express

The first shipping company we'll look at is Federal Express, or FedEx for short. The overnight delivery company has grown over the past 50 years into a global shipping partner that handles all sizes of accounts. When we sign up with FedEx, we're actually doing two separate things: We're creating a FedEx account, good for shipping packages with FedEx, and an account with fedex.com, which allows us to use their online Shipping Manager to create labels for shipments.

Click this link.

1. Go to `http://www.fedex.com`. When you go to FedEx's Web site, you should notice several links to help you establish an account. As of this writing, they're offering up to 15 percent discounts for online customers, as indicated in their Offers section. Click the Open a FedEx Account link to get started.

2. FedEx will review the account creation process with you. Since we're planning to use their Shipping Manager online capabilities, click the Sign Up for an Account with a 15 percent Discount link. If you're only going to use their retail locations, click the Sign Up for an Account Without a Discount link.

Click this link.

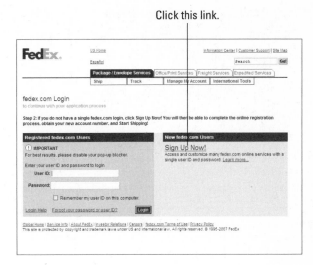

3. FedEx asks you to log into their Web site to continue. Unless you already have an account, click the Sign Up Now! link to continue. You're creating an account for fedex.com as well as a Federal Express shipping account, so this is a two-step process. Click the Sign Up Now! link to create your new fedex.com account first.

4. You'll be asked to create a user ID to use when logging into fedex.com. Your user ID and password must each be six or more characters long, and FedEx requires your password to contain at least one letter and one number. Pick something hard for others to guess for the password. Once you're done, click the Continue button to proceed.

5. Now you need to establish your FedEx shipping account, separate from the Web site. If you have already set up a FedEx account (perhaps for a retail business) and you want to use it for your Web store (or you want to combine your retail and Web store operations), simply input your existing FedEx number in the box provided and you do not need to create a second account. I'm assuming you don't have a FedEx shipping account, so if that is the case, select the Open a New FedEx Account option and click Continue to proceed.

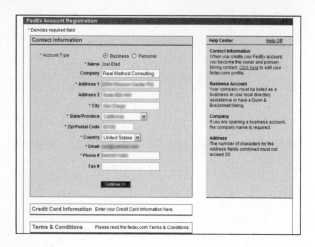

6. FedEx asks for your Contact Information for the shipping account. Confirm or change the contact information you gave them in Step 4 and click Continue. If you're using a warehouse for your packages, you probably want to associate that address with your FedEx account, and you can input that here.

7. The next step involves providing your credit card information to be linked to the account. Here, you're asked to keep a Visa, Mastercard, American Express, or Discover credit card on file for your account, so FedEx can bill you automatically instead of receiving a bill in the mail. Fill out the appropriate fields and make sure you give your billing information that matches the credit card you are putting on file, then click Continue to proceed.

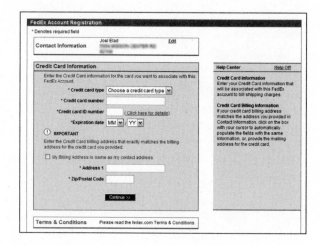

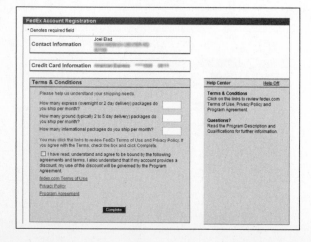

8. FedEx asks for your estimated traffic, in terms of packages being sent per month, in three categories: Express (1–3 days air), Ground (2–5 days truck), and International/Overseas. Put in your estimated numbers, review the Terms and Conditions set forth, and click the Complete button to finish your account creation.

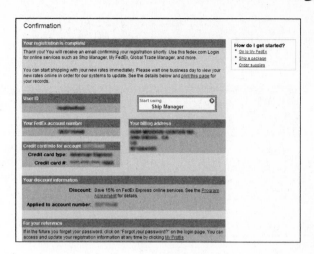

9. You have now created your FedEx shipping account number and your fedex.com user ID to use when creating labels. You should see a confirmation screen with all your valid information. Be sure to print this screen out and keep the information handy, as it contains your fedex.com user ID and your FedEx shipping account number.

Signing Up with UPS

Stuff You Need to Know

Toolbox:
- An estimate of your shipping activity per week
- Business contact information
- Business credit card

Time Needed:
20–30 minutes

The second shipping company we'll look at is United Parcel Service, known as UPS. The company has become the world's largest package delivery service and has an extensive department to help with logistics and enterprise shipping needs. They created their own software system called WorldShip, which you can access through their Web site to generate labels for your packages. Similar to FedEx, we'll be establishing two types of accounts: a UPS account number and an account to use on their Web site to generate labels for shipments.

Click this button.

1. Go to the UPS home page at www.ups.com and select your country. Once you get your country's home page, click on the Register button to get started. From here, you can access and read more about lots of different UPS functions, based on your needs. To sign up for an account, look for the Register button in the top-right of the screen.

2. In this part, you're setting up an account for access to their Web site. Fill in the blanks as prompted to put in your name, e-mail, user ID, and password. Your password needs to be between 6 and 10 characters long. Once you're done, click the Next button to continue the process.

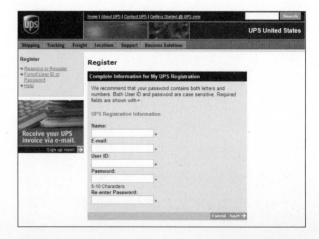

3. In order to create your account to use UPS online, they need to have your full set of contact information. Fill out the different fields as prompted, as the required fields are marked with the diamond character.

4. As you scroll down from the Contact Information section, you'll see the areas to indicate your preferred shipping method, e-mail contact options, and payment options. Your Service and Packaging options here are simply going to be the defaults when you log into your account to make labels. Pick the options you plan to use most often, but know that these can be changed for any shipment.

2 Shipping Defaults

Save time by selecting your most frequently used shipping options. The options you select will appear as defaults each time you ship.

Service ⓘ
Select One

Packaging ⓘ
Select One

3 Select E-mail Options

E-Mail:
joel@joelelad.com

Select which e-mail communications you would like to receive.

E-mail Options: ◆

○ Send me the following UPS e-mail communications:
☐ New Product Announcements/Enhancements
☐ Promotions and Offers
☐ Newsletters
☐ Service Updates / Regulatory Changes

○ Remove me from UPS e-mail communications*

Need more information?

View Examples ⊠

4 Payment Defaults

How will you pay for your shipping?
No Payment Default

Note: After completing registration, you can change your payment defaults in Shipping Preferences.

4 Payment Defaults

How will you pay for your shipping?
Open a New UPS Account

Note: After completing registration, you will be given the opportunity to open a UPS Account.

5 Primary Role

Which of these statements best describes you? ◆
Select One

6 Technology Agreement◆

UNITED PARCEL SERVICE

UPS TECHNOLOGY AGREEMENT
Version UTA1072006

PLEASE CAREFULLY READ THE FOLLOWING TERMS AND CONDITIONS OF THIS UPS TECHNOLOGY AGREEMENT. BY INDICATING BELOW THAT YOU AGREE TO BE BOUND BY THE TERMS AND CONDITIONS OF THIS AGREEMENT, YOU HAVE ENTERED INTO A LEGALLY BINDING

☐ By selecting this box and the Next button, I agree to these Terms and Conditions.

Cancel | Next →

5. At the bottom portion of the form, UPS wants to know the decision-making level of the person creating the account (onscreen this is Section 5) and then asks for that person to review the Terms and Conditions of having a My UPS account. Check the box indicated to signal your approval of the terms and click Next to continue.

* Note: You may continue to receive certain e-mail from UPS if you select this option. UPS uses e-mail to deliver information that you and others request (example: UPS Quantum View Notify shipment alerts). UPS also uses e-mail to provide details about your account(s) and operational information regarding existing products, services and systems.

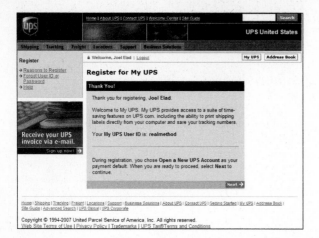

6. You have created your account for accessing My UPS online and are presented with a confirmation screen. Now you need to create your UPS shipping account that will be used when you ship with UPS. Click the Next button to proceed.

7. In the first step of this part, UPS needs to know your average shipping needs. Fill in the blanks based on your estimated packages per week sent and any other shipping-related questions. Click the Next button to proceed.

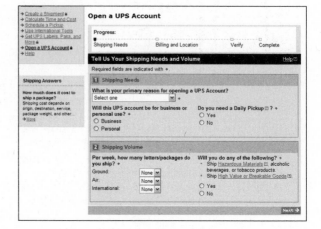

TIP

When letting UPS know your average shipping needs, **do not** sign up for a Daily Pickup unless you think you have the volume to justify it, which is about 3-5 packages per day. You can always work with your UPS account representative to add this later.

8. At this stage, UPS needs to set up the billing profile for your UPS shipping account. You can either file to have UPS send you a bill every week, which will require a credit check of your business or personal assets, or you can put a valid credit card on file, which UPS would use to bill you weekly. Fill in the appropriate fields and click Next to proceed.

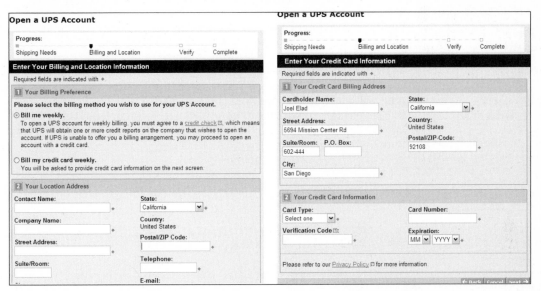

9. You'll see a summary screen. Take a look and make sure that everything you entered is correct, and make sure you've established the correct Location information based on where your packages will be picked up. You can click the Edit link next to any section to go back and make changes. When you are done, go down to the bottom of the page and click the blue Next button to create your account.

10. Your new UPS shipping account has been created! You'll see a confirmation screen, and be sure to make a note of your new account number. You've now completed the process and can log into UPS and create shipping labels that will be billed against your UPS shipping account.

Signing Up with the US Postal Service

Stuff You Need to Know

Toolbox:
- Business contact information
- Business credit card

Time Needed:
20–30 minutes

The last company we'll look at is the United States Postal Service, or USPS for short. The Post Office is the only shipper that can guarantee you can mail a package to any country in the world. They also have a Web site where you can generate your own shipping labels for packages. Unlike FedEx or UPS, however, you don't get a special account number to use whenever shipping packages, and there is no concern about average shipping volume, because the Post Office already comes to your door every day to deliver mail, regardless of your package volume. Be aware that not all shipping methods are available through printing a label online, such as First Rate International.

Click this link.

1. Go to the USPS Web site at `http://www.usps.com` and click the Sign In link at the top-right of the screen. When you get to the home page, you can click on the Business button and see all the various options you can perform on the Web site.

2. From the Sign In screen, if you've already registered with USPS for any reason you can log into their Web site in the spaces provided. Otherwise, click the Sign Up button so you can create a new account on their system.

Click this button.

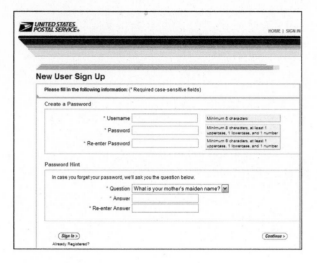

3. In this step, choose a user ID and password to access the USPS Web site. The US Postal Service has slightly stricter standards for creating a password than other shipping companies. Your password must have at least one upper case character, one lower case character, and one number. Click the Continue button to proceed.

4. In this step, you're asked to identify your account as a Personal or Business account. If you plan on taking advantage of certain business services, like Business Reply Mail or bulk mail features, then sign up as a Business account now. If you're just starting up, selecting a Personal account will allow you to create labels and do all the essential functions. There are no extra fees for picking either option, so you may want to go ahead and select Business.

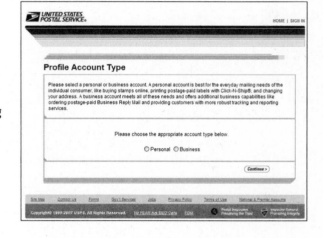

5. This step is about gathering all the contact information necessary to create your account. Fill out your personal information and location information. I highly recommend putting in your location where packages will be picked up from, not necessarily your mailing address. When you are done, click the Continue button to proceed.

Company Profile Summary

Please review the company information below. If you need to edit this information, select Edit below.

Company Account Information

Username: realmethod

Title: MR
First Name: Joel
Last Name: Elad

Company Profile Information

Company Name: Real Method Consulting
Address 1:
Address 2:
City:
State:
ZIP Code™:
Country:
Business Phone:
Email:

Communication Preferences

☐ Other USPS programs, products, or services
☐ Products or services of USPS partners that you may find of interest

< Edit | Continue >

6. You're presented with a summary screen. Make sure every entry is correct, and if anything is incorrect, click the Edit button to go back and make any necessary changes. Otherwise, click the Continue button to proceed.

7. The last step in the sign-up process is to review the USPS Privacy Policy and agree to their terms. Review the policy, click Yes to agree to the terms, and click the Continue button to create your account.

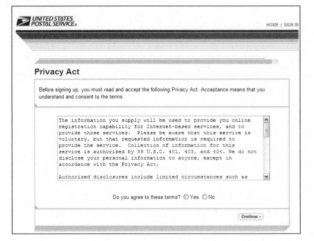

Privacy Act

Before signing up, you must read and accept the following Privacy Act. Acceptance means that you understand and consent to the terms

> The information you supply will be used to provide you online registration capability for Internet-based services, and to provide those services. Please be aware that this service is voluntary, but that requested information is required to provide the service. Collection of information for this service is authorized by 39 U.S.C. 401, 403, and 404. We do not disclose your personal information to anyone, except in accordance with the Privacy Act.
>
> Authorized disclosures include limited circumstances such as

Do you agree to these terms? ○ Yes ○ No

Continue >

Your Options

Welcome Joel | Edit Your Profile

Take a look at the USPS Services available to registered customers like you.

Create and mail letters and cards:

NetPost® CardStore
Keep in touch with customers and business partners with customized greeting cards, gift cards, postcards, and letters from NetPost®.

NetPost Mailing Online™
Attract new business or strengthen existing relationships by sending postcards, letters, flyers or greeting cards delivered directly to your customers' doors.

NetPost Premium Postcards™
Spread the word about your business with customized postcards-in one simple online transaction.

Buy stamps and shop:

The Postal Store™
Save a trip to the Post Office by ordering stamps and mailing supplies online.

Prepare to ship:

Carrier Pickup
Have your carrier pick up your packages at no charge.

Click-N-Ship® (Print a Shipping Label)
Need to send packages but don't want to leave the office? Print labels at your desk with Click-N-Ship®, now with international mailing options.

Customs Forms
Complete customs forms online to declare the contents and value of your international shipment.

8. That's it! Your USPS account is created. You can log in, create labels, and start shipping with them! You will be taken to a very plain looking confirmation screen that serves as a launching pad for all the different USPS Web site applications. When you log in to create shipping labels, they will prompt you to add a credit card to your profile so you can be billed for creating these labels.

Printing Out a Sample USPS Label

Stuff You Need to Know

Toolbox:
- ✔ USPS account information
- ✔ Attached printer with paper or labels available

Time Needed:
5–10 minutes

In order for your new USPS account to be useful, your first action with the account should be to print a sample label, so you're not diagnosing problems when a pile of packages is sitting waiting to be dropped off. The USPS uses a programming language called Java through your web browser to generate a window with your label, which you can send to your printer. Be aware that, when printing labels through USPS, you will need to allow popup windows to occur from usps.com.

1. Log into your USPS account (at www.usps.com) and click on the Click-N-Ship link. You're taken to the Click-N-Ship page. Notice there is a link to print a sample Domestic or International label. Click either of those links.

Click either link.

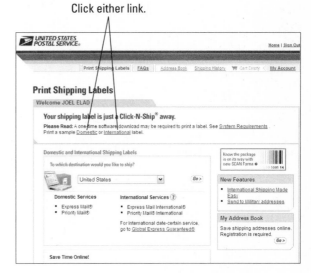

Printing Out a Sample Label

Once you've gone through the trouble of setting up an account, you want to make sure that you can print out your shipping labels without any trouble. Of course, before we can test anything, you should decide what kind of printer you want to use to create your shipping labels. Every shipping company can now print labels on your regular inkjet or laser printer, so if you already have a printer and don't plan on a heavy volume this will satisfy your needs.

However, if you expect a large volume of orders and you're still buying equipment for your shipping station, you may want to look into buying a *label printer*. These are specialty printers (from companies like Zebra, Eltron, and Pitney-Bowes) that are designed for functions like printing shipping labels. Companies like UPS will even provide you with rolls of these specialty labels to use in printing your shipping labels. These printers are designed for large volume operations, and the peel-and-stick nature of these labels means one less step for your shipping team.

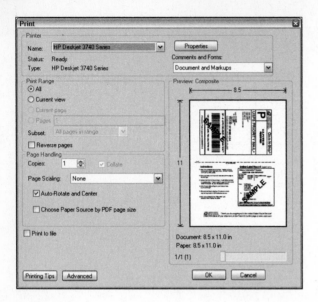

2. USPS will detect if you have the right software installed to handle their labels. If not, they'll prompt you to do a one-time software download. USPS uses Adobe PDF technology to create their domestic labels, and Java technology to create their international labels, with customs forms integrated into the label.

3. Once the software is on your system, USPS will automatically open a print window showing you a sample of the printout. Make sure the correct printer is selected that will handle your labels, and click the OK button to test it out.

4. Review the label that comes out and make sure it printed correctly. If everything is fine, click Yes to the question the USPS asks you about the label and they'll know your printer is ready to handle their labels.

Printing Out a Sample UPS Label

Stuff You Need to Know

Toolbox:
- ✔ UPS account information
- ✔ Attached printer with paper or labels available

Time Needed:
5–10 minutes

In order for your new UPS account to be useful, you should take some time to ensure that you're able to print UPS package labels from your computer. UPS does interface with specialty label printers, or you can use a regular inkjet or laser printer to print labels on paper as well. Be aware that UPS will also require pop-up windows to be allowed from ups.com.

Click this link.

1. Log into your UPS account (at www.ups.com) and click on the Create Shipment link. You're taken to the Create a Shipment page. This is the screen you'll complete to set up a shipping label manually. Look for the Set Preferences link along the left-hand side of the page and click it.

Click this link.

2. You're taken to the Preferences screen for your UPS account. As you scroll down the page, stop when you see the Printing Preferences header. In that section, you'll find the link to Print a Sample Label. Click that link when you are ready.

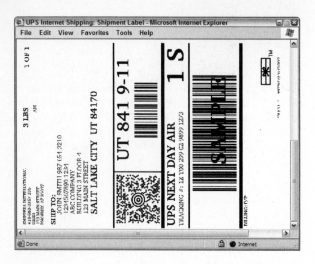

3. UPS will automatically open a label window, showing you a sample of the printout. Then a print window opens where you pick your printer and click OK to send that label to the printer.

4. Review the label that comes out and make sure it printed correctly. If everything is fine, you're done and ready to print UPS labels.

It is advisable, before or after you print your sample label, to spend a few minutes on the Preferences screen and set up your UPS account the way you'd like so your preferences automatically come up every time you prepare a label. The more time you can save by automating this process, the more time you have for the rest of your business.

Part IV
Finalizing Your Web Store

The 5th Wave   By Rich Tennant

"I can't really explain it, but every time I animate someone swinging a golf club, a little divot of code comes up missing on the home page."

In this part . . .

In this part, I cover the essential steps for you, a Web store owner to take right before you launch your store on the Internet. I discuss tactics to organize all of your online and physical materials to point to your new Web store. I then move into the process of quietly opening your Web store to test all the bugs and functionality and inviting a select group of shoppers to sign on and try to order something.

Finally, I go through all the last-minute steps you should take to proof-read and double-check your Web store for accuracy and professionalism. I also recommend steps to verify your Web store design looks the same, regardless of Internet browser or operating system used by your clients.

Chapter 13

Putting Your Web Store at the Hub of Your Sales

Tasks performed in this chapter

- ✔ Announcing your new Web store

- ✔ Using your Web store to increase your online presence

- ✔ Creating e-mail signatures in Microsoft Outlook or Yahoo! Mail

- ✔ Linking from other Web sites or stores

After spending time doing the "heavy lifting" of designing and implementing the core of your Web store, it's time to start focusing on the "last touch" elements — the parts of the process that will promote your overall business and not just necessarily affect your catalog or one product category.

In this chapter, we discuss one of the simplest, but most important parts of your business success — getting your business name mentioned in as many places as possible. Specifically, we want to promote your Web store URL, or Web address, that customers will type in to get to your Web store. So, we look at ways and places you can promote your store in the real and virtual worlds, as well as how to mention your Web store in any online sales activities.

Updating Your Literature and Signs

In order for people to know about your Web store, they have to see your Web store name or URL so they can go to your Web store and see it for themselves. Therefore, you need to use every avenue you can to make your URL known. Thankfully, there are a lot of mechanisms you already use and control that require a simple update or addition to accomplish this.

With all the technology we use every day, there is still a lot of paper (and plastic and canvas and more) that we use, hand out, interact with, or see on a daily basis. Any "physical" or tangible material that you create and use to promote or do your business can be updated to mention your Web store URL, so next time you plan to order more business cards or catalogs, don't forget this addition. We've put together a checklist of places where you can take advantage of this opportunity to promote your Web store, so check it out!

When including your Web store URL, you can typically drop the `http://` part and just focus on including your actual domain of `www.yourname.com` instead.

✔ **Business cards:** This is probably the easiest and most obvious mention, but interestingly enough, many Web store owners overlook this one. If you don't have business cards yet, go get some, and make sure your Web store URL is included. Typically, they can go at the bottom of the card, as shown in Figure 13-1.

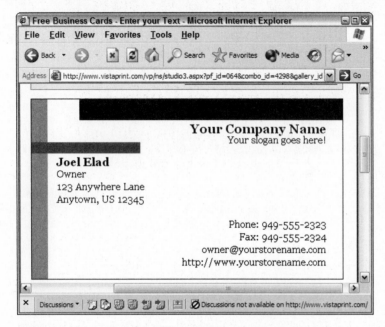

Figure 13-1: Include your Web store URL in your business cards.

✔ **Sales or promotional flyers:** If you are going to promote a sale on your Web store, people have to find it, right? In this case, you may want to promote a specific Web page or subdirectory of your Web store, so here you might put: `www.yourname.com/sale` instead of `www.yourname.com`.

✔ **Brochures:** Whenever putting together any company literature, regardless of who the end customer is, you want to put your Web store URL in there. The point of a brochure is to give someone a set amount of information and then encourage that person to learn more by taking an action. Today, the easiest action you can take is pointing someone to your Web site.

✔ **Catalogs:** If you already publish print catalogs, or are planning on publishing print catalogs to supplement your Web store, you *definitely* have to promote your Web store, even if the catalog is mail or phone order. The more options you give your customers, the more likely they are to order from you, and if you are training people to shop from you via a catalog, they're the easiest to transition to a Web store because, let's face it, a Web store is simply an online catalog.

✔ **Newsletters:** Print or e-mail newsletters are an excellent way to keep in touch with your customers, employees, partners, and/or vendors. Even though the newsletter will typically be about you or your Web store, it never hurts to remind people of your Web store URL somewhere (or in two or three places) in your newsletter.

✔ **Physical displays/signs:** If you've got a physical retail store, or perhaps set up a booth at a trade show or convention, don't forget to advertise your Web store on any physical displays or signs you have. Even though the customer is in front of you for that first sale, you want them to become a repeat customer, and the best way for that to happen is to remind your "offline" customer that you're also available online, 24-hours a day, 7 days a week.

✔ **Shopping bags:** Have you ever noticed the free advertising companies are getting just by putting their name on a plastic bag? It's most obvious at trade shows and conventions, where companies give away bags so people will carry around their logo and trademark to thousands of impressionable customers. Take advantage of this mechanism by branding your shopping bags with your Web store URL. You never know who'll see it and check it out.

✔ **Shipping/packing boxes:** Your Web store will typically involve sending out products in boxes to your customers. Use that (usually empty) space to brand your business and put your Web store URL (and logo, if you have one) on the boxes. Not only does it signify to your customers that their order has arrived, but everyone else, from the neighbors to the postman, see that box as well. The best example is Amazon.com, which brands all their boxes, mailers, and envelopes.

✔ **Company delivery trucks or cars:** You'll be surprised by how much people pay attention to advertising on the road. I had a client who operated eBay drop off stores, so the company vans had the Web site URL and phone number. We had people drive up next to us, even bus drivers, and ask us about our business while we were both stopped at a traffic light. It's free advertising (besides the cost of painting the vehicle, that is) that can become your free, mobile billboard.

✔ **Packing slips/receipts:** If you run a retail store, update your cash register or POS system to add a small mention about your Web store at the bottom of the receipt. Some companies go further and print a special discount code on the bottom of their receipts. Don't forget to add your URL to your Web store packing slips too. As obvious as it sounds, even though a customer knew your URL to place an order, putting your Web address on the packing slip simply reinforces the message.

✔ **Display, magazine, and classified ads:** If you are already paying to advertise your business in a newspaper, magazine, or trade journal, it should be very simple to add a URL to mention your Web store. Similar to the sales flyers, in this case you may consider adding a subdomain or subdirectory so you can track the effectiveness of this ad.

If you are paying by the word, simply end the ad with www.*yourname*.com and pay for 1 additional word.

✔ **Yellow Pages and newspaper ads:** Even though the point of a Yellow Pages (or local newspaper) ad is to inform local customers about your retail location, it never hurts to include a Web store URL so people can go there at their own schedule to get more information about your business. Like a display ad, you're paying to promote your business, and your URL is another way to promote your business.

✔ **Invoices:** When doing business with other companies, it never hurts to include your Web store URL to remind the other party of what you offer. Sometimes, the value of including your URL comes when the receiving party researches the invoice and learns more about your business.

✔ **Stationery:** While many small companies don't invest in their own company letterhead, it's an easy mention to identify your online component with a Web store URL. It can go at the top of the page below the company logo or slogan, or along the bottom of the page in the footer.

✔ **Fax cover sheets:** While many companies don't use letterhead, most of them still require the good old fax machine to do business, which means your cover sheet is simply another branding mechanism when communicating with other companies.

✔ **Address labels:** Your Web store should have detailed contact information about your business, so including the URL on an address label is simply another way of identifying your business for anyone who sees that letter. It's another reinforcement of your Web site name, which should eventually lead to name recognition.

✔ **Business checks:** Like your invoices, your business checks speak about the image of your business, and including the URL in your business checks reminds your partners and vendors that you participate online.

✔ **Coupons:** If you are using print or e-mail coupons to encourage traffic to your business, don't forget to include your Web store URL in the coupon somewhere. The only exception to this is that, if the coupon is only valid at a retail location and not on your online store, putting the URL is wrong because it could confuse the buyer.

✔ **Gift certificates:** If you are giving someone currency to spend with you, they should have as many options to spend it as possible, which means including your Web store URL somewhere on the certificate. Once again, if it is a retail-only certificate and has to be kept separate or away from your online operations, then exclude the URL to avoid confusion.

✔ **Voicemail/answering machine:** Advertising your URL isn't limited to things you can see. As part of your company greeting, you should include, "To find more information, check out our Web site at www.*yourname*.com." If nothing else, it gives an after-hours caller something to check out if they have a question or concern.

✔ **TV, radio, and billboards:** Your Web store is part of your overall business, so whether you are taking out TV, radio, or outdoor billboard advertisements for your retail location, including your Web store URL is a small way to make a big impact on your online sales.

Updating Your Online Presence with Your Web Store

We've talked about updating your "offline" presence with your Web store URL, which is everything that isn't related to your (or your customer's) activities on the computer. Before you launch your Web store, however, you should also integrate this new information with your "online" presence.

This means that all your online activities, from e-mail to discussion forums, should include a mention of your Web store. Therefore, let's detail the major steps you should take for these mediums:

✔ **E-mail:** Advertising your Web store through e-mail is best accomplished by creating something called an *e-mail signature file,* which will sit at the bottom of every e-mail (or whichever e-mails you select) that you send out. This e-mail signature typically contains your name, preferred e-mail address, a Web site URL, and perhaps a quotation or slogan that you like. Some people add logos, graphics, and even a scanned representation of their physical signature.

✔ **Discussion forums:** Every time you contribute to an online discussion forum or message board, you're typically allowed to have your own signature block after your message. Similar to an e-mail signature, this forum signature block usually contains your name, e-mail address, Web site URL, and any additional information about yourself.

✔ **Networking Web sites:** From social networking sites like MySpace and Facebook, to business networking sites like LinkedIn, there are new Web pages being created that talk about ourselves. Each of these sites allow you to build something called a profile page, and on that page you're allowed (and encouraged) to mention and link to Web sites that you use and like, and in some cases, asked to input your profession. Don't forget to log into each site where you have a profile and add a line that you are the "Owner of www.*yourstorename*.com" or something to that effect.

We'll cover this in more detail in Chapter 16, but if you sell on other Web sites such as eBay or Amazon, don't forget to update your profile page on those sites with your Web store URL as well.

Creating a Microsoft Outlook Signature File

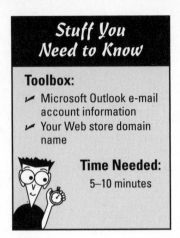

Stuff You Need to Know

Toolbox:
- ✔ Microsoft Outlook e-mail account information
- ✔ Your Web store domain name

Time Needed:
5–10 minutes

It's very easy to create your own e-mail signature file. This section looks at adding a signature file to an e-mail program that sits on your computer, specifically Microsoft Outlook. When you create a signature file in Microsoft Outlook, that program will automatically append every e-mail you send out with your signature information, reminding everyone you contact about your new web store.

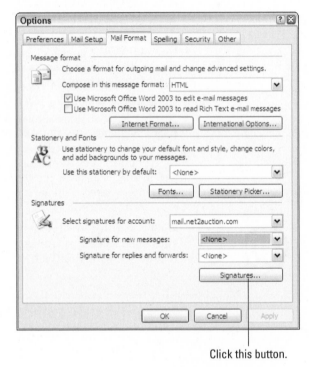

Click this button.

1. In Outlook, select Tools➪Options, then click on the Mail Format tab. Click on the Signatures button to create your new e-mail signature.

Click this button.

Create Signature

Signature:

[Edit...]
[Remove]
[New...]

Preview:

Unable to preview selected signature, or no signature selected.

[OK] [Cancel]

2. You will be taken to the Create Signature window. From here, you can create and review different e-mail signatures for use in different situations. Click on the New button to create your e-mail signature.

3. Create a name for your e-mail signature file. If you're going to create multiple e-mail signatures, be sure to use a name that reflects the situation where you want to use that signature. For example, you could create a "Work" signature and a "Personal" signature and only include your Web store URL in your Work signature. Once you assign a name for your e-mail signature file, you can retrieve a previously created file to use as a template, or leave the option selected to start with a blank signature, and then click the Next button to continue.

4. In the Edit Signature window you can type in your basic information. You can use the buttons below the text box to enhance the font or text settings, or click the Advanced Edit button to add things like your company logo. When you are done, click the Finish button to save your work.

5. Click OK to close the Signatures window, and then click OK a final time to close the Options window. By clicking OK and not the Cancel button, you are telling Outlook to save your changes, not abandon them.

Creating a Yahoo! Mail Signature File

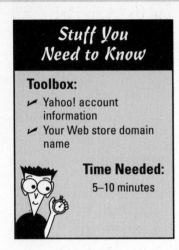

Think about all the e-mails you send out, whether it is for business or pleasure, and you begin to realize the exposure that a signature file can create for your new Web store. The value of a signature file is that the information will automatically be appended to every e-mail you send out. Since we're using Yahoo! Merchant Solutions as our example throughout this book, let's discuss how to create a signature file in Yahoo! Mail.

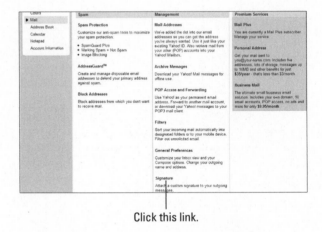

Click this link.

1. Log into your Yahoo! mail account and click the Options link from the top-right of the screen. You should be taken to an e-mail options screen. Under the Management header, look for the Signature link and click it to continue.

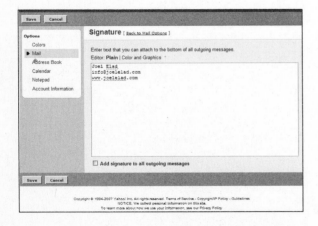

2. The system will default to a plain editor window. Simply type in your e-mail signature. You can also click the Color and Graphics link to bring up a set of buttons you can use to configure your font, color, and text size, and add fancier elements to your e-mail signature. If you want to have your e-mail signature appear in every e-mail you write, then click the Add Signature to All Outgoing E-mail checkbox. When you're done, click the Save button.

3. You're done! You should be taken back to the Mail Options screen.

Creating a Discussion Forum Block Signature

Stuff You Need to Know

Toolbox:
- Discussion forum account
- Your Web store domain name

Time Needed:
5–10 minutes

Discussion forums exist on many different sites, so visitors can discuss popular themes of the day, products they like or dislike, or their opinion on matters large or small. Many sites that sell direct to the consumer, like eBay and Amazon, have discussion forums about different concepts. In the example below, we're going to create a forum signature for one of the biggest social networking sites on the Internet, namely MySpace.

1. Go to MySpace by visiting www.myspace.com, and log into your account. Once you've logged in, click on the Forum link from the MySpace header.

2. Once you're looking at the MySpace forum home page, click the button marked Settings near the top right of the screen.

3. When you click on the Settings box, you should see the screen grayed out, and a new white text box appear in the middle of the screen. In the text box provided, type in your signature. Try to keep the length of your signature block to no more than two or three lines of text.

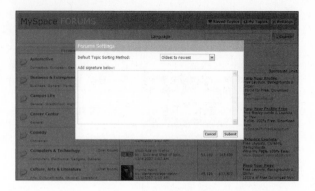

4. When you're done writing your signature block, click the Submit button at the bottom right of the text window to save your signature information. Once you do this, every time you post something on this discussion board your signature will be automatically appended to your entry.

Chapter 14

Hard Facts About Your Store's "Soft Launch"

In the retail world, a *soft launch* is when you start conducting business before your Grand Opening to test all your processes and systems to make sure that you can handle the business once you officially open your store. This practice exists in the virtual world as well, and is highly recommended for those of you opening your first Web store. It's very easy to build the different pieces of a Web store and assume that, since all the individual Web pages and store elements are functional, everything will work well as one integrated Web store. The reality is quite different, unfortunately, as some sites open for business with lots of inconsistencies, some of which dramatically affect sales.

In this chapter, we discuss some of the basic actions you should take to perform a soft launch for your Web store. Remember, this step is meant to be one of the last activities you take before your official Grand Opening, so don't worry about this step if you're still filling your product catalog, for example. We look into checking over every page of your Web store, going through the steps to order a product, and creating a special group of people to preview and test your Web store for you.

Visiting Every Page of Your Web Store

When you're ready to open your virtual doors for business, your first action before hanging any "Open" signs should be to go through and visually inspect every single Web page within your store. Think of it as walking down every virtual aisle, making sure the presentation and appearance are the same regardless of where you are in the store. After all, you don't want your customers to feel like they're in a rag-tag collection of differently-colored market stalls, do you? You want your customers to know where they are doing business, from the first visit to the final checkout page.

The easiest way to do this step is with something called a *site map,* which contains a listing of all the Web pages within your store. Yahoo! Merchant Solutions, for example, creates a site map automatically for you, so you can pull it up on your screen and start clicking links, one by one, to inspect the various Web pages.

When you're done going through the site map, and you know there is one (or more) Web pages on your store that you didn't visit, don't forget to add those pages to your site map before you finish.

If you don't have a site map, then perhaps this alternative is for you. Bring up the home page for your Web store and print out a copy. Then, one by one, click on all the links available from your home page. Any time you click on a link and get brought to another Web page with lots of different or new links, print out that page and do the same actions with that Web page. Eventually, you should've clicked through all the different Web pages you have on your store.

If you've clicked through all the links and you know you haven't reached every page on your Web store, you need to go back and find the appropriate page and add a link to it. Your goal is that every page on your Web store (unless it's a private or members only page) is accessible through a link that starts on your home page.

How do I know I'm ready for this step?

Once you know how you are going to perform your page-by-page search, you should know when and how to perform this exercise. Therefore, ask yourself these questions before inspecting your Web store:

- 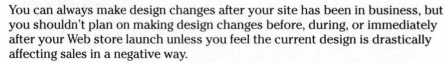 **Am I satisfied with my Web page design and layout?** If you're still planning on tweaking or fixing your Web site design, page design, or catalog layout, it doesn't make sense to inspect your Web site now because any changes you make to your design could affect a part or the whole Web site. You may make changes that fix bugs or problems after this process, but don't inspect your site thoroughly until you know the Web site design for your store is the one you want to launch.

  You can always make design changes after your site has been in business, but you shouldn't plan on making design changes before, during, or immediately after your Web store launch unless you feel the current design is drastically affecting sales in a negative way.

- **Have I allowed enough time to do a thorough inspection of my Web store?** Some people are so busy getting their store ready and putting a promotional campaign into place that they run out of time and forget to budget any time for a soft launch. While you can rush this process and quickly inspect each page looking only for the most severe problems, you risk letting small- and medium-sized problems reach the end customer, who could see these inconsistencies negatively and never return to your store. Make the time to do an accurate review job, so you convey the right level of professionalism.

- **Are all my files available on the server yet?** While you could test your Web store with a subset of items, you want your soft launch to be as close to your actual opening as possible so you can spot any potential problems early. Therefore, you want to make sure that all of your templates, files, databases, and images are uploaded to your storefront provider and are available on the Internet.

If you are worried that customers and search engines will find your soft launch Web site ahead of the grand opening and start using it when you're not open yet, consider creating a "development" server or section of your Web store that requires a user ID and password to enter. Talk to your store-front provider about whether you can create a "development" or "test" environment for your store.

What to inspect on each Web page

As you make your journey, page by page, here is a list of things you should look for on each page and check off every time the answer is good:

- Is the navigation bar in the same place on every page?

- Is the company logo in the same place on every page?

- Do any of the links I click on this page go to a Web page that doesn't exist (known as an HTTP 404 error)?

- Do I get any sort of error when I click a link?

- Does every Web page have the same (or consistent) background color and design?

- Do all the images and graphics load properly on the screen?

- Are there any misspelled words or grammatical errors on the page?

- Is the correct pricing information being shown on each page?

- Is any information being "cut off" or obscured on the page?

- Does each page have the correct and corresponding page title?

- Is there any "dummy" or place-holder text that needs to be updated or removed?

- Does every button or function work on the page? In other words, can I add a product, complete a guestbook entry, or fill out a form?

- Does the "lock" appear at the bottom right of my Web browser when I visit a secure Web page using SSL technology?

- Does every drop-down list have all the correct options presented?

- Does every product in my catalog have at least one image or picture associated with it?

- Are the ALT and META tags completed for each Web page? (View the Source of the Web page to check for this.)

- Are my contact information and shopping cart links visible from every page?

You should place a simple copyright notice at the bottom of every Web page on your store, to protect your design. Simply write (C), the current year, and the name of your company, on a single line at the bottom of every Web page, like this:

© 2007 NewComix.Com

Inviting a Select Group to Shop Before the Grand Opening

Okay, you've gone through your Web site, you've placed an order, and hopefully you feel ready to release your Web store to the masses. One good way to test out the system during your soft launch is to invite a small group of people to go into your store and check it out first. Not only does it make sure the system can handle multiple orders in a short amount of time, but you're getting test users that haven't lived and breathed this Web store and have zero preconceptions beyond a normal customer.

In some ways, you can spin this as a positive to your select group. Perhaps you've already been doing business in some form. This is a way to "reward" your loyal customers or a way to make past customers feel more special by giving them premier access to your Web store ahead of anyone else. Not only are you testing your Web store, you could get extra sales and customers out of it!

As far as the logistics, if you're worried about the general public and/or the search engines finding this "live" store, you can either set up a required user ID and password to block uninvited guests from getting to your store, or sometimes, simply creating an alternate URL and separate subdirectory that isn't linked to anywhere on your store is enough to keep people out. If no one knows where the door is located, how can they enter?

As far as who and how to do it, here are some thoughts to consider:

✔ **Friends and family:** If you can't ask your friends and family a favor, who can you ask, right? This is the easiest group to ask in terms of getting participation without an overt reward or hurting your brand. If you go this route, the main thing to consider is that you should make this as easy as possible for them. Specifically, you do this by:

 • Providing detailed instructions or guidelines in your request.

 • Providing a sample credit card number and/or profile information so they don't have to give up their information.

 • Requesting feedback on the experience, perhaps with a follow-up e-mail questionnaire that they can respond to, or print out, check off, and mail back to you.

 • Following up on the feedback request by offering to "interview" them so they have zero writing to do.

✔ **Past customers:** Inviting past customers (eBay auction winners, previous retail customers, and so on) to check out your new store can be a great way to build your first group of loyal customers. You benefit by already having a relationship with these people, so hopefully they'd be eager to shop from you again. There is some level of trust so it's not a blind or out-of-left-field request for them. But this does require some guidance on your part for success. Specifically, you might:

 • Offer some sort of reward or incentive for them to check out your site early (a discount, free shipping, or bonus gift).

- Tie the reward or incentive into a required feedback form of their experience (without the feedback, testing it early is just shopping) that asks for positives, negatives, and problems.

- Ask for testimonials or promise to highlight your new customers in an upcoming newsletter (people love to see their name in lights, real or virtual) if they participate.

- Don't promise any drastic changes or updates based on their feedback, unless it's a serious problem that will affect sales (don't change your business on the whims and likes of one or two customers) or a problem that you hear from virtually everyone.

✔ **Business colleagues/potential customers:** While you may not have done business online before, or have a past set of customers, hopefully you have some contacts from doing business and you have their e-mail addresses. Perhaps you know of potential customers from your professional career, non-profit activities, or extracurricular activities or hobbies. You can solicit some help and give out some benefits as well. Here, you should consider doing the following:

- Spend more time explaining your new Web store and this pregrand-opening opportunity to this crowd.

- Definitely consider offering some sort of reward or compensation for being able to act first, but make sure they have to provide some feedback to get that reward.

- Thank them early and often for their time and commitment.

- Provide a direct line of communication for them to contact you immediately for any concerns.

Inspecting Your Store for Multiple Web Browsers

Stuff You Need to Know

Toolbox:

✔ An idea of which Web store pages are the most important to inspect

✔ An idea of which browsers you should test for your Web store

Time Needed:

20–30 minutes

When you develop your Web store, odds are you're viewing your Web store with the same Web browser and operating system for your computer throughout the process. This means that you know exactly how your Web store will be portrayed . . . for anyone using your particular operating system and Web browser version. But what about other users? You don't want to isolate a large percentage of your potential customer base because they use a different Web browser that may not display your Web store correctly or properly.

Therefore, you want to test your Web store to see how it will be displayed on different Web browsers that use different operating systems from your development computer. Thankfully, there are companies that will go out (using different setups) and analyze your Web site with different operating system and Web browser combinations. As of this writing, one such site, BrowserCam (www.browsercam.com), currently has a free trial option on their Web site.

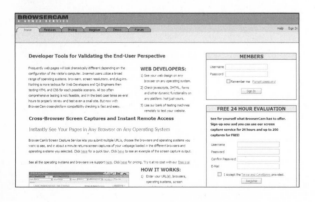

1. Go to BrowserCam's home page at www.browsercam.com. On the BrowserCam home page, take a look at the Free Evaluation window along the right side of the page, and complete the fields to begin to sign up for their free trial.

2. Go to your e-mail program (the one you listed when signing up for the free trial) and look for an e-mail from BrowserCam. BrowserCam sends the e-mail to verify that the address you provided to them is legitimate and that you own the account. If the e-mail doesn't arrive in 3–5 minutes, check any Bulk or Junk Mail folders, and if necessary re-register for the trial. When the confirmation e-mail arrives, click the activation link or cut and paste it into a Web browser.

TIP

Don't click the activation link until you're ready to do your work. Your trial account is only valid for 24 hours from the time you activate your account.

3. Once you click or use the activation link, you should see a confirmation screen on BrowserCam's site that your account has been created. Even though your account has been created, BrowserCam wants you to load a current version of their Web site by closing down your active Web browser sessions and starting a brand new session.

4. Start a new Web session and go back to BrowserCam to log onto their site. When you log onto their site using the Members section of their home page, you will be taken to your Plan Summary page. This page reviews your current account status with BrowserCam and gives you the details on how much time and how many *browser shots* (a picture of your Web store in a particular version of a Web browser and operating system; for example Windows XP, Internet Explorer 7.0) you have left in your account. Typcially, your trial account will let you take up to 200 shots of a window in a specific browser combination that you designate.

5. Click on the CAPTURE link to set up your Web site test shots. When you click this link the Screen Capture Service window will open. First, you have to give a name to your new Project or test scenario. You can also decide if you want other BrowserCam users to be able to view these shots, and if you want these screen shots publicly available over the Internet. Once you have set up your project name, you have two options. For the first option, you can enter your URL Web address(es) manually in the boxes provided. You can click the bulk URL link to provide a list of individual Web pages, or click the Enter More URLs link to add up to 10 individual Web pages. Click the Continue button when you're ready to proceed.

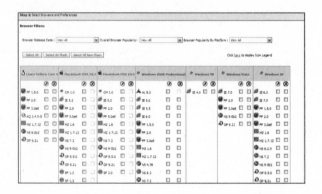

6. For your second option, you can select the Crawl a Web Site for Multiple URLs option. There, you can designate whether the program should crawl through the entire Web site or only through a set number of sublevels. Additionally, you can have the program take screen shots of links that go outside your Web site, or stay within your own domain name. Click the Continue button when you're ready to proceed.

7. You're now taken to the Browser Filters window. You can see there are a lot of options to choose from, as BrowserCam can test for all the major and mid-level versions of Internet Web browsers and the Windows, Mac, and Linux operating systems. Pick the browser/OS combinations you want to test. One option you have in narrowing your choices is to take advantage of the filter questions on top of the page, selecting based on release date, popularity, and popularity for the platform. For example, if you went to Overall Browser Popularity and picked 5 percent or greater, you'll notice there are fewer options in the list than there were in the default window. You could display browsers with 10 percent or greater popularity and get a more refined list.

When picking either of the options in Steps 5 and 6, you should specify a user ID and password if you want BrowserCam to take a picture of a password-protected site. (If the site requires no userid/password, leave these fields blank.) Click the Continue button when you are ready to proceed.

When choosing your browser filters, your goal is to try and test your Web site against the main options that your customers may be using to shop your site. Your trial account has 200 views, and you can subscribe to get as many as necessary, which could be worth the investment. You should definitely test for Internet Explorer and Firefox for the most popular versions of Windows, and you should include some testing for the Macintosh OS systems with Firefox and Netscape, meaning if you stick to the trial account, allocate at least 5-10 percent of your views for testing the Macintosh OS X operating system with Firefox and Netscape.

8. Once you have selected your browser and operating system combinations, scroll down to review your final options for this test. Before you start your test, you need to configure your test shots so BrowserCam knows what to do and how to deliver the results to you. Your options are Browser Size (unless you have specifically geared your website for a specific resolution, you should leave this box alone), Capture Area (unless you are testing to see if pop-up windows are being created successfully, stick to the Browser Only option), Format (it is recommended to leave this on the default setting, JPG, as most programs can display this file the easiest), Delay (this option is recommended if you have some sort of Flash or other animation, or some event that will be over in a matter of seconds, and you want to see the webpage after that initial event), Page Down (if you need BrowserCam to scroll down the Web page before taking the test shot, you can designate in the box provided how many times the program should Page Down before stopping to take the screen shot), Save Page Source (if you want to see the resulting HTML page source of your file as well as the screen shot), and E-mail Notification (if you want BrowserCam to send you an e-mail notifying you when all the test shots have been created). Click the Continue button when you're ready to proceed.

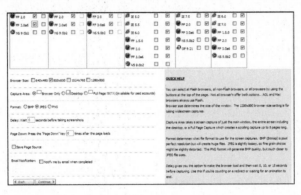

9. You've completed your order for your screen shot test. Depending on the size of your screen test request, you should wait a few minutes (or longer) before clicking the link to view your screen captures. If you chose e-mail notification in the previous step, you should wait until you get your e-mail before going back to view your screen test shots.

10. You will now see a summary screen for the test captures. Each screen shot is associated with the level of Web browser and operating system running on the computer that took that screen shot. Go through all your various test scenarios and make sure that your store loads correctly in all of them. If you see a flaw, make a note of the browser level and operating system and let your Web site designer or storefront provider know, since they may be using incompatible HTML commands to build your pages.

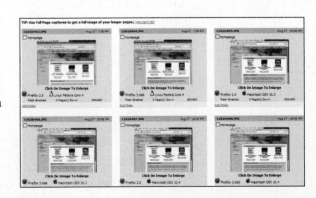

Testing Your Check Out Process

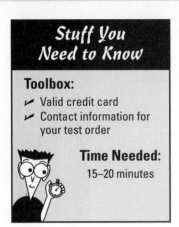

Once you know everything looks fine, it's time to test the cash register. After all, the coolest looking e-commerce store means nothing if your customers cannot process their orders, right? Therefore, the next step after testing the design of your Web site is to test the main functionality by placing a sample order on your Web store.

The first thing you should check is to see if your shopping cart software has an option to place a sample order. If you read Chapter 4, Yahoo! Stores, you saw that they actually require you to place a sample order before they will publish your Web store. If this function is available, it's useful to use that feature so it doesn't affect your accounting or inventory management after the sample order is placed.

When you do place your order, it is recommended to pick a non-credit card option, so your card isn't charged, or, to be thorough, pick one of your credit cards to use, and then you can arrange for a refund after the sample order is placed. In this task, we're going to test the checkout process using a Yahoo! Merchant Solutions Web store.

1. Use your Web browser to go to the home page of your Web store. Read the home page like you have never seen this before, and try to browse through the catalog. Click on the first or middle category from your navigation bar to see the category page of products.

2. Once you're on the category page, click on any of the products on that page to bring up the product detail page. At this point, you should see the Item photo, price, and Product Description. Here, click the Add to Cart button to add this product to your shopping cart.

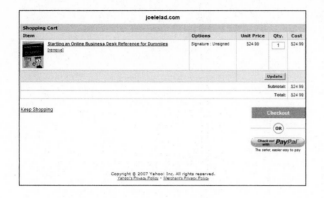

3. Now, you should be on your shopping cart page. If you want to test other products, then click on the link Keep Shopping near the bottom-left of the order page, and repeat Steps 1 and 2 to add more products to your shopping cart. However, one product is sufficient to test the check out process. When you're ready, click the blue Checkout button, or the orange Check Out with PayPal button, if you want to test your PayPal setup.

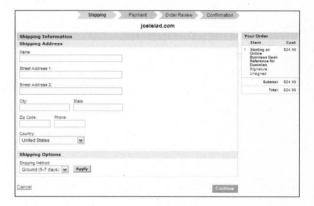

4. Enter your shipping information in the fields provided on the shipping screen. You can use your own home or business address, but make sure to complete every field (Street Address 2 field is optional) before clicking the Continue button.

5. On the billing page, you're asked whether your billing address is the same as your shipping address. Scroll down to enter either your credit card information or link to your PayPal account to pay for this order. Make sure to enter a valid e-mail in the E-mail confirmation box, so you can ensure the e-mail receipts your customers get are set up correctly. Click the blue Continue button when you are ready.

6. Review all the order information on the next screen, and click the blue Send Order button when you're ready. You'll see a confirmation screen that thanks you for your order and displays the shipping and billing information again.

7. To be thorough, you should probably go into your Yahoo! Merchant Solutions and delete this order, so you or one of your employees doesn't accidentally try to fulfill this order. Log into your Merchant Solutions account, and from the Merchant Starter page, click on Orders from the Process header. You should see "1 New Order" and the order number.

8. Click the View button to see your order. From the order page, click the radio button marked Cancelled on the right side of the page, and click Update to cancel this order from your system.

Sending Out a Grand Opening E-mail

Stuff You Need to Know

Toolbox:

- List of e-mail addresses of people to contact
- An idea of 1–3 products to feature in the e-mail

Time Needed:
20–30 minutes

What better way to get the cash registers going on your new web store than announcing your Grand Opening in an e-mail to family, friends, and customers! Yahoo! Merchant Solutions has a Grand Opening e-mail function that you will see after you launch your store. You will need to think of a list of people who you plan to get this e-mail, which we talked about earlier in this chapter.

1. Log into your Yahoo! Merchant Solutions account. Scroll down to the Promote section and click on the Simple Promotional Email link.

2. You'll see the Create your Email page load. In the From field, use the pull-down menu to select one of your Yahoo! Business e-mail accounts that handle customer service inquiries for your Web store. That way, if someone replies to this e-mail, it will go to the correct e-mail account.

3. In the To field, enter the e-mail addresses of the people you want to send this announcement. Use commas to separate multiple e-mail addresses. Look over the subject line to make sure it reads the way you want it. You may consider including your name in the Subject line so people know who it's from, if they are unaware of your Web store. Finally, make sure that your Store Name and URL are showing up correctly.

4. Now it's time to edit your message. Yahoo! gives you a template that you can follow, or you can delete everything and write your own message. The point of this e-mail is to introduce your Web store, so talk about the goals or mission of your store, what products or information you plan to carry, and why customers should click through and see what you have to offer.

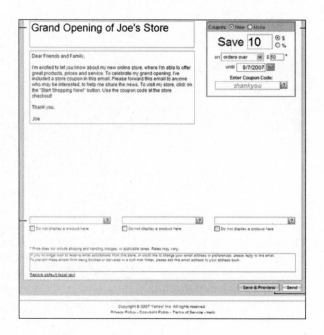

5. If you scroll down, you'll see three drop-down list boxes. Those are included so you can pick up to three of your products to feature in this Grand Opening e-mail. Simply click the down arrow and pick a product from your catalog to include, or click the checkbox marked Do Not Display a Product Here.

6. Click the orange Save and Preview button at the bottom of the form to review your e-mail before it is sent out. Make sure the e-mail appears exactly as you want your customers or friends to see it, and when you are ready, click the Send button to e-mail it off!

Chapter 15

Load, Look, and Launch — Final Steps Before You Open

Tasks performed in this chapter

- Verifying your catalog is uploaded and accurate
- Making sure all the information is up to date
- Doing a final check before launch
- Checking your load times
- Making a backup copy of your store

You've reached the final step. You've designed, created, uploaded, and tested your Web store. Your catalog is ready, your categories are created, and all your photos and descriptions are sitting and waiting to be displayed. You've gone through and verified all your Web pages are correct and look sharp. You've reached that magic moment, the readiness to go "live" and open your Web store to the public.

In this chapter, we cover the final steps you should take before and during your Web store launch. In many situations, as the time passes from initial store design to store launch, things change in your Web store that aren't reflected in the Web pages (like the accurateness of a description or the exact inventory level of a product). Therefore, we go over your catalog and inventory levels, as well as your product descriptions, and look now for accurateness, not spelling or grammar. Finally, we go over some common things to check for as you launch your store.

Verifying Your Catalog Is Uploaded and Accurate

As you've developed your Web store, odds are the more time between your initial gathering of data and the time to launch, the more of a chance that the catalog needs to be updated. While you were busy coming up with your store design, uploading all the information, and building all the functionality of your Web store, product descriptions may have changed, inventory levels may have fluctuated, and pricing information may be different.

Therefore, I recommend performing the following checks before your Web store goes live:

✔ **Check to make sure that all your pictures were uploaded correctly and associated with a product.** If you did something called a *bulk upload,* where you sent a lot of information, all at once, to your storefront provider, there is a small chance that perhaps one or more of your picture files may have gotten scrambled or uploaded incorrectly and is not visible on your Web store. Log onto your storefront provider and check your directories where your images are located. If you've got lots of pictures, do a random check (perhaps every fifth or sixth picture) by clicking on it and make sure it loads properly into a Web browser window. If you see any graphics representing a broken image, as shown in Figure 15-1, go back and upload that picture again.

Additionally, even if the image was uploaded correctly, sometimes it won't get assigned to the right product, or any product for that matter. If you have a product that doesn't have an image associated with it, your system may show "No Image Available," as shown in Figure 15-2. Check to make sure the image association is correct, as one misspelled letter or extra keystroke could have thrown off the system.

If you're going to re-use pictures for more than one product listing, make sure you display the picture at the same size for each listing. Otherwise, if you try to enlarge a small graphic (see Figure 15-3), you get a blurry and unattractive picture that could dissuade some buyers.

Figure 15-1: A broken picture typically shows up as an X in a box.

Figure 15-2: Make sure there is a picture associated with every product.

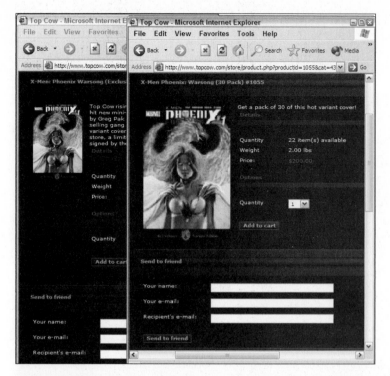

Figure 15-3: Keep instances of the same picture the same size throughout the catalog, or risk having a blurry enlarged image.

✔ **Check your pricing information against competitors on the Internet.**
Sometimes, a month (or even a day) is all it takes for a product to ignite (or fizzle) on the Internet. If you're selling sports memorabilia, for example, you might want to check your prices again, because I can guarantee that merchandise related to Barry Bonds sells for higher prices *after* he breaks a record, compared with before he breaks the record. If you're dealing with celebrity merchandise, then current events may dictate if you have to update your prices. Of course, any event-related merchandise is priced differently before and after the event, and sees either a sliding scale decrease the further away from the event, or a rising increase in price if the supply was limited and/or popularity is high. Finally, the manufacturer may announce or roll out a price cut, like Microsoft did in August 2007 on their X-Box 360 video game system. If all the major retailers update their prices, and you don't, then you become the high-price alternative and risk losing customers.

✔ **Read through your product descriptions for accuracy, not just spelling and grammar.** In the previous chapter, we recommended you scan through your Web site content to look for misspelled words or grammatical errors. This time, we want you (or someone on your staff who is very familiar with the products) to read through the product descriptions to make sure they're accurate. Sometimes, when you get information from the manufacturer, if the product hasn't been released yet then you get only a partial description. Look for any notes of "Missing Information," "Coming Soon," or "TBA (To Be Announced). Do some research with the manufacturer or on the Internet to see if you can replace these notes with current data.

In some cases (see Figure 15-4), you may find an item where the picture, title, and pricing information have uploaded correctly, but there's no description. It's your job to ensure that every product in your catalog has at least one paragraph of description for the item.

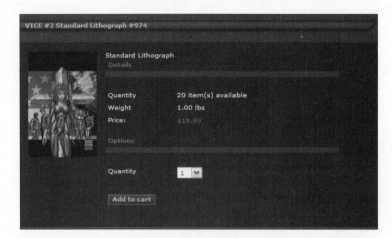

Figure 15-4: Make sure your catalog items aren't missing a description.

✔ **Make sure your category structure is complete and accurate.** It's encouraged to do some random sampling of the products in your catalog and make sure they're assigned to the correct category. Otherwise, if the product isn't in its logical place, then customers may not find it and therefore can't buy it.

Finally, you want to make sure that the categories created on your Web store catalog are properly filled in or are going to have hot merchandise soon. It's very easy during the planning stages of a Web store to create a list of desired categories and then find out (when the store is going to launch) that certain categories won't be filled with any merchandise (or only one or two secondary items). You don't want a customer clicking on a category to see zero items created for that category, as that looks like poor planning on your part.

Making Sure Your Store's Information Is Correct

Once you've verified your catalog data to be correct, up-to-date, and complete, it's time to inspect the rest of your Web store. Things can definitely change between your first initial plan for your store and the final implementation, and sometimes we're so happy to see the light at the end of the tunnel that we forget to go back and update our Web pages with the final decision of how your Web store will be executed.

Therefore, it's recommended to go back and review all the Web pages of your store. This time, however, instead of looking for obvious spelling and grammatical mistakes, pay more attention to the content on the pages, and make sure that the policies, guidelines, and rules stated are the same as your goals for running the Web store.

Here are some questions to get you started:

✔ **Did I finalize my store policies, including return/refund and privacy policies?** We talked about store policies way back in Chapter 2, and usually some boiler plate documentation is thrown in and then never reviewed again . . . until your initial customers start calling you on it once their orders are placed and expect you to honor the policy they read on your site when they placed an order. Therefore, go back and make sure you agree with the policies you previously stated. Perhaps, while building your store, you decided to focus on closeout or used merchandise and forgot to update your refund policy to state "No returns. Items sold as-is." The key is to make sure you're consistent in your policies.

✔ **What shipping methods and rates am I going to offer my customers?** Depending on the series of steps you took to build your Web store, you may have had to build your shipping options in first, and then go back and think about a shipping company and sign up for an account, like we did in Chapter 12. However, you may not have reviewed your shipping terms since that initial setup and you may be charging your customers incorrectly, and that could mean you're charging too little or too much.

Go back to your shipping options and make sure that your shipping totals are being computed based on weight of the package, distance between you and the customer, and the speed of delivery, whenever possible. You won't survive as an e-commerce merchant charging too little for shipping, unless you've decided that shipping will be a promotional cost to encourage customers to try you out.

✔ **Do I mention any events or dates as upcoming when they have already passed?** This is a common mistake for Web sites that have news, events, or press release sections where they plan to promote an upcoming event as they're building their Web store but by the time the website is ready to launch, the event has already occurred. When customers see this mistake, they assume you don't update your Web store often and will probably not get their order in a quick or expedient manner either.

✔ **Is my contact information current and up-to-date?** As people build their Web stores and set up their infrastructure, sometimes they experience change before the Web store has been launched. Perhaps you realize early that you have to set up in a warehouse to handle your new operations, or you have decided to relocate to a place with favorable tax benefits. Whatever the reason, before you go live make sure that the Contact Information page on your Web store is up-to-date with the correct e-mail address, postal address, and telephone number that you want your customers or visitors to use when contacting you. Let's say that when you set up your Web store you initially put one of your personal e-mail addresses, but since then you've established a stand-alone customer service e-mail address. Don't forget to go back and put that address in the right places on your Web store. (By the way, a customer service e-mail address is *highly* recommended.)

✔ **Have I left any of my store pages completely blank?** This may sound like a strange question, especially if you've been clicking through and reviewing all your Web pages. But sometimes, the pages we think about the least (like the About Us or Company History pages), get put off. The thinking is usually "Oh, we will get to that later," and then the Web site gets launched and you end up with an About Us page like the one in Figure 15-5. Make sure that every page without product has some content as well, and either fill the page with some content, or, if you don't have time and it doesn't affect the navigation bar, remove the page until you have the time to create something worthwhile.

Figure 15-5: Don't leave any Web page on your site without content.

Other times, perhaps you created a "place-holder" for a store page, with the hopes and intentions of filling it in later, like putting TBA in a product description (see previous section). The last thing you want your customers to see, besides an empty page, is a page with a placeholder like "Coming Soon" or "FAQ goes here" (see Figure 15-6), so fill that page or remove it from sight until you can properly fill it.

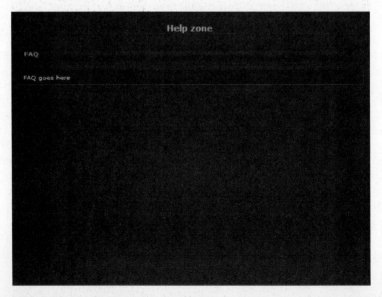

Figure 15-6: Placeholders should be removed and replaced, or hidden from view.

The Final Checks — Countdown to Launch

Once you're finished with adding your products to your catalog and creating all the various Web pages that will make up your Web store, and you feel that you're ready to open the doors and start generating traffic, I recommend doing a "final sweep" of your new Web store and getting everything ready for your launch. Once you have orders to fill, and customers and visitors asking questions, you probably won't have the time to go back and do these checks, so do it before the traffic begins.

✔ **Check your load times:** The *load time* is known as the amount of time it takes for a Web page to fully display on someone's computer screen. Depending on how much information and graphics are on the page and how the user is connecting to the Internet, the load time can be less than a second or several minutes. If your Web site is loading slowly on other people's computers, you need to figure out a way to decrease that time, as customers will not be patient enough to wait for the page to load — they'll simply go to a competitor's Web store. Some things you can do if your Web store load times are high are:

  • Reduce the amount of graphics on your page.

  • Reduce or eliminate unnecessary functions like animated Flash presentations.

  • Reduce the size or optimize the graphics you are using on your page.

  • Try to re-use the same graphics on different pages so the computer can use a locally-stored copy when your customer goes page to page on your site, thus saving time re-loading graphics.

✔ **Get your final pieces from your developer:** If you're going to use any outside contractors to help you finish your Web store, it's advisable to meet with them to receive your final deliverables (goods) and sign an agreement that you approve of the quality of work and accept it. This way, you're not launching your Web store and then having to go back and integrate a piece you just received, as that integration could cause problems down the road if not fully tested. When you launch your Web store, it should be with all the elements you planned (and paid) to execute.

✔ **Make a full backup copy of your website:** Some store-front providers do automatic backups of your system. If they don't provide this function, it's useful to prepare a file that has all the Web pages, images, and catalog information, and store it somewhere safe in case anything happens to your Web site. It's also useful to have a "snapshot" of your original site when it's time to plan for the next version, for example.

✔ **Check your custom programming:** If you're using advanced scripts or programming languages in your Web store, sometimes you can't fully test these scripts until the Web store is live and ready to go. Once you upload the code to your Web store, you should immediately start checking any advanced functionality to make sure it's working as designed.

✔ **Test your search engine criteria:** If you have a search engine for your Web site, go ahead and type in some sample searches as though you were a customer. If you have an advanced search engine (as shown in Figure 15-7), test the different criteria. For example, if you offer your customers a chance to search between a minimum and maximum value, try entering $1 for your minimum and $50 for your maximum and make sure the results contain only items in that range.

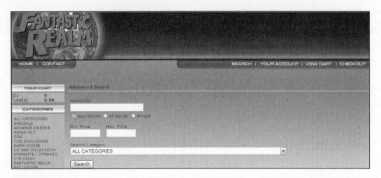

Figure 15-7: Test the different elements of your store search engine.

> ✔ **Transfer your files to the server:** With some e-commerce software packages you have to manually "turn on" your Web store by telling the software to transfer the Web pages you have created to the "live" or "real" server, so the public can access it over the Internet. In those cases, you prepare your Web pages on a "development" portion (that is only accessible to you and your provider) of their Web server so you won't have to worry about anyone accidentally coming across your Web store and placing an order too soon. Depending on your storefront provider, you may see one of the following phrases as the link to click when you want to "turn on" your Web store:
>
> • Upload your Web site
>
> • Publish your Web site
>
> • Open my store
>
> • Send to live server

You've reached a very important milestone — the official launch of your Web store! It's a time to celebrate, but also a time to shift gears. Think of this launch not as an end, but as a new beginning, because a Web store (like any Web site) requires constant tending and maintenance to stay viable. Look forward to your future and keep an eye on your store. The fun and profit has only begun.

Testing Your Load Times

Stuff You Need to Know

Toolbox:
- Access to a Web browser
- Stopwatch/timer

Time Needed:
10–20 minutes

It's important to view your Web store on a computer connected live to the Internet, not to look for technical or functional accuracy, but simply to study how long it takes each page to load on your computer. This will be an estimate for what your customers may experience when they use your Web store. If you're planning to open a large, enterprise-scale store, you may want to do an Internet search for Web site load testing and use a software program to test your load times. For most Web stores, you can measure your load times manually, which we do in this exercise.

1. Using your Web browser, type in the URL for your web store. You can either use a stopwatch or just monitor the page as it loads on the screen. If you use a stopwatch, once you type in the URL and hit the Enter button, start your stopwatch and don't stop it until your Web store home page fully loads. If it takes more than 5–10 seconds for your home page to load, you should consider reducing the number of images or data on the home page.

2. Click the Site Map button to view a full list of all the Web pages in your store. (Depending on the template you picked, the Site Map link could be along the top, left, or bottom of your page.)

3. Click the first item on the list, and study how long it takes for that page to load. Then, click the Back button on your Web browser to go back to the Site Map page and click the next page on the list. Repeat this process until you have clicked on every page in your Web store.

4. In many cases, your page will load so quickly that you won't get an accurate stopwatch reading, which is great. Once you've clicked through your entire Web site, if you notice one or two pages that seem to load slower than the others, go back to those pages and consider ways to reduce the load time, like eliminating large image files.

Creating a Backup Copy of Your Web Store Catalog

Stuff You Need to Know

Toolbox:
- Yahoo! account information
- Access to a local computer to store your backup catalog

Time Needed:
5–10 minutes

Yahoo! Merchant Solutions does an automatic backup of your entire Web site every four hours. They call this system "Snapshot Backups" and it is automatically activated when you start designing your Web store. The function takes a copy, or snapshot, of your Web site every four hours, nightly, and weekly, by recording changes to your files. These snapshots are saved and dated and made available to you. However, you can go one step further by making a backup copy of your product catalog, so you can upload it at a future date in case of an emergency.

1. Log into your Yahoo! Merchant Solutions account at `http://smallbusiness.yahoo.com` by clicking on the Small Business button next to the Manage Your Services header. When you get to your Merchant Starter page, click on the Catalog Manager link to load that page.

2. From the Catalog Manager home page, click on the Upload Items link to go to the Upload page.

3. From the Upload page, click on the button marked Download on the right-side of the screen. This will take you to the Download Table page. From here, you can pick the table that contains your catalog data and click the Download button to save a copy on your computer. Unless you have a complex product catalog, the "default-table" is the table you want to backup.

4. When you click the Download button, you'll see a window asking you to save a CSV file on your computer. Pick a directory and give this file a meaningful name, like `backupmmddyy.csv`. Once this file is saved to your computer, you may consider saving that file on another device, like an external hard drive or a tape drive, in case your computer's hard drive experiences a problem.

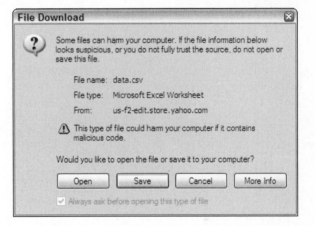

5. If you would ever need to restore your catalog, simply follow Steps 1–3, but during Step 3 click the Upload button and follow the instructions to indicate your backup file on your computer to restore your Web site.

Part V
Promotion and Outsourcing of Your Web Store

"Sales on the Web site are down. I figure the server's chi is blocked, so we're fudgin' around the feng shui in the computer room, and if that doesn't work, Ronnie's got a chant that should do it."

In this part . . .

In this part, I cover the essential steps that a Web store owner should take after the store has been built and launched on the Internet. First, and foremost, you need to think about bringing as much traffic to your Web store as possible. I start by discussing different mechanisms for generating buzz about your Web store online, from blogs to newsletters to using sites like eBay to announce your new Web store.

Then, I move into more traditional advertising mechanisms for your Web store, like pay per click advertising and submitting your store to the search engines.

Finally, I talk about how you may want to take your Web store to the next level, by outsourcing pieces of your business like shipping and fulfillment or store redesign, or how to use Internet sites like Prosper to get additional funding to grow your Web store.

Chapter 16

Getting the Word Out — Drawing Attention to Your Store

You've built your Web store, but will they come? That is the dilemma every Web store owner faces — the hope that their efforts will be rewarded with a steady stream of customers, a healthy profit margin, and a growing business to sustain. Building the Web store is very important, which is why we dedicated so many pages to talk about all the various steps and functionality. But your work is not over yet. It's time to tell the masses, get them fired up, and drive that traffic to your Web store.

In this chapter, we talk about many different ways you can use the Internet to get the word out about your store. One of the newer technologies, the Web log, or *blog,* has grown in popularity the last few years and is now a great way to build a dialogue and relationship with your customers while promoting your store and the various pages within your store. We show you two sites in specific that offer free blogs you can create. From there, we talk about the next great way to build that ongoing relationship — the newsletter (or *e-newsletter,* for Web stores) you should send out. We discuss the important elements of a newsletter and tips to consider. We finish up by discussing how you can use other Web sites to sell merchandise that will point customers to your own Web store.

Using a Blog to Promote Your Web Store

The blogging phenomenon has taken the Internet by storm, with reports of 80–100 million blogs in creation, and more being started every day. While many of the blogs out there focus on one area of discussion, from politics to marketing to entertainment, a small but growing number of blogs have been created by companies, large and small. Companies are creating blogs to have a dialogue or give more information to their customers about what goes on in their business, and how these events can help or impact their customer base.

In essence, having a blog is like having a conversation with your customers if they came through your door in a retail setting. Many store owners use their blog to discuss new inventory purchases, upcoming events and sales, and trends that they've noticed that could affect their business. Some blogs allow comments, where their customers can comment on a store owner's postings and give their enthusiasm, comments, or feedback.

Blogs have other features besides the increased communication between you and your customers:

- ✔ It's much easier to add a blog entry about an upcoming product category change or news announcement than to constantly add notices and reminders on your Web store pages — potentially having to redesign your site to include this new element.

- ✔ Your blog allows you to highlight individual sections of your Web store without having to completely re-design your navigation bar for a temporary promotion. You can feed people with targeted links to a different section every day, week, or month.

- ✔ The extra links that a blog makes to your Web site are seen as additional references that help your search engine ranking.

- ✔ Your blog gives your customers an additional media source to learn about the products they are purchasing, and a chance to learn from other customers via the feedback/comments section.

Since the goal of your blog is to connect with your potential customers, one strategy for using a blog could be to go where your customers are already reading blogs. If your Web store category falls into a big niche, like electronics or toys and games, you could look for a blogging portal that caters to that customer set and see if you can add a blog through their portal or site to reach the same customer set. This way, you can take advantage of the established traffic of a popular blogging portal or be included in a network or collective of blogs.

The other main strategy when it comes to blogs is to have the blog actually reside on your Web site. This way, customers have to come to your Web store to read the blog and, hopefully, get valuable information and become more "emotionally invested" in your operation. The hope is that they'll check out a new product, take advantage of a sale event, or simply be encouraged to place a new order. Talk to your storefront provider about what options currently exist to have the blog appear on your Web store.

Some of the options below will allow you to redirect people from a subdomain on your Web site directly to the blog page.

There are a number of free and paid blogging solutions to choose from. The main choices available today include:

- ✔ **Blogger** (www.blogger.com): Created by Google, this Web site allows you to build any number of blogs with built-in tools to make blog maintenance as easy as possible. We discuss how to sign up with Blogger later in this chapter.

- ✔ **Yahoo! 360** (360.yahoo.com): As part of Yahoo's effort to generate and organize more content on the Web, they've created the "360" pages as a way to blog and share photos, information, and more with others. You need a Yahoo! ID to take advantage of this, which you already have if you're using Yahoo! Merchant Solutions. We show you how to sign up with Yahoo! 360 later in this chapter.

✔ **WordPress (**www.wordpress.com**):** This company became well known for a powerful blogging software they developed through a concept called *open source,* where anybody can download and update the software code on their own while keeping the software free to use. They created a .com site to offer people free blog accounts.

✔ **TypePad (**www.typepad.com**):** This company is probably the most famous of the paid blogging sites, as big-name personalities like Seth Godin, Dilbert creator Scott Adams, and Andrew Sullivan use TypePad's powerful blogging tool to maintain their blogs. If you want an advanced blog that sits on your Web site and offers lots of options, TypePad has packages starting at $4.95 per month that may interest you.

✔ **MSN Spaces (**spaces.live.com**):** Microsoft will not only offer your business a free Web site through their Live service, but they have a Spaces feature that is, in essence, a free blogging tool that would integrate with your Web site. The downside is that Microsoft controls the advertising to pay for the service.

If you want to use your blog to generate some real buzz for your business, check out *Buzz Marketing with Blogs For Dummies* by Savannah Gardner (Wiley Publishing, Inc.) for more information.

Utilizing a Newsletter for Your Store

As a business owner, one of your responsibilities is to figure out how to stay in touch with your customers, keep them informed about your business, and encourage that all-so-coveted repeat business without annoying, turning off, or isolating your customer or visitor base.

One of the most popular ways for Web stores to accomplish this is to write and publish their own newsletter, which combines information and product announcements to remind people about the business and give them useful information in exchange for their time and attention.

Newsletters are quickly becoming popular for many reasons (low cost, quick set up time, improved customer loyalty, and typically a great conversion rate of visitors to paying customers) compared with other means. It's important to note that the online newsletters contain at least one article of useful, practical, or interesting information that would matter to your customers, along with a few product promotions or highlights, and perhaps some business announcements or promotions, like specialty eBay auctions or charity fundraising. As an example, let's look at Lynn Dralle (a.k.a. "The Queen of Auctions") who publishes a weekly newsletter (shown in Figure 16-1) that gives her readers valuable tips for selling online while promoting her own books, DVDs, and coaching seminars that she sells herself.

If you send out a newsletter that has no useful information, simply product announcements and business promotions, that's not a newsletter — it's a sales flyer. People typically agree to a newsletter because it brings them some value, which is why they choose to allow it and spend their valuable time reading it. You'll lose customers and business value by passing a sales flyer off as a newsletter.

Lynn Dralle
The Queen of Auctions
eBay with Heart

**Lynn's eBay ezine Volume III,
issue number 31**

Hi!

I can't believe that summer is almost over. I think more people
are back inside and thinking about back to school. My eBay
business has started picking up again. Thank goodness! I hope
yours has also.

👑 In This Issue

- Lynn Recommends: La Quinta Boot Camp
- Special Announcement: My Interview with Janelle Elms
- Feature Article: A Dirty Pan Can Sell for How Much?
- The Queen's Update: Our 25th *100 Best* Story from YOU

This ezine is published once a week.

Figure 16-1: Use newsletters to give information and build relationships.

Just like with blogs, newsletters take some time on your part, so think carefully
before you decide to promote this feature and collect customer names to be on your
newsletter list. This doesn't have to be a huge time-consuming effort, but set aside
some time on a regular basis to handle the newsletter creation, or designate an
employee to handle the newsletter for you.

Putting together the parts of your newsletter

When you want to create your Web store newsletter, it's helpful to understand the
basic anatomy of a newsletter and the elements needed to make this happen.
Therefore, let's go through each part of your store newsletter and talk about what
to consider:

✔ **Articles:** At the heart of your newsletter should be at least one article that
contains some useful information. You have many options here, depending
on the intent you want your newsletter to convey. Some store newsletters
feature tips and tricks related to the products they sell. For example, a Web
store that sells digital cameras could fill their newsletters with digital photography tips and how their customers can maximize their investment.
Other newsletters could highlight product reviews or detailed how-to

guides. You could also comment on the state of your industry and discuss overall product trends or important news items that would interest your customers. As far as who will write these articles for your newsletter, you have several choices:

- **You:** After all, who knows product lines better than the person who sells them, right? If you're setting up a Web store because you've got experience with your products, then share that knowledge by writing short articles for your store newsletter. You can write articles that focus on "Top 10 Tips for Using Product *X*," "Five things to watch out for when trying to do *Y*," or "Three Unexpected Uses for Item *Z*." You can use your newsletters to write columns about your experiences as a store owner, or the lessons learned from retailing in your particular industry.

  Publish your newsletter articles on your Web store as well. Adding content to your Web store will improve your search engine rankings. (We discuss this in more depth in the next chapter.)

- **Your customers:** By having customers relate their experiences with your products, whether it's a product review, interesting story, or questions about the product that you will answer, you get not only some original content for your newsletters, but an increased connection between you and your customer base. Every time your newsletter comes out, your customers will open it up looking to see if their names are in (virtual) lights. It also gives you legitimacy in customers' minds when they see other customers using your business.

  If you go this route, have someone look it over first to make sure the content is appropriate, as well as free of spelling and grammatical mistakes. You may also want to build up several entries of reserve, in case customer submission is light for a period of time.

- **Other people:** There are numbers of people who are looking for increased exposure for their own efforts, whether it's their own Web site, consulting service, or business. These people write articles that are freely distributed on the Internet with the goal of increasing their status due to the required biography and Web links attached to the end of these articles. You can go to Web sites known as *article directories* and find free articles that relate to your industry that you can include in your newsletter. Some places to get started can be found include Ezine @articles (www.ezinearticles.com), GoArticles.com (www.goarticles.com), ArticleTrader (www.articletrader.com), Articlesbase.com (www.articlesbase.com), and ArticleCity (www.articlecity.com).

✔ **Product Offers:** Once you've gotten your customer's attention and provided some good information, there's nothing wrong with reminding them of some of the products for sale in your Web store. You should definitely include the title of the product and a direct link to the product detail page on your Web store. Depending on the format of your newsletter, you can enhance your product offer with elements like a thumbnail photo, short description, current price, and more. If you're wondering which products to feature in your newsletter, here are some possibilities:

- **Brand new products to your store.** You can create excitement and buzz by highlighting the newest arrivals to your store, and labeling them as Just Arrived, Newly Available, or Brand New! This way, you're not only promoting them, but informing customers of your newest product offerings.

- **Items that you are putting on sale.** If you've decided to discount one of your products (perhaps it's not selling as quickly as you expected, or you want to reduce your inventory of a given product), then help that promotion by featuring that sale item in your newsletter.

- **Items that are mentioned in the newsletter's articles**. For example, if your article was a review of three different digital cameras that you carry in your Web store, perhaps offer a newsletter-only discount if they click the link from the newsletter and buy it.

✔ **Announcements or news updates:** Since the goal of a newsletter is to stay in-touch with your customers, it's perfectly acceptable (and preferred, actually) to mention any news updates regarding your Web store in the newsletter. You can announce an upcoming sale on your store, let people know that you plan to carry a new category in a few months, or tell people that you added a new payment method to your store. These are best suited for the end of the newsletter, but you can lead your newsletter with a featured news update and then introduce your article, like the Hero Initiative, a non-profit organization dedicated to helping comic creators in need, did in their newsletter (see Figure 16-2).

Figure 16-2: Introduce your newsletter with a featured news item.

Deciding on the mechanics of your newsletter

Once you have your content for your newsletter, it's time to figure out the process of how your newsletters will be generated and sent. Therefore, here are some questions you should ask yourself to get ready for this process:

TIP

- ✔ **What format should I use to publish my newsletter?** You have two options here, plain text and HTML . A *plain-text* newsletter is just that, plain old text. You can include Web links with your text, but no graphics, formatting, or anything special. The advantage of plain-text is that any e-mail reader can handle them, and they are quick to load and distribute. The disadvantage is that it is hard to capture a reader's attention with just text. *HTML (Hypertext Markup Language)* newsletters allow you to precisely format your newsletter and add graphics, color, and other HTML elements so it resembles your Web store. While some e-mail programs can't handle a fully formatted HTML newsletter, many of them will display these properly.

  When in doubt, make two versions of your newsletter, HTML and plain text, and let your subscribers choose their preferred method when they sign up.

- ✔ **How often should I send out my newsletter?** You have several options in this case. Most people prefer either a weekly, monthly, or bi-monthly/quarterly schedule. The important thing to remember here is to be consistent once you decide on a schedule. If you promise a weekly newsletter and only deliver one every few months, your readers will lose interest and confidence in your abilities as a retailer. Conversely, if you promise a monthly schedule and rapidly fire a few newsletters into their e-mail inbox every week, the customers will feel overwhelmed and abused. Pick a schedule where you know you can comfortably deliver quality.

- ✔ **How do I get people to join my newsletter?** The answer here is simple — as many ways as you can. This is an ongoing promotion mechanism for your e-commerce Web store, so getting people to sign up will be an ongoing effort as well. Some techniques retailers have used include:

  - Offering a discount or free shipping if a previous, current, or new customer joins the newsletter list.

  - Encouraging sign-ups from a link on the Web store home page.

  - Inviting people who have purchased from them to sign up for the newsletter.

  - Including a sign-up card (with enrollment instructions) in the package when an order is shipped out.

  - Partnering with similar companies (not direct competitors) and inviting those members to join your newsletter list in exchange for a free gift or bonus.

- ✔ **How do I manage my newsletter subscriptions and cancellations?** This is best handled by a newsletter service or list management service. The last thing you want to do is manually update your newsletter list and go through to take out a name when someone sends you an e-mail to get off your list. Later in this chapter, we discuss some companies that will help you build and distribute your newsletter, and those companies can help manage your subscription information. If you plan on building and e-mailing your newsletter yourself, you can use list management software from Freelists.org or start and maintain your own Yahoo! group at http://groups.yahoo.com.

Selling on Other Sites

As we discussed in Chapter 13, your Web store needs to be the hub of your sales activity. However, that doesn't mean it has to be the *sole* location of your sales activity. Shoppers take advantage of the wide variety of retailers and sales sites to find goods and services, and the most successful retailers will reach out to be wherever their customers may go.

It is important, when setting up some products for sale on other sites, to remember the reason why you are doing this. The end goal of doing business on these other sites is not necessarily to make money while selling on these sites, but rather to promote their business and refer any customers to their own Web store. Therefore, some Web store owners will sell promotional items, or sell regular products below their cost, simply to attract attention, gain new customers, and point those customers to their Web store.

In addition, every time you do business on another site, you typically have the chance to set up your own profile page, which can include information and links to your Web store, and this will raise your Web store profile online as well.

Here are some Web sites to consider putting up some items:

- **eBay:** With over 240 million registered users around the world (as of this writing), eBay is the number one e-commerce site on the Internet. They're one of the top 10 most popular Internet sites in general, and the highest ranked commerce site. More important, however, is that the average eBay user spends almost 2 hours per visit on the site, looking for merchandise in over 50,000 distinct categories and sub-categories.

- **Amazon.com:** Earth's Biggest Bookstore has branched out to include up to 41 different categories, as of this writing. They have 65 million customers in various countries around the world, and they created the Marketplace where anyone can get an account and sell items like books, DVDs, CDs, electronics, and video games to Amazon buyers using the Amazon infrastructure. In addition, they have an Advantage program where publishers can list their own books, DVDs, CDs, and other media to be sold on Amazon.

- **Yahoo! Shopping:** Independent of Yahoo's other offerings, like Merchant Solutions, Yahoo! Shopping offers a directory of products available for sale across the Internet. Retailers provide Yahoo! Shopping with a catalog or list of products available for sale, and Yahoo! Shopping organizes this information in a directory-style format, where browsers can look up various products and see which retailers are selling that item and each retailer's price for that item.

- **uBid:** This site is looking to become an alternative to eBay, where small and large sellers offer a variety of brand-name goods in a more focused and controlled atmosphere that is conducive to completing the transaction. uBid has a seller registration form that allows your business to register and take advantage of this up and coming marketplace.

As I mentioned, eBay is the top shopping destination on the Internet as of this writing. One of the reasons that eBay became so popular is because many of the products sold on eBay are sold via an auction-style format. Buyers place bids on the items to compete for the right to buy that item from a seller. When the clock runs out on an item (going once, going twice, sold!) there is known to be some frenzied bidding activity as eBay users log in and put their final bids. This has turned shopping into entertainment, as people compete instead of browse and get the sense of victory when they "win" an item.

This excitement can translate into new customers to check out your own Web store, if you put some auctions on eBay that relate to your Web store in some way. Simply having an account with eBay allows you to build a profile page to advertise your business. Previously, it was called About Me, but today it is referred to as My World, and later in this chapter we detail how you can create this page.

The My World page is the only Web page within eBay where you are allowed to link or mention the URL of your Web store. You can't link from your individual auction pages to any outside URL for commerce purposes, including your own Web store.

You have several options when it comes to picking items to sell on eBay:

- ✔ **Products from your Web store:** Since you're already selling products in your Web store, you could pick one item from each category and list it for sale on eBay at an introductory price. You can also start the bidding at the minimum price you need to break even, or a fixed price based on your cost or Web store price.

- ✔ **Promotional or one-of-a-kind items:** If you have any unique offerings, or perhaps can create an experience or something similar, then eBay is the perfect place to let customers compete for this rare item. Some companies have auctioned off everything from a dinner with the company CEO to the original desk used by the founder. Toy companies have been known to auction off one-of-a-kind prototypes of an action figure to coincide with the retail launch of that action figure line in stores. Some companies have even sold the chance to own the first of a new product. One example is Dr. Pepper, which auctioned off unopened 12 pack soda can boxes of their new flavors like Berries and Cream to enthusiastic buyers before those flavors were available in retail stores. Some of those 12 packs went for as high as $60-80 each and gave Dr. Pepper some extra publicity.

- ✔ **Damaged or "hurt" inventory:** Perhaps there is some inventory in your Web store that isn't exactly new and unused that you don't feel comfortable selling to your regular customers alongside other new, unused products. eBay has become an excellent place to sell your used, damaged, scuffed, or otherwise "hurt" or non-new inventory at a separate price on a separate channel from your retail sales. Companies such as the Sharper Image, Kodak, and Olympus have made big bucks selling this kind of merchandise directly to their end user customers without upsetting their retail channel partners.

- ✔ **New product lines:** Sometimes, if you want to judge the popularity of offering a new product line in your store, you can test it out by having an eBay auction for the item first and seeing how popular and how many bids the item received. Auctions allow you to gauge some customer demand to help you set good prices for your customers, since you can see how much people are willing to go, monetarily speaking, to get the product.

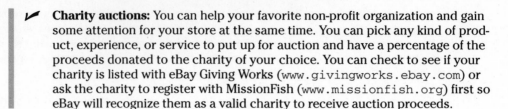

✔ **Charity auctions:** You can help your favorite non-profit organization and gain some attention for your store at the same time. You can pick any kind of product, experience, or service to put up for auction and have a percentage of the proceeds donated to the charity of your choice. You can check to see if your charity is listed with eBay Giving Works (www.givingworks.ebay.com) or ask the charity to register with MissionFish (www.missionfish.org) first so eBay will recognize them as a valid charity to receive auction proceeds.

If you need more information about how to set up an account on eBay or general tips on buying or selling on the auction site, I recommend either *eBay For Dummies* or *Starting an eBay Business For Dummies,* both of which were written by Marsha Collier and published by Wiley Publishing, Inc.

Signing Up with Blogger

As of this writing, Blogger is definitely the biggest name in blogs today. This free service is owned by Google and has a streamlined process for getting your own free blog on their site.

1. Go to Blogger's home page at www.blogger.com. When you get to Blogger's home page you'll see their 3-step process of creating an account, naming your blog, and picking a template from their selection of pre-designed templates. Click the orange Create Your Blog Now button to get started.

The Sign In First link.

2. The first part of the sign-up process involves getting a Google account. If you haven't signed up yet for an account, fill in the fields including your e-mail address, password, display name, and the word verification test, so Google knows a computer isn't automatically trying to sign up. Click the box to accept their terms of service and click the orange Continue arrow to proceed. If you already signed up for a Google account (perhaps to enroll in Google Base, like we discussed in a previous chapter), then click the Sign In First link and enter your e-mail address and password when prompted and click the Continue button. Then, enter your display name and click the box to accept Terms of Service, and click the orange Continue arrow to proceed.

3. In the second step, you need to create a blog title and a blog URL. Fill in the boxes as prompted, or click the Advanced Blog Setup link for other options. If you click the Advanced Blog Setup link, you can have your blog reside on your store URL name or a third-party site. For simplicity sake, you can enter your blog title (make sure your store name is in the title) and create a blog URL that is similar to your store name as well in the boxes provided. Click the orange Continue arrow to proceed.

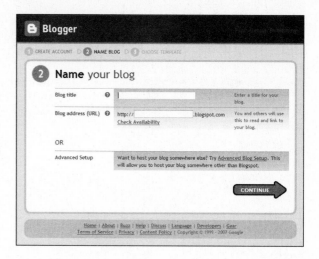

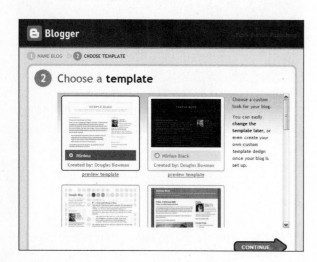

4. In the last step, you need to scroll through the list of pre-programmed design templates and select the template you want to use for your blog. You are presented with a list of dozens of pre-programmed templates available to you for free on Blogger. Use the scroll bar to go through the list, and when you see the blog template you like, simply click the radio button next to the template name and then click the orange Continue arrow to complete the sign-up process.

5. Your blog has been created on Blogger and you will see a confirmation screen. While these steps have gone through the basics of creating your blog, we recommend continuing so you can input your store information and make it part of your blog. Click the orange Start Posting arrow to define your profile and start posting.

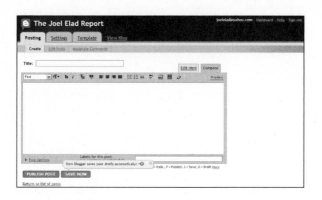

6. You are taken to your main control window for your Blogger blog. To create an introductory post announcing your presence as an extension of your Web store, enter your first post in the box provided. Every blog entry consists of the title of the post, the text of the post, and any attachments or photos you wish to include in your post. Fill in the boxes provided to create your first post welcoming people to your blog and announcing your new Web store. Click the Publish Post button if it's ready to be read. If you're unsure and want to come back to it later, click the Save Now button.

Enter your Web store description here.

7. Did you notice the three tabs along the top of the main control window in the previous step? Click the Settings tab to set up your profile information with Blogger. When you click the Settings tab, you will see the Basic settings window. As you can see from the newly displayed sub-navigation bar, there are a lot of settings you can configure for your blog. In the Basic setting, be sure to enter a description that describes your new Web store and all the keyword phrases you want to promote regarding your main products.

You are limited to only 500 words in your blog description, so choose your words carefully and make them count. Also, make them readable and not just a collection of keyword phrases.

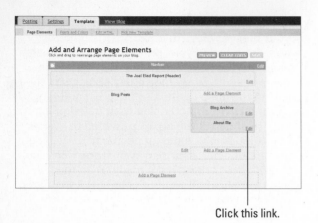

Click this link.

8. Click the Templates tab to set up your About Me information. When you click the Templates tab, you will see the Templates setup window. What you're interested in first is the About Me window, which will be somewhere on your blog screen, depending on the template you have selected. Click the Edit link in the About Me window to input your profile information.

9. In the About Me window, enter your name and description, as well as your location information. Even though you just finished writing your blog description, now you get the chance to write another description about you, the blogger. Use this opportunity to promote yourself as the owner of your Web store, which gives your store another mention and link. You can use the Location fields to put in your actual location or Web site location. Click the Save Changes button to save your work and exit this process. You have now gone through the basic set-up of your own Blogger blog! Add content, links, photos, and whatever else helps you promote your store. The key to a successful blog is fresh new content on a regular basis. Don't ignore your Blogger blog, and if you have time learn about their new features and how to promote your blog.

Signing Up with Yahoo! 360

Yahoo! is expanding upon their Groups concept with a new offering called Yahoo! 360. Designed to give the viewing public a full picture of yourself, Yahoo! 360 allows you to build your own blog, as well as share photos, interests, and connections with other people, drawing upon the popularity of social networking from sites like MySpace and Facebook. The Yahoo! 360 offering can add a layer of personal interaction between you and your Web store customers and visitors, so in this exercise we start a Yahoo! 360 page for your Web store.

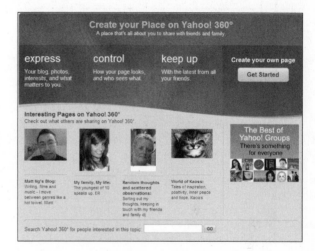

1. Go to their home page at 360.yahoo.com and click the yellow Get Started button. When you go to their home page, you'll see a variety of people that currently use their service, and you can search their directory to see the many categories of blogs that they represent, in the text box provided.

2. You'll see their Join Yahoo! 360 page. Enter a nickname in the box provided that will reflect the intent of your Yahoo! 360 profile as being associated with your Web store. (As my example, I chose "The Joel Elad store.") Click the yellow Continue button to proceed.

3. You'll be taken to your Yahoo! 360 home page. From here, you can view statistics about your page, look at other people's examples, and start to construct your Yahoo! 360 page. Click the yellow Start My Page button to enter the details of your page.

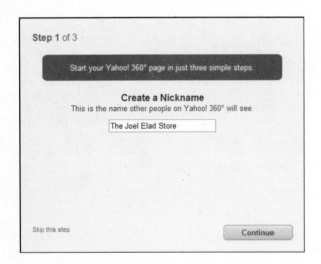

4. Yahoo! has a three part process to start your 360 page. The first part is to confirm the nickname you picked in Step 2. If you want to change your nickname, enter it in the box provided. Once you are happy with your nickname, click the Continue button to go to the second part.

5. In the second part of this process, Yahoo! will ask you to pick a background for your page. You'll be able to change the background after your page is created. Try to pick a background that matches the theme of your store. (For example, if you sell pet supplies, a dog or fish background might be more appropriate. A safe choice for a general Web store is the Classic background.) Once you've picked your background, click the yellow Continue button to go to the third part.

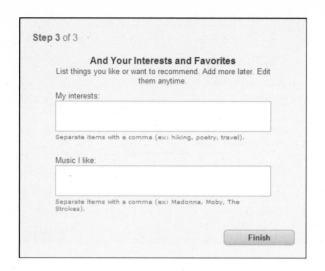

6. You'll be asked, in the third part, to enter your interests and favorite music. You could use this opportunity to indicate your favorites, in order to connect to your customers, or gear your interests to your web store product selection. Click the yellow Finish button to create your page.

7. You'll be taken to your newly created Yahoo! 360 page. From this page, you can upload a photo of yourself, write reviews, and most importantly, start your blog page. Click on the words "Start a Blog" in the middle of this page to activate your new Yahoo! blog.

8. You'll be taken to your Yahoo! Blog Setup page. Your blog title has defaulted to your newly created nickname, but you can change your title in the box provided. In the Description field, you have 120 characters to describe the purpose of your blog, so pick your words (and keywords) carefully. If you want to activate the Simple URL for your blog, so you can easily point people to your new blog, click the checkbox under the Simple URL header.

9. If you scroll down the page, you can finish setting up your blog. First, you should leave the Who Can See Your Blog setting as Public, so any new customers or visitors can read it. Secondly, if you want people to be able to subscribe to your blog via an RSS feed, leave that checkbox checked. Third, you should decide whether you want anyone to be able to leave comments (Public) or if you want to restrict comments to yourself or selected friends. Once you're done with these settings, click the blue Begin Blog button to start your blog.

Building and Distributing a Newsletter

Stuff You Need to Know

Toolbox:

✔ An article or short guide of information that pertains to your store products

✔ A list of any sales or news announcements

✔ A list of 2–4 products you wish you promote in your newsletter

Time Needed:
30–60 minutes

Thankfully, there are a number of feature-rich e-mail newsletter services that will help you piece together your content, format it properly, and manage the mechanics of your newsletter as well. Five such services are Constant Contact (www.constantcontact.com), Campaigner (www.gotmarketing.com), E-mail Publisher (www.email-publisher.com), iBuilder (www.verticalresponse.com), and ListApp (www.server.com/WebApps/ListApp). For this task, we are using ListApp to build and distribute our newsletter.

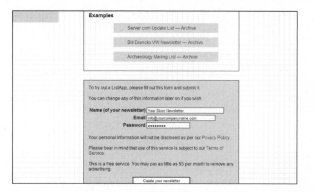

1. Go to ListApp's home page at www.server.com/WebApps/ListApp. When you go to ListApp's home page, scroll down and you'll notice that they offer a simple form to get started. Simply enter your newsletter name, e-mail address, and create a password. Then, click on the Create Your Newsletter button to get started. It will prompt you again for the password you just created. Enter that password and click Continue.

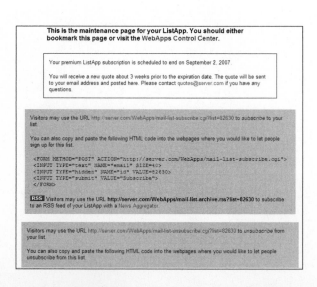

2. You'll see the ListApp maintenance form. In the shaded boxes, you'll see HTML code that you can insert into the Web pages of your store that will allow customers to click a button and either subscribe or unsubscribe from your newsletter. You should also see a Web link that you can distribute in e-mails that will accomplish the same task. Use these functions to start building up your mailing list. Scroll down the page and click Create Message to build your newsletter.

3. When you click Create Message you'll see the message page. Ignore the text in the To: field, as that is more of a placeholder than anything else. Enter a subject line for your newsletter, and then enter your newsletter text in the box provided. If you have an HTML newsletter, you'll need to copy all the text and HTML tags, except these tags: <HTML>, <HEAD>, <BODY>, <FORM>, </HTML>, </HEAD>, </BODY>, and </FORM>. When you're done, click the Preview Message button to review your newsletter.

To:	NewComix.Com_Newsletter@server.com
Reply-to:	order@newcomix.com
Subject:	

Content type: ⊙ text ○ HTML

If you select text content, use the ENTER key for each line or your recipients will get a single line of text. If you select HTML, do not include HTML, HEAD, BODY, or FORM tags.

Message (max 64K):

[Preview Message] [Return to Main Form]

4. You will be presented with a sample of the newsletter you wish to send out. Read through the newsletter message you've just created. If you created an HTML newsletter, don't be afraid to click any of the links embedded in your newsletter to make sure they go to the correct destination. If you need to change or update anything, click the Edit Message button and you'll go back to Step 3 to update your newsletter. If everything looks good, click the Send button. If you're happy with the newsletter but not ready to send anything out, click the Return to Main Form button. Once you have your starter mailing list defined (think of the list you used in Chapter 14 for your Grand Opening e-mail, for example), click the Send button to have ListApp mail out your newsletter.

```
To: NewComix.Com_Newsletter@server.com
From: order@newcomix.com
Subject: Sample Newsletter
Content-Type: text/plain

Welcome to the NewComix.Com Monthly Newsletter!

Here is where I would put my feature news announcement about a new giveaway available at NewComix.Com!

<HERE IS WHERE I WOULD INSERT MY ARTICLE FOR THE NEWSLETTER>

<HERE IS WHERE I WOULD INSERT MY PRODUCT OFFERINGS FOR THE NEWSLETTER>

<HERE IS WHERE I WOULD INSERT ANY OTHER UPDATES FOR THE NEWSLETTER>

Thanks for shopping! We look forward to seeing you every month!

Joel
NewComix.Com
```

[Send] [Edit Message]
[Return to Main Form]

5. ListApp will put your newsletter in the queue and send out the newsletter at the next scheduled batch. Usually, messages go out starting at midnight EST, so once your message is ready for sending it will sit in a queue until that time occurs. If you need the newsletter to go out sooner, click the "Click Here to Send Your Message Now" button. Your newsletter will be moved up the queue and go out almost immediately.

Your message has been queued for delivery. Messages will be delivered beginning at midnight EST.

It is currently Sat Sep 1 01:07.44 2007

Do not send any more messages until the current message has been processed, otherwise the current message will be deleted.

Please let us know of any problems.

[Return to Main Form]

[Click here to send your message now]

Creating Your eBay My World Page

Stuff You Need to Know

Toolbox:
- Description of your Web store
- List of main product keyword phrases
- eBay account information

Time Needed:
10–15 minutes

Once you have an eBay account that you want to use in promotion of your Web store, it's time to build your profile page (previously known as About Me) called My World.

1. Go directly to the eBay My World home page at `http://myworld.ebay.com` and log into eBay. When you get to the MyWorld home page, you'll see a variety of options that you can include in your profile, like blogs, wikis, and reviews and guides. Depending on the time you have, you can pursue any of these options. For now, we're going to stick to creating a basic profile page for your business.

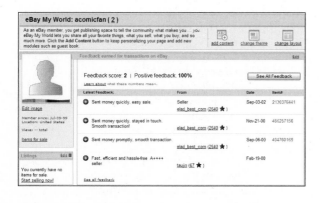

2. Click the View My World button to update your profile on eBay. When you click the View My World button, you will be taken to the default My World page that is created for your account, consisting of your listings, current eBay feedback, and any picture you have associated with your account.

Making Your eBay Auction Stand Out

When it's time to list something for sale on eBay, you want to make sure that your auctions stand out as much as possible. Therefore, here's a checklist of tips to follow when you set up your eBay auctions:

✔ **Research the product using eBay's search engine before you start listing it.** So many people just dive into creating an eBay listing without checking to see how similar items have performed on eBay in the past. That's like buying a share of IBM stock without knowing its closing price, 52 week range, or other key financials. The beautiful thing about eBay is that you can perform a free search of eBay's records for the past 15 days to see how the item has previously sold. When you search for completed listings, you can learn many things to help you sell your product.

✔ **Leverage your product catalog by re-using pictures and descriptions whenever possible.** If you're selling products from your catalog, don't reinvent the wheel. Simply copy and paste your product photos, description, title, and any other information into your eBay listing. This way, you can put an item up for sale and retain the same information that customers would see on your Web store. Try to add a watermark to your pictures that has your Web store name in it. Not only does this prevent your competitors from re-using your pictures, but it lets customers see the name of your business!

✔ **Make sure that your product descriptions are both comprehensive and organized.** When someone takes a look at your eBay auction page, your goal is to have enough information in that auction description that the buyer has zero questions and is ready to place a bid. Therefore, you need to create a structured approach to your description, using white space and formatting to lay out the information in a way that doesn't overwhelm the reader. Additionally, there needs to be enough information to answer any potential customer's concerns without becoming tedious or overbearing. When they come to your Web store, the average customer is more focused and knows what they want. On eBay, they love to click around and browse, so you have to do more to hook them and convince them to buy.

✔ **Include your Web store "look and feel" into your auction descriptions as much as possible.** When a customer goes to your auction description, it should feel like they're on a part of your Web site. That means you should try to include your store logo, colors and buttons as part of the auction description section. Simply copy and paste the HTML code from one of your Web store pages and put the essential elements in your eBay auction description section. Remember: don't put any direct links to your Web store from your eBay auctions.

✔ **Introduce every one of your eBay winners to your Web store after they win an auction.** Once you have a successful auction with a new customer, that relationship is yours to mold, which means that you can talk about more than just the eBay auction. When the auction ends, you will get an e-mail with the results of the auction, including the high bid amount and, most importantly, the e-mail address of the high bidder. You could use eBay's invoicing tool, but it is recommended to send your own e-mail, welcoming that new user to your Web store and describing what you have for sale.

3. Click the Add Content link in the top-right of the screen to add your business information into your profile. When you click the Add Content link, you will be taken to the My World module list. Initially, the only module that is added is the Listings module, which details your eBay sales. On the right-hand side, you should see the other five modules you can add to your page. The one you are interested in is Bio, as that one allows you to define your Web store and talk about your product offerings with some detail. Click the Add link below Bio to add that module to your My World page. Feel free to add any other sections you would like, as well. Once you have added a module, you can click the Edit link to go in and update your information.

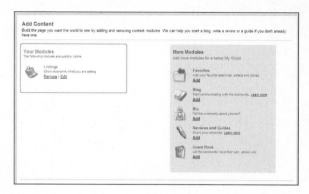

4. Click the Edit link for the Bio module to add your business information to the My World page. You'll be taken to a long form entitled Edit Bio Module. The first section of fields relates to your About Me section of the Bio. First off, under Module Title, you probably want to select My Business from the options given so customers know this is about your business, not necessarily your personal hobbies. Feel free to treat the About Me section to talk more about your Web store, or about you as the store owner. As you fill in information and scroll down the page, you should come to a header entitled Business Information. This section should be fully completed, telling users all about your Web store, like the hints I typed in each box for that section. You are free to advertise and promote your business URL on this page, so don't be shy. Definitely emphasize any keyword phrases you wish to promote for your Web store, as eBay sends the information from the My World pages to the search engines. When you are done, click Save at the bottom of the page to save your work.

5. You'll be taken back to the My World home page. Review the page to make sure everything is displayed correctly. If you want to move the content around on the page, you can click on the link marked Change Layout to move the Bio section to the top, for example. If you added any other Modules to your list, be sure to click the Edit link next to that module and add information about your business there as well.

Chapter 17

Online Marketing Campaigns

Sometimes, if you want to get attention you have to pay for it. In the previous chapter we talk about ways to promote your new Web store that are free (or very cheap) to use and required some effort. There are other ways to get attention for your store, and it has to do with the main way that most people use the Internet nowadays — the search engines. Studies have been done that show a majority of people start their Internet session by going to a search engine, typing in some keywords, and clicking on a link from the results screen to get started. Therefore, being on that result screen can be very lucrative to your business. It's like building a gas station at a highway off-ramp to attract customers from the busy freeway overhead.

In this chapter, we talk about how your business can position itself within the search engines to get traffic for your Web store. In the first part, we look at a concept called Pay-Per-Click. Secondly, we demonstrate how to send your Web store information to many different search engines to help influence your "natural" or "organic" search results that are not advertising-based. We also touch on banner advertisements and coordinating your promotional campaigns. Finally, we walk you through the two main programs set up for businesses to advertise on the search engines, namely Google Adwords and Yahoo!'s Overture tool.

Understanding Pay Per Click (PPC) Advertising Campaigns

If you've used a search engine to find anything online, you're probably familiar with how the results screen looks after you type in your keywords and click Search. It's probably something similar to Figure 17-1, with the main part of the screen filled with *organic* or *natural* search results that the search engine had in their database, and the top and right sides of the screen filled with various advertisements.

Advertisements sections

Figure 17-1: Advertisements are put on the top and right of the page.

These advertisements are determined by the keywords typed in by the user. The search engines accept advertisements that are tied into specific keywords or keyword phrases. Any time that keyword or phrase is entered into their system, they will display all the advertisements that are tied into the input. This way, it allows the search engine to provide targeted advertising since they're targeting specific users who are more inclined to look at those ads than something chosen at random. For example, if someone is looking for golf clubs, the search engine displays ads that are written specifically for golf clubs.

Years ago, advertisers would have to pay for every *impression* (every time the ad is simply displayed on the screen). However, they couldn't afford to pay for ads that most people ignored, so advertisers demanded a new system based on results. Therefore, today's system is based on how many times someone clicks on the advertisement. This allows the search engines to collect more money per click, and allows the advertiser to only pay for people who get sent to their Web site. Thus, we have *Pay Per Click* advertising, or *PPC*.

Now, depending on how much an advertiser is willing to pay per click, the search engines will give their best spot (a.k.a. the top spot on the screen) to the advertiser who pays the most per click, and will determine the order of advertisements, from top to bottom, based on the per click amount. Therefore, the higher you want your ad placed on the screen, the more you have to pay for that position. Because you are competing with other businesses for the same advertising spots, there is no fixed price for a particular spot, as businesses are constantly changing their pay per click amounts to improve their ad position. You don't get to see your competitor's bids either, so it's better to place your PPC bid based on your budget first.

PPC campaigns provide several advantages for today's business owners:

- ✔ **They are quick to establish and maintain.** You could set up your campaign and have traffic coming to your Web site within hours or a few days at most.

- ✔ **You don't need a big budget to participate.** You can set up a campaign for $10, $100, $1,000, $10,000, $1,000,000, and any number in between. You set up the rules so the ad campaign matches your budget, not the other way around. When the money is spent, your ads no longer show up on the screen.

- ✔ **You can monitor your costs down to the penny.** You establish your per click rates, daily budgets, and total ad spending, and you can watch your costs per day.

- ✔ **You can monitor the performance of your campaign.** By encoding the links your ads carry to send users to your site, you can monitor exactly how effective each campaign is by studying how many visitors who clicked to your site actually placed an order, signed up as a customer, and so on. You can then compare your profit from those orders to the cost of your ads and know the benefits of this campaign (and how much to spend for future campaigns).

- ✔ **You can create multiple, highly focused campaigns.** Instead of one big flyer or catalog to promote all your items, you can create multiple ad campaigns to focus on specific niches. Let's say you sell electronics. You can create one campaign for digital cameras, another for scanners, and yet another for flat-screen TVs.

The biggest disadvantage to this type of advertising is when your sales don't show any improvement. You can pay to divert thousands, or even millions, of potential customers to your Web site, depending on your budget. However, if all these people are coming to your Web site and then leaving before they place an order, you just paid to have a lot of window shoppers mill around without a cent of profit. Companies have spent thousands of dollars getting the traffic and never did their homework to realize that the traffic never equated to sales, orders, or profit. Don't fall into this trap!

For more information about PPC advertising, be sure to check out *Pay Per Click Search Engine Marketing For Dummies* by Peter Kent (Wiley Publishing, Inc.).

Submitting Your Store to the Search Engines

In addition to PPC campaigns that get your advertisements on the search engine results screen, your store can also have a presence on the result screens in the natural search results section. The goal of any Web store owner is to see his or her store in the top 10 results page for a Google or Yahoo! search. This way they aren't paying for results but getting an excellent placement which should lure more people to their store.

The area of expertise in this field is called Search Engine Optimization (SEO), and there are many books, for example Peter Kent's *Search Engine Optimization For Dummies* (Wiley Publishing, Inc.), and Web sites that can guide you on how to make your Web store more friendly or receptive to the search engines. There are consultants who will charge you to make over your entire Web site to get better results in the search engines. It's a growing field as more and more people try to outguess the search engines and position their Web site for greater visibility.

Therefore, I'm going to leave this area as a task for self-study, as you could spend two or 2,000 hours on this topic, depending on your free time. I recommend several Web sites where you can read up on this topic and get lots of advice, as you can see in Table 17-1.

Table 17-1	Search Engine Optimization Information Sites
Name	*URL*
SearchEngineWatch	www.searchenginewatch.com
SearchEngineForums.com	www.searchengineforums.com
WebMasterWorld	www.webmasterworld.com
HighRankings.com	www.highrankings.com
About.Com SEO	websearch.about.com/od/searchenginemarketing/

The real answer about "getting in" to the search engines is that, sooner or later, they'll find you! The search engines have these computer programs known as *bots* or *spiders* that crawl around the Internet and send information about every single Web page that it finds back into the search engine database to be cataloged and ranked. These computer programs go from Web site to Web site, following every link provided, and if you're doing enough marketing where other sites are linking to you, then the search engines will find you.

When you're launching your Web store, however, you can take some action to speed up this automatic process and hopefully get indexed into the search engines quicker. You can, in some cases, submit your Web site information to the search engines, so they'll specifically send a computer program to look at your Web site and catalog your pages. That's what we're going to discuss in this section.

Now, your first question should be, "Which sites should I submit my Web site to?" The answer is, "As many as possible." To get started, it's helpful to get an idea of which Web sites people are using to search the Internet. Go online and do a search for search engine rankings, and eventually you'll find a report like Nielsen/NetRatings top search engine providers for the month, as shown in Figure 17-2. The top three will almost always be Google, Yahoo!, and Microsoft's MSN AdCenter, but pay attention to the others on the list, as we discuss the "other" search engines later in this section.

Now that you know where to go, the next question should be "How do I do it?" Let's start with the big kahuna, Google, and work our way down.

Top 10 Search Providers by Searches, July 2007		
Provider	Searches (000)	Share of Total Searches (%)
Google	4,143,752	53.3
Yahoo	1,559,745	20.1
MSN/Windows Live	1,057,064	13.6
AOL	407,988	5.2
Ask.com	143,513	1.8
My Web Search	69,145	0.9
BellSouth	40,374	0.5
Comcast	37,311	0.5
Dogpile	25,675	0.3
My Way	24,534	0.3
Other	264,073	3.4
All search	7,773,174	100.0
Source: Nielsen//NetRatings, 2007		

Figure 17-2: The top 10 search sites as of July 2007.

Submitting your site to Google

Ah, you want to be loved and included by Google. Okay, how about included? As mentioned earlier, sooner or later Google will stumble onto your Web site and catalog your Web pages into their system. However, if you want to try and speed that up, there are a couple of things you can do.

First, you can directly go to Google and use their Add URL function to add a mention about your Web site to their computers, so their computer programs will go and scan your Web site. There is no guarantee that doing this will speed up the process, but it can't hurt, and it's free to use.

You simply go to `www.google.com/addurl/` and you should see the Add URL page, as shown in Figure 17-3. Then, you simply:

- ✔ **Put in the home page of your Web store in the URL field**. Don't forget to add the `http://`. Only include the name of your Webpage if it is *not* `index.html` or `default.html`.

- ✔ **Add a one-sentence description in the Comments field**. Pick your most important keywords from your store description and put one elegant, flowing sentence here.

- ✔ **Enter the squiggly word into the box provided**. This action is known as security verification or human verification, because when you input the word that appears in the graphic Google knows that a person is performing that action, not a computer.

- ✔ **Scroll down and click on the Add URL button to submit your page.**

- ✔ **Repeat the process for a few main category pages on your Web site.**

    Do *not* perform this function for every Web page on your store site, only your main pages. Once Google sends a software robot or spider, they'll pick up all the pages on your Web site.

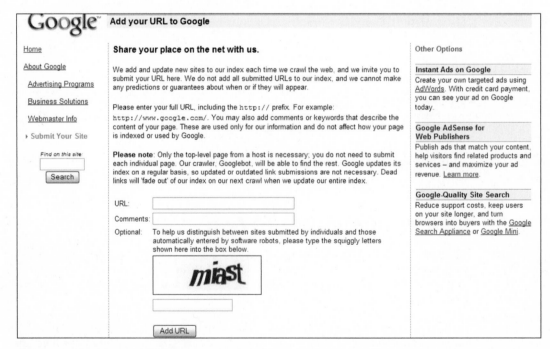

Figure 17-3: Add your URL to Google's database.

The second thing you can do is feed Google an entire Site Map of your Web site, so they know every single Web page that exists on your site. They have created something called Google Webmaster Tools, which you can sign up for free at `http://www.google.com/Webmasters/tools/` and get access to tools that can improve your Google search position. They offer a tool called SiteMap Generator that will help you build a Site Map if you haven't already done so. Check with your storefront provider to see if you can install this tool on your Web store account. (It requires a programming language known as Python to be readable on your Web store account.)

Read more about Google's list of Webmaster tools at `https://www.google.com/Webmasters/tools/docs/en/about.html`.

Finally, the quick way to check and see how many of your Web store pages are already in Google's database is to go to `www.google.com` and type in this code in the search box:

```
site:www.yourstorename.com
```

In the above code, `www.yourstorename.com` is the name of your e-commerce Web store. When you do this, you should see a results screen similar to the one in Figure 17-4, which will show you all the different Web pages in your site that Google has already cataloged. (If your site is brand new, Google says it can take up to a month before you will appear in their database.) By running this "site" command, you get an idea of which pages are cataloged and, by process of elimination, find out which pages need to have better links.

How many pages Google already has cataloged.

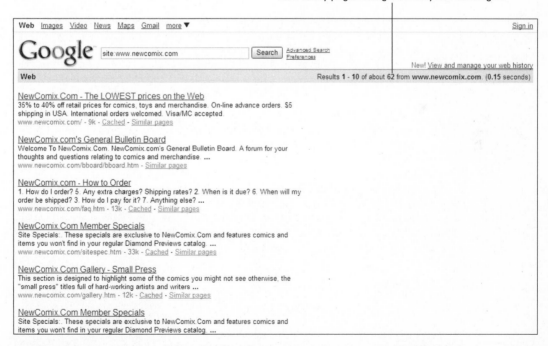

Figure 17-4: Find out how many Web pages of your store site are in Google's database!

Submitting your site to Yahoo!

Yahoo! is very similar to Google, in that their search engine robots will most likely find your Web site eventually. They've also built some functionality to let you alert them as to your Web site's presence. Unlike Google, however, they have some paid programs where you can pay Yahoo! a fee to include your Web store in their search and/or directory. Like the PPC advertising campaigns discussed earlier in this chapter, you are paying for placement, but unlike those programs you pay one fee (or a yearly fee) for improved search results across the board.

When you are ready to submit your Web site to Yahoo!, go to their Submit Your Site page at `http://search.yahoo.com/info/submit.html` (see Figure 17-5). There are several options on this page, but the ones you mainly need to know are:

- ✔ **Submit Your Site for Free:** This allows you to send your main URL information to Yahoo!. They may (or may not) send a spider program to read your site after you fill out this form. There is no guarantee.

- ✔ **Search Submit:** You can guarantee that your Web site will be inserted into the Yahoo! search index within four business days, and they'll refresh their index of your Web site every seven days. The cost is a recurring fee of $49 per year, per URL submission, and there's a limit of five URL submissions per person.

- ✔ **Yahoo! Directory Submit:** You can guarantee that Yahoo! will consider including your Web site in their core directory index within seven days. There is no guarantee that your site will be accepted and included, but they'll review your site. The cost for this service is $299, and if your site is accepted there is a recurring annual fee of $299 to keep your site in the directory index.

If you're a Yahoo! Merchant Solutions customer, you get a $50 discount on Directory Submit and, sometimes, a discount on Search Submit. Log into your Store Control Panel and check the Promotions section for more information.

If you click on the Submit Your Site for Free link, you'll be taken to their Site Explorer page, shown in Figure 17-6. Enter the URL of your Web store in the box provided, and if you are using RSS or Atom to feed information from your Web store automatically, you can enter your feed file in the other box provided. When you click the Submit button, the information will be sent to Yahoo!.

Yahoo! Search Submission

<u>Submit Your Site for Free:</u>
- Suggest your site for inclusion in Yahoo! Search (requires registration).

<u>Submit Your Mobile Site for Free:</u>
- Suggest your xHTML, WML or cHTML site for inclusion in Yahoo! Search for mobile phones (requires registration).

<u>Submit Your Media Content for Free:</u>
- Add your audio, image, and video content to Y! Search using Media RSS (<u>learn more</u>).

<u>Search Submit:</u>
- Guaranteed inclusion in Yahoo! Search index.
- Frequent refresh-every 48 hours.
- Reporting to track and optimize performance.
- Ranking based on relevance.

<u>Sponsored Search:</u>
- List your business in sponsored search results across the Web.
- Control your position by the amount you bid on keywords.
- Set your own price-per-click and pay only when a customer clicks through to your site.

<u>Product Submit:</u>
- Submit your products for inclusion in Yahoo! Shopping.
- Have your products appear in Yahoo! Product Search and on Buyer's Guide comparison pages.
- The price-per-click is based on the category of your products.

<u>Travel Submit:</u>
- Promote your offers in Yahoo! Travel's Deals section where users search for timely deals and offers.
- Pay only when a customer clicks through to your site.
- Price-per-click based on category.

Yahoo! Directory Submission

<u>Yahoo! Directory Submit:</u>
- Submit your site for review and inclusion in the Yahoo! Directory

Figure 17-5: Yahoo! gives you different ways to submit your site.

As for the premium services, let me say this. One of the ways search engines judge Web sites for their relevance and ranking is by how many other Web sites have a link to your Web site. More importantly, the search engines look at the quality of that link, meaning they rank those incoming links based on the reputation of the Web site linking to you, the length of time that Web site has been registered, the popularity of that Web site, the position of the link, and so on. If your store gets included in Yahoo!'s directory, that is one of the most respected and powerful links your store can have, in terms of popularity, and that'll increase all your search engine results for Yahoo!, Google, and all the other search engines. Trust me, there's a reason why it costs $299 per year, and that's why.

Google's most trusted directory source for their search engine rankings seems to be a human-powered directory site called The Open Directory, at `www.dmoz.org`. To find out more about submitting your site to the Open Directory Project, simply go to `http://www.dmoz.org/add.html`.

Submit Your Site

▶ **Submit a Website or Webpage**

Enter the URL for your website or webpage you would like to submit.
For any URL (directly submitted or obtained from a feed) our crawler will extract links and find pages we have not discovered already. We will automatically detect updates on pages and remove dead links on an ongoing basis.

| http:// | | Submit URL |

Please include the **http://** prefix (for example, http://www.yahoo.com).

▶ **Submit Site Feed**

Enter the full URL of the site feed you would like to submit:

| http:// | | Submit Feed |

Please include the **http://** prefix (for example, http://www.yahoo.com).

You can provide us a feed in the following supported formats. We do recognize files with a **.gz** extension as compressed files and will decompress them before parsing.

- RSS 0.9, RSS 1.0 or RSS 2.0, for example, CNN Top Stories
- Sitemaps, as documented on www.sitemaps.org
- Atom 0.3, Atom 1.0, for example, Yahoo! Search Blog
- A text file containing a list of URLs, each URL at the start of a new line. The filename of the URL list file must be urllist.txt; for a compressed file the name must be urllist.txt.gz.

Figure 17-6: Submit your site to Yahoo! for free.

Submitting your site to everyone else

At this point, many people think that they've covered their bases by submitting to both Google and Yahoo!, as those two search engines make up a large majority of people's Web search queries. However, those two don't make up 100 percent of the searches done on the Internet, so it's worth looking at some of the other major and minor players.

In fact, there are great reasons to go ahead and submit to the other search engines. Google and Yahoo! go out and see what the other search engines have cataloged, so when your Web site gets included in these other search engines, it'll be seen as a reference for Google and Yahoo! and help you in your standings.

Therefore, if you have some time go through Table 17-2 and add your Web site URL (like the Google and Yahoo! free submissions above) so you cover as many bases as possible. While some sites like Ask.com have removed their submission page, others like Microsoft have kept theirs open for submittals. Other sites that draw on multiple search engines, like Dogpile and MetaCrawler, have no internal database of their own, so there is nothing to submit to in those cases.

Table 17-2	Other Search Engine Submittal Pages
Name	**URL**
MSN	http://search.msn.com/docs/submit.aspx
Alexa	http://www.alexa.com/data/details/editor?type=contact
InfoUSA	http://dbupdate.infousa.com/dbupdate/index.html
SearchIt	http://www.searchit.com/addurl.htm

There are a number of paid search inclusion services, from sites like Enhance.com that allow you to advertise on Dogpile, Metacrawler, and other search sites, to services that offer to submit your site to tens or hundreds of the search engines for you automatically. Do your homework on those services, and decide if you want to pay the money to have these services promote your site.

While you can never reach every Internet site on your own, submitting your site to the major and mid-level players is typically enough to get your store noticed. Your goal should always be to keep your Web store updated and keep your customers happy. Your marketing techniques and efforts will be reflected as customers mention you and other Web sites link to you.

Creating a Google Adwords Campaign

Stuff You Need to Know

Toolbox:

- An idea of your ad budget
- A list of keyword phrases you want to use for your ad(s)
- Address(es) of your store Web page(s) connected to your ad(s)
- Business credit card

Time Needed:

30–60 minutes

When it comes to search engine advertising, the reigning king of search (as of this writing) is Google. They derive over 80 percent of their revenue from placing ads on their search engine results screens which means they take this very seriously. They've created a robust program called Google AdWords to manage these advertisements, which allows any size company to participate.

Click this button.

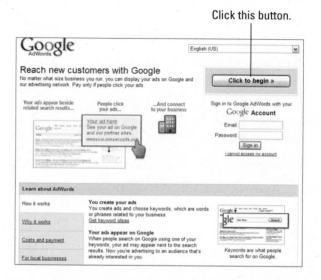

1. Go to the Google AdWords home page at `http://adwords.google.com`. You can learn specific information about the AdWords program from their home page. You can use the same information from your Google account to create your AdWords account, or you can use a different e-mail address for your AdWords login. Look for the Click to Begin button in the top-right corner and click it to start the signup process.

2. When you get to the first screen, Google wants to classify your account as a beginner account, with their Starter Edition, or their advanced option, the Standard account. If you're already familiar with AdWords, you could go for the Standard edition now, but I highly recommend going for the Starter Edition. You can always move later to Standard, so you're not shutting yourself out by picking Starter Edition. Also, let Google know that you have a Web page (your Web store home page) and click Continue to move on.

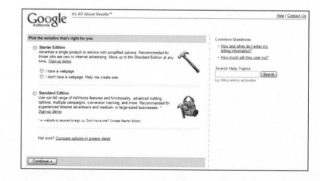

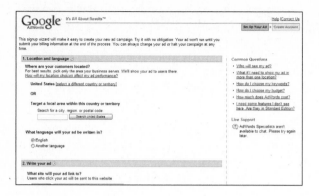

3. When you get to the Build your ad page, you're going to see six different sections on this page that'll help you build your search engine ads for your account. In the first section, Location and Language, you are asked to identify the location of your target customers. You can pick customers based on country, or narrow it down to a specific state or province, a city, or even a zip code. Additionally, you are asked what language you're using in your ad (the default is English, but you can pick whatever language you'd like to write your ad).

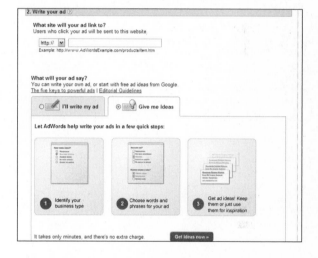

4. Scroll down the page to the second section, Write Your Ad. First, you are asked to provide the specific URL that your customers will be sent to when they click on your ad in the box provided. It doesn't have to go to your home page, especially if you are creating a campaign for a specific product or category. Also, if you want to track the effectiveness of your ad campaign, you can direct it to a special page only available from this ad, so you can monitor the results.

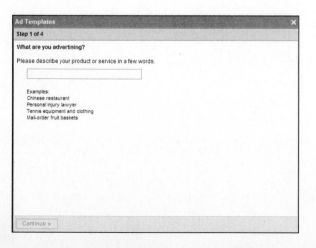

5. In the What Will My Ad Say area, you'll find two options for developing your search engine ad. You can click the I'll Write My Ad radio button and come up with your own title, text, and URL display, or you can leave it on Give Me Ideas and click the blue Get Ideas Now button to follow their prompts and develop an ad. If you click the Give Me Ideas button, you'll see four separate windows, the first one asking for a summary of your product or service. Enter a few key words for your primary item for this campaign, then click the Continue button and go to the next step. If you click I'll Write My Ad, enter your ad text and proceed to Step 9.

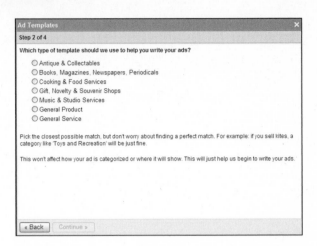

6. In the second window you'll be asked you to pick a template to help you write your ad. This selection is based on your product, but doesn't affect your actual ad. It acts like a guide to help you pick something appropriate for your category. When you're done, click the Continue button to move on.

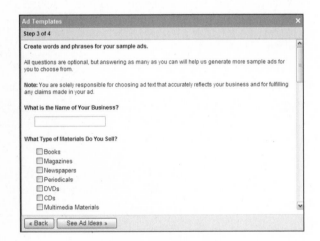

7. The third window involves you giving the name of your business and picking from a list of products that you actually sell, in order to help build your ad. When you're done, click the See Ad Ideas button.

8. The fourth window will show you ad ideas that Google has generated, based on the information you gave in the previous windows. If you see an ad you like, simply check the box marked Choose below the ad you like. You can select up to five of these ads to put in your account. When you're done, click the Finished button.

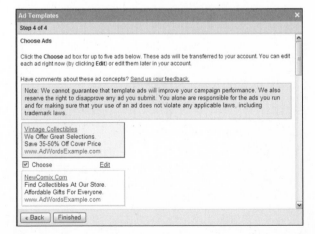

Once you pick your ad, you can always click the Edit link next to the ad to make any additional changes.

9. Scroll down to the third section of the form, Choose Keywords, where you pick the keywords that will trigger your ad to be displayed. Enter your list of keyword phrases in the box provided. When you get to your list of keywords, you may notice some phrases already in the box. If you used Google to help you build your ad, then they've already pre-filled the box with category phrases. You can simply click the Remove Category Keywords link to clear the box so you can enter your list. If you want to verify that you're selecting good keyword phrases, you can click the Check My Keywords button to have Google scan the list. If they find a phrase too generic, you'll see it appear in a window. You can choose to edit that phrase, delete it, or ignore the warning. When you are done, click the Finished — Recheck List button.

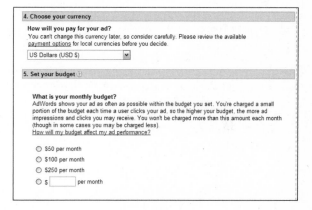

10. Scroll down the page to the fourth (Choose Your Currency) and fifth (Set Your Budget) sections of the form. You should pick the local currency of the country where you're doing business in, and then pick a monthly amount you're comfortable with spending. You can't change your currency option, but you can always go back and reset your monthly spending limit.

The more specific your phrases are, the better chance you have of redirecting a more serious customer. If someone types in DVD player, odds are they are just browsing for general information. If someone types in Sony BDP-S1 Blu-Ray DVD player, odds are they are ready or close to buying one. You may get less leads, but they are more "qualified" and should ultimately lead to better conversion rates.

You must pick a monthly budget limit or Google will continue to display ads and charge your monthly account indefinitely, which can cost you big bucks in a few months (or weeks) depending on your ad and keyword phrases.

11. Scroll down the page to the last section of the form, Future Contact. Google will prompt you with two communication options. Checking the first box will allow Google to send you occasional e-mails with ideas on how to improve your ad performance. Checking the second box will allow Google to send you regular AdWords newsletters, with tips, suggestions, and stories about their best practices. As a default, both are already checked. Decide if you want these or not, and click the Continue button to proceed.

12. Google will now ask you if you want to link your AdWords account with an existing Google account, or if you need a new Google account. If you want to link your accounts, pick the first option, and log into Google using the boxes provided. If you link your accounts, Google will give you the option to create a special login name and password just for your AdWords account, separate from all other Google account services. This is helpful in case you have employees or friends who use your Google account to help manage your business, but you don't want those people having access to your advertising account. If you don't want to link accounts, pick the second option and fill in the boxes shown to create a new Google account.

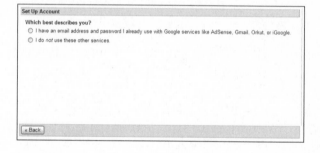

13. Your AdWords account has been created! Before Google will display your ads, they need to have a billing source, like a credit card, on file so they know you can pay for your ad campaigns. Therefore, click the Sign In to Your AdWords Account link to go into your new account, or use the link that comes in your activation e-mail to proceed.

14. When you log into your AdWords account, you should see a summary page with the ad you created. The summary page states that "Your ad is not yet running." When you are ready to start your campaign, click the Enter Billing Information and Activate Ad link.

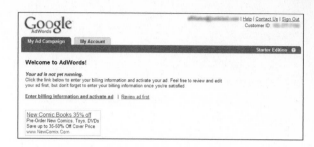

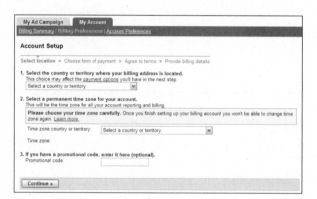

15. When you set up your billing account, Google needs to know which country your billing address is located in, as well as your specific time zone. Pick the appropriate options based on your billing address for the credit card you plan to keep on file, and click Continue to proceed.

16. You will see three choices for billing on the next screen. You can have Google bill your bank account directly through Direct Debit, bill your Credit Card for clicks that your account accrues, or fill your account by charging a Credit Card in advance before clicks come in. Pick one of these options, and click Continue to proceed.

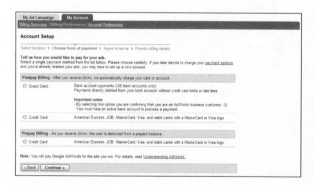

You can go to the My Ad Campaign tab and set a specific start date, allowing you to enter your billing information now and then set up your campaigns to start at a later date. This is helpful if you are timing your campaign with other promotional efforts.

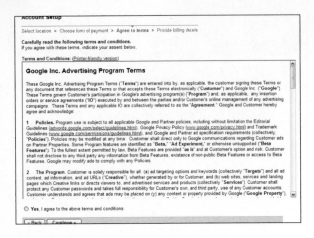

17. You will see the box containing all of Google Inc. Advertising Program Terms on the screen. Spend a few minutes to read through the terms, and when you're ready, click the radio button next to Yes, I Agree to the Above Terms and Conditions and then click the Continue button to proceed.

18. In this last step, Google asks you for the credit card number and associated billing address of that card in the fields provided. Enter a valid Mastercard, Visa, American Express, or JCB credit card information, scroll down, and click the Save and Activate button to start your AdWords campaign.

19. Your Google AdWords account is now active! Your advertising campaign information has been fed to Google and they will start showing your ads based on your monthly budget and the keywords that you selected. You can make further changes by going to your ad campaign. You should see a confirmation screen, and if you want to make any additional updates to your ad campaign, like setting a daily limit for each ad, for example, simply click the Go Directly to My Ad Campaign link.

TIP

If you really want to take advantage of Google AdWords, check out *AdWords For Dummies* by Howie Jacobson (Wiley Publishing, Inc.), as he walks you through everything you need to maximize your campaigns and be efficient.

Creating a Yahoo! Overture Campaign

Stuff You Need to Know

Toolbox:
- An idea of your ad budget
- A list of keyword phrases you want to use for your ad(s)
- Address(es) of your store Web page(s) connected to your ad(s)
- Business credit card

Time Needed:
30–60 minutes

While Google gets a lot of the press mentions and attention, Yahoo! still commands a sizable portion of the search audience, as they have tens of millions of members who use their various functions, such as Mail, Finance, and of course, Merchant Solutions. Back in 2003, they purchased a company called Overture (previously GoTo.com) that was using the pay per click method to sell advertising on their member networks. Now that Overture is a Yahoo! company, it is the tool that Yahoo! uses for its search engine result pages, as well as the advertising tool for all their functions and Web pages.

1. Go to Yahoo!'s Search Marketing home page at `http://searchmarketing.yahoo.com` and sign up for an account. You can read more about the program on their home page. If you're ready to sign up, simply click the Click Here link next to Ready to Sign Up? If you're a Yahoo! Merchant Solutions customer, log into your account to see if there are any special promotions for joining Yahoo! Sponsored Search. You may see an ad, and if you do click the link to sign up and receive bonus credit. Check with companies such as PayPal or your storefront provider to see if they partner with Yahoo! and offer you a bonus credit for signing up.

2. Currently, there are two levels of service: Self Serve, where you develop the ads yourself, or Assisted Setup, where Yahoo! works with you to craft your ads and develop a campaign. Pick the service that fits with your goals and budgets. For this example, we're going to go with Self Serve. Click the appropriate Sign Up button to get started.

3. In this step, you need to register for your
account by confirming your contact information,
credit card on file, username, and reviewing
their Terms and Conditions. You should see
the Registration page, and if you're already a
Merchant Solutions customer (or Yahoo! account
holder) then this information will be pre-filled. If
you're a new user, simply complete the fields.
When you scroll down, you'll see the section to
enter your credit card information, which Yahoo!
will keep on file to charge you based on your ad
campaigns. Below the credit card info is the
place to put your user ID (if you're not already
a Yahoo! user, this is blank) and below that is
where you review the Terms and Conditions.
When you have completed each section, click
the Order button to start your account.

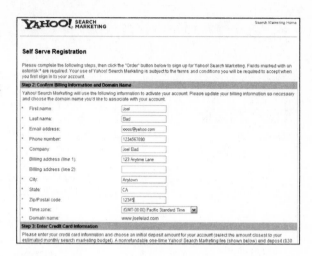

4. Once your account has been created, you will
need to complete a five-step process to start
your sponsored search campaign. In the first
step, you need to establish your geographic
location, as that will impact elements like your
reports and campaign management. Select your
country of business from the list provided, and
then select your time zone from that list provided. When you're ready, click the Get Started
button to continue.

5. You will see the first step selection in a window.
If you're operating any sort of local business, or
want to run a test marketing campaign for a certain region, you can select Specific Regions and
enter your specific target area in the fields that
are prompted. Otherwise, leave the selection on
Entire Market to make sure your ad is shown to
users in the entire region.

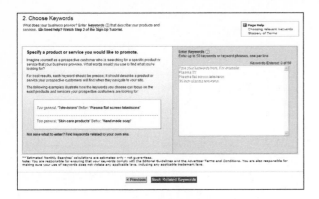

6. In the second step, you're asked to enter the list of keyword phrases that you want to trigger your advertisement. You want to pick the best keywords or phrases that customers would type in to find a store like yours, and type them in the box. You can provide up to 50 different keywords or phrases here. Click the Next button when you are ready to proceed.

7. Yahoo! will go through their search records and show you keyword phrases similar to the ones you entered, and, for each phrase they recommend you add, you'll see the estimated number of times that phrase is searched for per month. This way, you can get an idea of which phrases are the most popular and a rough idea of how many people will see your ad, based on the phrase(s) you add. When you are done, click the Next button to proceed.

8. In the third step, Yahoo! will ask for a daily spending limit. Yahoo! does warn you that they may go up to 10 percent above your daily limit if necessary, and if they go above that 10 percent threshold, you'll need to file for a refund with them. If you have a monthly budget in mind, adjust it for a daily amount. If you want to see an estimate of how many ads you'll get, click the Estimate button after entering your daily amount. You'll be prompted by Yahoo! for a recommended bid amount per phrase, and based on that bid amount, you will see an estimated number of monthly ad impressions (how many times your ad will be displayed per month) and clicks on that ad. If you change your maximum bid and click Estimate, you will see a new set of estimated figures. Click the Next button when you are ready to proceed.

The more specific your keywords and phrases, the better chance you have of redirecting a more serious customer. If someone types in DVD player, odds are they're just browsing for general information. If someone types in Sony BDP-S1 Blu-Ray DVD player, odds are they're ready or close to buying one. You may get less leads, but they're more "qualified" and should ultimately lead to better conversion rates.

9. In the fourth step, you are asked to Create your Ad. You'll see a window where you will develop your search engine ad. You will have a space to enter your Ad Title, your Ad Description, and the URL where your potential customers will be sent after they click your ad. Your key here is to highlight the important keywords that will grab your customer's attention and mention any important distinguishing features of your store. Look at your competitor's ads for inspiration (*don't* copy and paste their ads, though) and think about what you would need to see, as a potential customer, to click on that ad. When you're done, click the Next button to proceed.

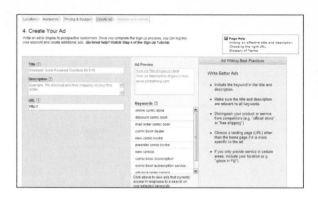

10. In the fifth and final step, you'll review and activate your ad on Yahoo!. You'll see the Review window. Look over the ad you created, and click the Edit button on the right-hand side if you need to go back and make any changes. Otherwise, go down and enter your account information in the boxes provided. Once you're done with that, scroll down the page and click the orange Activate Now button to get started.

11. You're done! The Yahoo! Sponsored Search account has been created for your business, and you'll be charged for the initial setup and deposit into your account. Your ads will start showing up on searches, and if you need to make any changes, log into your Search Marketing account to make any necessary updates.

If you want to track the effectiveness of your ad campaign, you can direct it to a special page only available from this ad, so you can monitor the results.

If you really want to study up on Yahoo! Sponsored Search, or PPC advertising in general, you should definitely consider getting *Pay Per Click Search Engine Marketing For Dummies* by Peter Kent (Wiley Publishing, Inc.), as he goes through all the leading programs in this area and provides lots of ideas, processes, and ways to manage your campaign.

Chapter 18

Outsourcing Store Elements — Going to the Next Level

Tasks performed in this chapter

✔ Handling order fulfillment

✔ Hiring someone to (re)design your store

✔ Creating an affiliate program for your products

✔ Placing your project on Elance

By this point, your Web store should be open to the public, taking orders, and growing in terms of popularity. You should be hitting several milestones as you operate your store, reaching your first month in business, first quarter in business, first year in business, and hopefully many more milestones to come. As you hit your milestones, and begin to handle a volume of orders and the joys of day-to-day operations, you may be giving some thought to the future — namely, "How am I going to handle everything if orders continue to increase?" At some point, you'll need to consider outsourcing elements of your store so you can focus on what you do best. After all, Jeff Bezos could only pack orders on his concrete garage floor for so long with his employees before he had to get his company, Amazon.com, some warehouses and distribution centers.

In this chapter, we discuss some of the more common steps taken by Web store owners when their businesses start to grow, in terms of outsourcing and re-design. We talk about questions to consider and how to evaluate someone before you bring them on. We discuss how to expand the reach of your store by looking at partnerships and, in some cases, how you can create your own affiliate program for the products you sell in your store. We then walk you through a site called Elance, where you can find contractors for jobs ranging from Web site redesign to writing new software for your store.

Finding Someone to Handle Fulfillment

When I've talked with various e-commerce store owners over the years, I noticed one common trend — almost all of them picked their order fulfillment as the first thing to hire employees for or outsource. Nobody really starts their business dreaming of all the time they'll spend packing and shipping out customer's orders. They just want to turn their business idea into a viable operation, and the fulfillment is simply a necessary piece of the overall picture. As business owners begin to run out of time and resources, they realize that in order to focus on what they do best, they should turn over fulfillment operations to someone else who does that function the best . . . or at least better.

When some people think of outsourcing fulfillment, they assume that only the largest companies can hire someone like UPS to re-route thousands of packages from far-flung warehouses in a fully computerized system. The truth is that there are a number of *fulfillment houses,* or companies who serve the small business community, by grouping together several companies' outsourcing needs into one warehouse with one staff.

Deciding whether to outsource

When you're ready to start the outsourcing process, the first step is deciding whether to hire an employee to handle the packing and shipping within your operation or to set up a contract with a fulfillment house and have that company do all the packing and shipping for you. As you try to decide, keep a few guidelines in mind:

- ✔ **Figure out a budget.** You can't go shopping if you don't know how much you can spend, right? Take a look at the orders coming in, figure out how much of a budget you can afford to handle the problem, and come up with an average amount per order that you can spend. This will help you decide whether an outside company will qualify as an option. Remember that you'll be freeing up some employee time with an outsourcing partner, so factor that into your budget.

- ✔ **Think about your physical space requirements.** For some companies, outsourcing becomes a necessity because they no longer have the physical space needed to accommodate inventory storage and a packing/shipping area. Look at your current space usage, and do some estimates based on past sales data on your future space needs. If you're operating a seasonal store, like selling Christmas gifts, then your space estimates should be based on your peak demand. The last thing you should have is a crammed warehouse in the middle of your critical order season.

- ✔ **Decide how much can be handled off-site.** If you sell products that require a lot of customization before being shipped, then perhaps you need to keep the fulfillment inside your company and hire some employees or independent contractors. If you're simply acting as a warehouse and perform zero customization, then you're more likely to benefit from a fulfillment house.

- ✔ **Determine the location of your customers.** As your company starts to grow, you should be building your customer database, and hopefully you'll be noticing some trends regarding your customer's location. If, for example, many of your customers are located in one region of the country, you could save money by locating your fulfillment center closer to that customer base. At the very least, the cost savings could pay for the labor required to outsource fulfillment, and it would speed up order delivery, which should lead to increased customer satisfaction. Remember to factor in the delivery costs from your product source to your fulfillment center. If your customers are wide-spread, then minimize costs by locating your fulfillment near your product source.

Finding an outsourcing partner

If you've decided to outsource your fulfillment, your first step is to locate a provider. Unfortunately, there isn't a handy tab in the Yellow Pages for Outsourcing or Fulfillment. Instead, you need to do some research online and find companies that fit your service needs or are located near you. I have compiled a list of some example fulfillment houses, which you can find in Table 18-1.

Talk to fellow business owners at chamber of commerce events, SBA workshops, or talk to your vendors or manufacturers to see if they can recommend a company. While an Internet search can turn up a lot of names, it's always recommended to do a search on message boards and forums to see if anyone has had a bad experience with one of those companies.

Table 18-1	Fulfillment Outsourcing Companies
Name	*URL*
eFulfillmentService	`www.efulfillmentservice.com`
ShipMyOrder	`www.shipmyorder.com`
PFSWeb	`www.pfsweb.com`
ProLog Logistics	`www.prologlogistics.com`
WeFulfillIt	`www.wefulfillit.com`

Talk to more than one company and get competitive quotes from each. Treat this like a job interview, but instead of hiring a direct employee you're hiring someone to do their work away from your watchful eye. As you talk to them, keep these questions in mind to help you find the right partner:

✔ **What kind of service level can you guarantee?** When a fulfillment house handles your packing and shipping, it's still your company name on the invoice, which means that any problems or inconsistencies get blamed on you, not the shipper. You need to know that this company will represent your company well to your customers, since the only point of physical contact in your business is when the package carrier hands over the box to your customer.

✔ **What is your complete fee structure, and what do you charge for additional services?** Many companies will easily quote you their per-order charge, and the most popular surcharges, like per item charges, one-time setup fees, and maintenance or storage fees. For example, eFulfillmentService.com lists their different fees on their Web site, as shown in Figure 18-1. However, you should try to get as complete a price list as possible so you're not surprised down the road when they hit you with a bunch of small fees that quickly add up. Sometimes, companies can offer low prices because they collect their revenue through a maze of fees. Add everything up in advance, and compare similar packages with all the fees included.

✔ **Have you or are you handling clients similar to my business?** Ideally, you would like a fulfillment house that has some experience in your type of Web store. This way, they may be able to identify potential problems because their similar clients experienced those problems first. If your products require special packaging or handling, a fulfillment company with past experience will handle those needs more effectively than someone who is learning at your expense. Some companies detail their niche expertise, as shown in Figure 18-2.

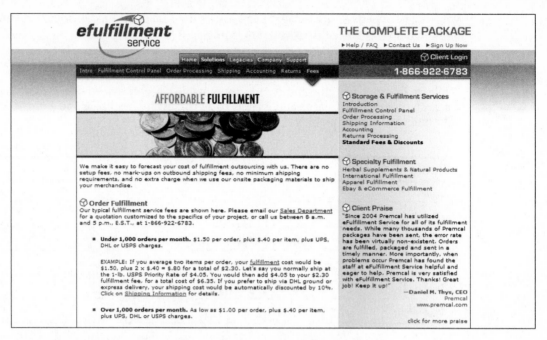

Figure 18-1: eFulfillmentService.com breaks down their different fees.

Apparel

We ship a wide variety of wearables from our fulfillment centers and work with a number of clothiers and garment importers. Email our Sales Department or call us between 8 a.m. and 5 p.m., E.S.T., at 1-866-922-6783 to discuss your special handling requirements. Apparel such as t-shirts, hats and dresses must arrive in our warehouse in individually-packaged plastic bags, with SKU numbers affixed to approximately the same spot on the outside of each bag. If your supplier is unable to bag and SKU individual items, our receiving team can do this for you at our $35 per hour assembly rate. When you take advantage of our returns processing service, you can count on our experienced personnel to exercise good judgment on returns, empowered by your pre-authorized returns policy. Our team inspects all items for wear, and carefully examines each article for stains or other damage. As your fulfillment partner, we look good only if you and your customers do, too.

Scrapbooking

The scrapbooking boom has reached eFulfillment Service centers. With an average of 11 items per customer order and more than 3,000 SKUs, scrapbooking fulfillment might have increased labor costs, if it weren't for the know-how of our software innovators. They found an automated solution that would expedite receiving, as well as pick and pack. Using pre-printed packing lists and labels generated from orders transmitted via our Fulfillment Control Panel, both departments have decreased labor costs and boosted their productivity.

eBay & Internet Commerce

eFulfillment Service exclusively offers fulfillment solutions for online businesses. We're a fulfillment company, not an online retailer, so we never compete with our clients for customers. We've carefully developed and continue to create outstanding software solutions based on our years of experience as an efulfillment partner. Some of those solutions include real-time order transmittal through merchant service partners like Yahoo! Merchant Solutions or UltraCart or customer tracking options for our eCommerce and eBay client customers.

Figure 18-2: Consider a company who's experienced handling your niche of business.

✔ **Can you handle product returns, and if so, what are the costs?** When there's shipping, there's usually a need for returns. Once you set up a fulfillment house to stock and ship your products, you most likely want them to handle your returns so the inventory can be re-shelved or discarded without inserting another step (you) into the process. Find out all the costs involved, including the sorting and evaluation time when a returned item is processed, and whether they'll ship a return label to your customer automatically.

✔ **How much experience do you have in this area?** You're looking for someone who's handled this kind of operation before, not necessarily some new startup that is hoping to learn as time goes on. If possible, ask for references of past clients who are satisfied, and talk to those people about their impressions of this fulfillment house.

✔ **What kind of reports or information do I get?** As time goes on, you want to be able to monitor the effects of this new relationship, and some fulfillment houses will be able to provide you with detailed reports about order turnaround, percentage of returns received, average cost per package, and so on.

✔ **What are your minimum levels for taking an account?** If you're still unsure, or want to see this process in action before you fully commit to it, ask if you can turn over a small portion of your fulfillment operations first and then evaluate their service after a determined period of time. When you find out their minimums, you can decide if you can give them a test run or if they'll only accept your entire business.

Hiring Someone to (Re)Design Your Store

Let's turn our attention away from packing and shipping and talk about another important element in any Web store — the Web site design. One of the unwritten rules of doing business online is that customers expect something new, fresh, and exciting as often as you can provide it. Perhaps that's why blogs are doing so well, because of all the new content that's added weekly, or even daily!

Web design is a constantly changing and evolving concept. If you've looked at the different styles over the past decade, you'll notice that some trends have come and gone, with popular sites such as eBay or Amazon rolling out brand new designs on an average of 12 to 18 months, with smaller changes happening all the time. The Web community learns from each other and studies the patterns and techniques that their fellow Web site owners are using.

Therefore, if you've been running your Web store for a while and your customers are looking for "the next level," you might consider hiring someone to redesign your Web site. Perhaps you may have implemented a simple design to get your store online, and now you want to portray a more professional image to attract a bigger audience. Whatever the case may be, consider hiring a professional to handle the job.

When you redesign your Web site, remember to keep the interface clean and fast-loading, regardless of what any hired professional recommends to add to your Web site design. If you completely overhaul the interface, make sure existing customers can "re-find" items in an intuitive manner, without too many Web "bells and whistles" getting in the way.

When it comes to specific jobs like Web site re-design, you don't need to hire a full-time employee to handle this job. You don't even have to hire someone who is local to your area, though you may want someone to discuss the project with face-to-face. There are lots of qualified freelancers around the world that can take on your assignment and deliver the results electronically, by uploading your Web pages and graphics to your Web site for you, as an example. You can post your job requirements on several different places on the Internet, including:

- Elance (www.elance.com)
- Craigslist (jobs.craigslist.org)
- Guru.com (www.guru.com)
- Rentacoder (www.rentacoder.com)

We take a look at how to post your project on Elance later in this chapter. When going to any of these companies, or using a local favorite, you should definitely keep a few things in mind, which will help control your costs and yield a better product:

- **Write down a plan of your major goals for this project.** While I don't expect you to be able to list the 25 specific commands your designer should integrate into your Web site, I do expect you to write down what you like to see when the project is done. It helps to give your designer a roadmap of your goals so they spend their valuable time doing the designing and not brainstorming with you. Ask them questions, draw from their experience, but remember that you're paying the bills, so have them fulfill your goals, not their own.

- **Develop a schedule with specific goals.** Talk with your developer to come up with a schedule or time-line that contains measurable milestones so you can monitor progress and agree on intermediate steps. This way, you don't get to the end of the project and find that you hate their entire effort. The easiest way to enforce these milestones and periodic reviews is to tie payment to these dates, so they get paid only when they achieve specific goals that lead to the overall success of the project.

- **Get everything written as a contract.** This contract should not only include the basic agreement of what tasks they will perform and the schedule, but there should be provisions that discuss what happens if overtime is required (and the costs associated with that), how change requests are handled, and what steps must be taken to dissolve the contract. It's better to talk about all potential circumstances first than to have a problem arise during the project with no way of handling it. Have your contractor sign the contract and sign it yourself, or at the very least, exchange e-mail agreements of the contract.

- **Establish ownership of the work they do.** Since they are performing this work on a work-for-hire arrangement, make sure that you and your business have sole ownership of the project work they provide. Have this stipulated in any agreement or contract you develop with them. They'll probably ask for the right to include this work in a portfolio they use to get new jobs, and that is fine. Just make sure they don't have the right to re-sell the work, or you may see your five big competitors with the same Web site as you!

Creating an Affiliate Program for Your Products

As a small business looking to grow to the next level, there is a way that you can increase your sales force without hiring extra personnel to go out and sell for you. In fact, you won't pay any additional money until your qualified lead or sale comes in the door. You can accomplish this by creating your own affiliate program. An *affiliate program* is where you pay another business (or person, or Web site) when they provide you with a sale or qualified lead, like a new customer who enrolls in your Web site. They help connect you with the customer, and in exchange for that effort, you pay the affiliate a commission, either a percentage of the sale or a fixed amount of money.

Because there are so many products available on the Internet, and eager marketers looking for something to sell, there are lots of affiliate programs out there today. You can join a clearinghouse of affiliates, like Commission Junction (`www.cj.com`) shown in Figure 18-3, or Shareasale (`www.shareasale.com`) and have your program available to thousands of affiliate marketers, or you can develop your own program in-house.

Figure 18-3: Commission Junction can build and manage your affiliate program.

An affiliate program can work with almost any product or service you provide, not just e-books or digital content. You can offer an affiliate program on any products that you manufacture or wholesale, or offer a referral bonus program for people who bring you new customers or leads.

If you're interested in starting up an affiliate program for your Web store, you can submit your interest to Commission Junction (CJ) by filling out their information request form at `http://www.cj.com/advertisers/information_request. html`, as shown in Figure 18-4, and someone at CJ will get back to you and schedule a consultation so you can get more information and, hopefully, get started with their program.

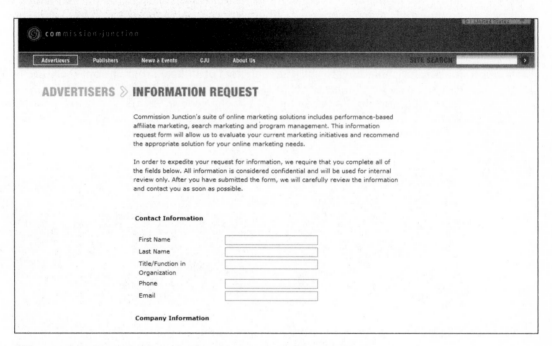

Figure 18-4: Get more information from CJ about their affiliate programs.

You can also check with your storefront provider and your shopping cart software to see if there is built-in technology that will allow you to create affiliate ID's on your own and establish your own program. You could also manually track the progress of a few selected trial affiliate members by supplying them with one of the following:

- ✔ **A special link they must use to send their customers to your Web site, as follows:**

```
<a href="http://www.yourcompanyname.com?id=xxx">Click here
       to buy from YourCompanyName!</a>
```

  This way, your server logs will keep track of the different ID numbers that are used to access your site, and you can manually compute how much you owe each affiliate from the number of times their ID appears in the server log.

✔ **A copy of your home page, in a different directory, and a link to that copy, like this:**

```
<a
        href="http://www.yourcompanyname.com/affil/name1.ht
        ml">Click here to buy from YourCompanyName!</a>
```

Similar to the first option, your server logs will keep track of how many people go to this Web page. Your storefront provider should have a report to show you the page views for each of these pages, so you can get an accurate count that way. Obviously, don't mention or link to this page from anywhere else, as you don't want people stumbling into someone's affiliate link and lose money on that sale.

✔ **A special promotional code or identifier that their customers must put in their order form before they can checkout.**

This option is much easier for you to track, since you have to go through only the orders received to track your affiliates' progress, and you can specifically tie an order to an affiliate. The downside to this option is that their customers may forget to enter the promotional code, which means affiliates may feel like they're not getting accurate credit.

The keys to providing a good affiliate program are this: good incentives and good promotional support. Make the reward worth your affiliates' time, and provide them with enough promotional material, banner advertisements, graphics, and support they need to promote your Web store products and get paid easily.

Placing Your Project on Elance

Stuff You Need to Know

Toolbox:

✔ 2–3 paragraph description of project request
✔ An idea of your potential budget for this project
✔ Proposed timeline and deadline date for the project

Time Needed:
20–30 minutes

Elance is a marketplace for people to find and hire service professionals for a variety of tasks that can be done over the Internet, from writing to Web design to computer software programming. You can either search their database for a qualified person who specializes in a given area, or create a request for the project you wish to have done. That request is then posted on Elance, and you'll receive bids on your project from people or companies who want to perform that task for you. Once you get several bids, you look through them, investigate the profiles of the people bidding, and choose one to handle your project. From there, Elance will help you monitor the status of your project and coordinate payment once the project is completed.

1. Go to the Elance Web site at www.elance.com and click the Post Your Project button. Be aware that when you go to Elance, they have created multiple categories to handle requests in different areas.

2. You'll see the registration screen. In the first phase, Enter Contact Information, you'll need to create a user ID and password that you'll use to access your Elance account, and provide your e-mail address, first and last name, and a phone number where Elance can reach you. This phone number will *not* be available for any contractors to see. Click Continue when you're ready to proceed.

Elance has developed Elance Packages which are fixed-price packages of specific tasks that they offer through preferred partners. The advantage to these is that they are fixed price, so you don't have to worry about cost overruns or a low rate designer charging you way too many hours for a simple task. The disadvantage is that the package may not fit your individual needs.

3. In the second phase, Select Your Project Category, you need to select the project category that fits the job request you are making. Elance has organized their project request database into eleven distinct categories, from Administrative Support to Writing and Translation. Pick the category that best describes your project. Once you've picked your category (in this case, we are picking Web site Development), you'll see a list of matching sub-categories for the selected category. Pick the sub-category that best describes your project (in this case, it's Web Design) and then scroll down the page to click Continue and proceed.

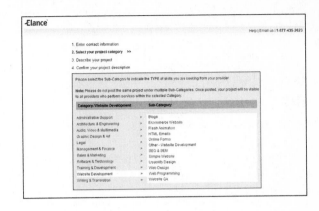

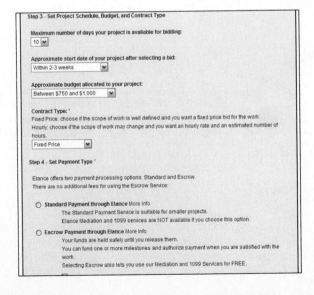

4. In the third phase, Describe Your Project, you'll need to describe your project in some detail. When you get to the Project detail page, you'll see a number of steps that Elance presents to get all the information needed for a project request. In Step 1, you need to create a Project Title that is meaningful and represents the type of work that will be done (for example "Website Redesign," "Update customer database," and so on). In Step 2, you have 3700 characters to describe the project you want performed. Remember, stick to high-level goals and actions, as this is not the space for specifics.

5. Scroll down to Step 3 and give Elance the parameters of the project proposal. You'll need to decide how many days you'll leave the project open for bidding, the approximate start date of the project, your estimated budget, and whether you want to pay your freelancer a fixed price or an hourly rate to work on this project. Step 4 of the process asks if you want to pay the freelancer directly, or use an escrow service through Elance. If you want to enforce milestone completion, then you will need to select escrow service.

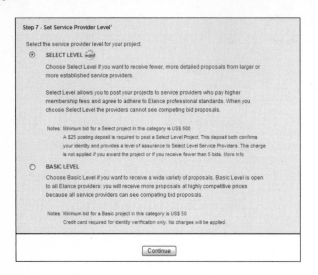

6. Scroll down to Step 5 and answer the demographic questions there. Step 6 asks you if you want to upload any files that better explain the project. Click the button if you've written up your proposal, and attach the correct file. In the final part, Step 7, Elance will ask you whether your project proposal can be filled only by select providers that are pre-screened by Elance and offer a higher level of quality proposals, as well as privately submitted proposals. You can also open up your project request to the entire community, where freelancers can see the competing proposals.

7. You'll see a credit card information screen. Provide the basic details for your credit card in the fields provided. There is a box to check for authenticating your credit card, if you plan to pay your freelancer with your credit card. By leaving this box checked, Elance will put two small deposits on your credit card and then ask you for those amounts. When you correctly identify the amounts, this verifies to Elance that you own that credit card, and you will be allowed to pay your freelancers with the credit card. Allow approximately four business days for this authentication process to be complete.

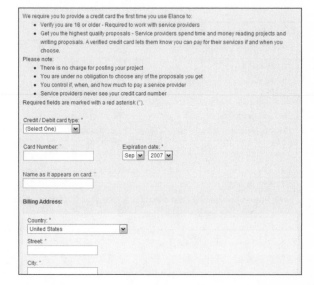

If you pick the Select Level of provider, Elance will charge you a deposit to make your project request, and require a higher minimum value of the project. If you successfully find a provider for your proposal, or very few people bid on your project, the deposit is refunded to you.

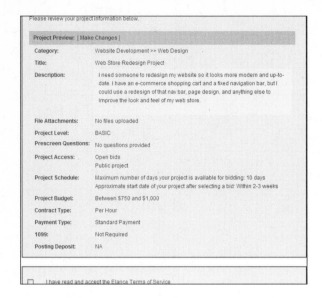

8. In the final phase of this process, Confirm Your Project Description, you'll see a summary screen based on the project proposal you have been entering. Look over the details to make sure you inputted everything correctly, since the proposals you'll receive will be based on the information you're giving them here. Click the Post Project Now button to submit your request. (You can also click the Save and Post Later button if your request is incomplete or you're not yet ready to accept proposals.)

9. You're done! Your request is added to the Elance database, and you should start to get some proposals soon, depending on the complexity of the project. You can monitor the status of your request by clicking the My Elance link and looking in your account to see if any questions or proposals have been submitted.

Part VI
The Part of Tens

The 5th Wave   By Rich Tennant

"Guess who found a Kiss merchandise site on the Web while you were gone?"

In this part . . .

In this part, I cover the final tips, tricks, and thoughts regarding your new Web store. I start by talking about the ten things every Web store needs, in terms of content and function. Then I discuss a variety of design tips that many different e-commerce professionals agree are the things that e-commerce ventures need to consider when building their Web store.

Finally, I discuss the things you should *not* do, as I outline the ten most common traps Web store owners fall into, and what you should do to avoid making those mistakes.

Chapter 19

Ten Things Every Web Store Needs

T he essentials of a Web store should be clear: You need shopping cart software, a catalog of products (or other items) to sell, a storefront provider to host your Web store, and at least one payment method of accepting credit cards over the Internet. I've gone over a lot of additional things that are a part of most Web stores, and functions and areas that can enhance any Web store.

In this chapter, however, I discuss the ten elements that every Web store *should* have, independent of the catalog, shopping cart, and so forth. These are the elements that customers are always asking about, and secretly (or openly) complaining about when they don't see these on a Web store they visit. Some of these are considered "deal-breakers" for lots of people, meaning if you don't have it, they move on to a Web store that does have it. Others are critical enough that it could mean the difference between a new order being placed and someone going off to buy from a competitor . . . and telling 20 people why they didn't shop with you.

Contact Information Page

Surprisingly, when I did an informal survey of different Web customers and developers, this was the number one thing mentioned that every Web store should have. Even if a customer will never have the need to contact a Web store owner to ask a question or make a complaint, it creates the sense of trust and legitimacy that a Web store owner can be contacted.

Additionally, the more contact methods provided, the better. Because the Internet gives your customer a disconnected experience, they want as many ways as possible to get in touch with a store owner or employee. If for no other reason, you should provide multiple contact methods because different people prefer different methods, and you don't want to isolate a section of your customer base.

You should consider providing as many of these as possible:

- Telephone number
- E-mail address (branded to your store; *yourstorename*@hotmail.com or @yahoo.com looks unprofessional)
- Fax number
- Postal mail address
- Instant Message (AIM, ICQ, and so on) or chat ID

In the next chapter, I cover a design tip related to the contact information page — make it as accessible as possible throughout your entire Web store.

Stellar Navigation

While contact information was the most popular item mentioned, a close second has to be excellent navigation for your Web store. You simply *must* have some sort of navigation bar or system to let people access different sections of your Web store. Some people use tabs, other people use buttons, while others simply use plain text. The point, however, is to have clear, consistent navigation that easily takes customers between sections of your Web store.

It's recommended that, regardless of the method you use to display your navigation bar (along the top or left-hand side of your screen), you include a second navigation bar in plain text only along the bottom of your home page. This way, the search engines can read your text navigation bar and access the different parts of your Web store, in case they can't decipher the buttons or graphics you use for your top/left navigation bar.

Clear and Complete Shipping Policy

Unless you're selling only digital or downloadable products, you'll have to ship out the orders to your customers. Obviously, you have to advertise the price of your products to your customers so they can decide whether to order from you. Additionally, however, customers want to know the full price of their order, including shipping, before they place their order or create an account with your store. Therefore, you need to have a clear, complete, and comprehensive shipping policy spelled out on your store for customers to access.

Not only is it important for customers to know the different shipping options (by the way, the more options, the better; if you haven't picked up the clues I've dropped, customers like choice), but you need to set up the correct expectations for shipping delivery times and arrival procedures, like whether the package will have to be signed for by a live person or left on the doorstep. This is not a retail environment, where you hand the customer a plastic bag containing their order and they walk away. The customer is counting on your shipping to be fast and accurate, and they want that product the moment they clicked the Order button.

Clear Return Policy

Before a customer decides to plunk down their money and purchase something from a Web store, they want to know their options in case the order isn't handled properly, the item doesn't work upon delivery, and any other scenarios that may occur. Therefore, you need to have a clear return policy that explains, in detail, what you'll provide and what situations you'll cover (and not cover) in case a problem arises.

At the bare minimum, your return policy should contain the following elements:

- Is the product returnable? If so, do they return it to you or the manufacturer?

- How long does the customer have to report a problem after the order arrives? A week? 10 days? 30 days?

- Who pays for return shipping? If the item arrives broken, who pays for return shipping?

- Does the customer have to pay a restocking fee if they return the item for any reason? (A *restocking fee* is a charge that a retailer implements to cover the cost of receiving an opened item and putting it back in their inventory.)

- Are there any products or conditions where the return policy does not apply?

Security (SSL Certificate)

Given all the fraud and identity theft concerns that have plagued Internet customers these past years, your customers are going to demand that any sensitive information, especially financial information like credit card or bank account data, be transmitted securely using a Secure Socket Layer (SSL) certificate on your Web store that encrypts the data being entered.

Never have your customers send you their sensitive information in an e-mail! Most won't do this anyway, but never offer this as an option.

If your storefront provider or payment processor doesn't offer an SSL-protected Web page for you to gather financial data from your customers, then you'll need to create your own SSL certificate and make your own secure page to get the data. Discuss the details with your Web host or storefront provider, as the steps vary depending on your individual setup.

You can also check out THAWTE at www.thawte.com to have them help you create the right SSL certificate for your Web store.

Fast Loading Pages

Internet users want their shopping experience to be fast, easy, and convenient. After all, they could get into their cars, drive in traffic, hunt for a parking spot, walk into a mall or department store, fight the crowds, walk aisle by aisle, grab different items, try or inspect them, walk to the checkout area, wait in line, pay for their item, walk back to their car, fight traffic again to get home, and then get into their house with the shopping bag(s) in hand.

On the Internet, they want a smooth process. If they go to your Web store and have to wait for pictures to display or functions to start up, and they're staring at a blank page or a page that is slowly drawing the picture, it's like they're stuck in their car, put on hold when calling someone, or waiting in a long, slow line at the store. When customers have to wait, and every other Web store is just a click or some typing away, guess what will happen? Yep, you guessed it — they'll take off and try someone else.

Customer Testimonials

Your Internet customers will typically not be able to see you, which means they need a level of trust to do business with you. A professional-looking Web store, with a great selection, competitive prices, and maybe some additional functions, is the first step to building that trust. If you want to build an additional level of trust to help ease your customer's minds, let them know that other people were in their situation and had a great experience. You can do this by showing or displaying customer testimonials on your Web store.

This accomplishes several goals in building that extra level of trust. When someone reads that another customer enjoyed getting a product, it's like giving that product an unofficial thumbs up or seal of approval. The testimonial gives new customers confidence that you have been in business awhile and are not planning on running away with their money. It lets customers know that someone else was pleased with how you, the store owner, handled their order, so they have more confidence that their order will be handled the same way. Finally, it gives current customers a chance to shine and feel recognized, which can lead to increased loyalty and repeat purchases.

Confirmation Page After an Order

At first glance, it sounds simple enough. If someone places an order, they want to actually see the words "Your order has been placed." They want some confirmation that their order was placed successfully and the product is being sent to them. After all, there could have been an issue with the Internet connection and perhaps not all the information was transmitted successfully. Yes, they'll see the charge on their credit card, but the customer wants to know that their order was received and it will be processed.

While you may be concerned with streamlining the process, it is wise to include that final step in the ordering flow that acknowledges the order was received. It doesn't necessarily have to be a separate Web page that displays this, but an additional sentence added to an existing page, in boldface or in a larger font. The confirmation message is an excellent place to reinforce the expected shipping time of the order, and can include a reminder that their order information is accessible from the customer information section of your Web store.

Clear Product Descriptions

For some Web store owners, the descriptions that they get from the manufacturer seem to be complete. However, this is typically because the owner is familiar with the product already. The question you have to ask yourself is, "Is the description clear enough for my customer?" Some customers need more than a one-sentence description or a laundry list of indecipherable bullet points that spout some jargon they may or may not understand. They're looking for clarification, for reassurance, for proof that this product solves their need.

Therefore, you may need to go back and update or add information in the product description, so it is clear to anyone what they're purchasing. The first paragraph alone should contain all the vital information necessary to know what they're purchasing. You can also include information on the benefits of the product, not just the technical features. Remember, you're not just selling a product, you're selling a solution to a problem.

Third-Party Certifications

No doubt you've spent a fair amount of time constructing your Web store, so you know it's good. You've tested it, checked for accuracy and function, and you're ready to take orders and go live. However, as I mentioned before, you need to build that level of trust so customers are ready to give you their money and order from you. One way to do that is to approach third-party companies who can verify that your company or business is legitimate and safe for doing business.

Some examples of certifications or companies to approach include:

- **Verisign** (www.verisign.com)
- **The Better Business Bureau** (www.bbbonline.org)
- **Shopzilla**, formerly BizRate (merchant.shopzilla.org)
- **SiteSafe from Network Solutions** (www.networksolutions.com)

Chapter 20

Ten Tips for Designing Your Web Store

When it comes to design tips, your overall goal is always to provide an easy and clear experience for your customers to interact with you. If your store fits the needs of your buyers they'll consider shopping from you, and if you serve them with good products at a good price with excellent customer service you'll hopefully retain them as repeat customers. Therefore, after discussion with lots of different Web store owners, customers, and design professionals, these were the ten things I heard over and over that you should think about when designing your own Web store. Enjoy!

Keep It Simple and Professional

By far, this was the number one thing I heard when talking to anyone else about how to design your Web store. While I discuss adding functionality and content to give your customers a reason to come back and use your business often, you should never let your Web store look like an overgrown, unmanageable mess of pictures, text, and functions. At any time, any visitor should be able to come to your Web store and understand what they are seeing, whether it is their first or their 100th visit.

Understand, however, that simple can sometimes evolve into amateurish, and that's not something you want either. When someone is planning to spend their hard-earned money with you, the last image you want to convey is a Web store that looks like it was thrown together in 30 minutes by a second grade student. You want to convey a professional image, with clean lines, crisp graphics, and a straightforward interface.

Make the Contact Information Easy to Find

I mentioned in the last chapter that a Contact Info page is one of the top ten things you should have for your Web store. When you're designing your store, however, there's another cardinal rule to consider: Your contact information should be easily accessible from *any* page on your Web store. Yes, you should have your contact info prominently featured on your home page. But you may think, "Why would they need my phone number if they're browsing my catalog or reading an article?" The answer is simple: If they have a question, problem, concern, or even a suggestion, they want to be able to immediately contact you while they're thinking about it. If they have to click around and hunt for that information, many of them will get upset, leave your Web store, and most likely never return.

In a retail store, you can approach the customer before they storm out the door. In a Web store, you don't get that physical opportunity, so make it as easy as possible for that customer to find a way to contact you, no matter where they are on your site. You'll never be able to guess every single time someone has a question, so make that contact information accessible anywhere they can be, and make sure that link or button is in the same place on every page, too.

Simple, Organized Navigation Bar

I know we cover this point in detail in the book, but it bears repeating because it's become so important. You need to have a simple, organized navigation bar that customers use to find their way around your Web store. If a customer can't find their way around, they'll leave and go to another Web store where it is easy to navigate. While it takes a lot to impress your Web customers, it's very easy to annoy them and turn them away from you. Take a look at your navigation bar and ask yourself these questions:

- **Are there too many options on the main navigation bar?** You should have an average of 4–6 options. If you have more and you should add sub-navigation bars.

- **Does the navigation bar look the same on every page?** It can shake a user's confidence if the order of options gets mixed around when they go from section to section.

- **Can I tell from the navigation bar what section I'm in?** Many Web sites use a marker or a highlighted tab to indicate the section they're currently browsing.

- **Is it obvious what each link from the navigation bar represents?** Your users should be able to intuitively figure out where they're going with each click from the navigation bar. Use specific language and avoid any obscure or "cute" references. If you survey your competition, you should see the same option names used over and over.

Let Customers Get to the Merchandise Quickly

Believe it or not, some e-commerce store owners begin to "forget" their main purpose is to sell things, because they start adding so much content and functionality and get caught up in presenting that "cool stuff" to their customers. When someone comes to your Web store, ask yourself this question: Can they access my product catalog, buy something, and leave quickly? If you force them to go through several screens before getting to your products, you're slowing down a portion of your buying public who wants to get at the goods fast.

Try to remove any unneeded or extra Web pages or processes between your customers and the ordering process. If someone uses your search box, make sure they can order a product from the results page, not browse through summary statements first. If you promote a product from your Web store home page, make sure they can click once to either read more about the product, or add it to their shopping cart. Someone summed it up for me by offering a popular slogan — "Give the customer what they want." When it comes to e-commerce and convenience, what they want are your products.

Offer a Smooth Checkout

It's important to focus on the smooth checkout portion. Some Web store owners think that, once someone adds a product to their shopping cart, that desire to get the product will carry the customer through any process. Wrong. Make it too difficult to check out or place an order and that customer will take off, leaving behind an abandoned shopping cart. There are entire books and studies that focus on the abandoned shopping cart phenomenon and how to reduce that occurrence. The easiest way is to make the checkout as smooth as possible:

- **Don't ask for every piece of information under the sun right away.** Let them check out with the minimum amount of information to process their order. Later on, if you offer customer accounts, surveys, or feedback forms, you can gather extra information, at the customer's leisure.

- **Break up the process into manageable steps.** If you present one, long, never-ending form for customers to complete, they may take one look and say, "Forget it." But ask them for their name and address first, then take them to "Step 2" and get their Credit Card information, then go to "Step 3" for anything else, and now it's manageable. Show the number of steps and the customer's progression along the top of the screen.

- **Reuse information as much as possible.** If you have to collect billing and shipping information, offer an option where the customer can identify that both are the same, so they don't have to type in the same address twice. If you know what state they're in by asking them earlier, fill in that info on the checkout screen. If the customer has an account on your Web store, fill in as much information as possible when they go to check out again.

Choose Your Colors Wisely

Believe it or not, the colors you use on your Web store speak volumes in the eyes of your customers. Most importantly, the colors have to make the text readable on the screen. If you put white or light colored characters on a black or dark background, your customers can't read anything. If the text and background colors clash, it is very distracting for the customer to read the instructions or product descriptions.

Load your Web store in any Web browser and go from top to bottom yourself. If possible, have other people read through your Web store and get their opinion, especially if you're color blind and have trouble distinguishing different shades. Some people recommend more muted colors that aren't as harsh on the eye. Some users are very specific — red text on a blue background is horrible, for example.

Optimize Your Pictures and Web Pages

Have you ever gone to a Web page where you can actually see the image being drawn on the screen, line by line? It's like getting put on hold, and most customers will wait a maximum of 3–5 seconds before going on to the next Web site. You need to make sure that your pictures and your Web pages load in a reasonable amount of time. More specifically, the faster the page loads, the better.

When it comes to your pictures, make sure that you resize the pictures so they're no more than 600 by 800 pixels, on average. If you need to offer detailed pictures, then use a thumbnail photo first, and allow the user to click on the thumbnail to bring up a detailed version of the picture. Some people do the reverse of this rule, and *only* offer the thumbnail version of the picture. That is a mistake as well — offer a low resolution or thumbnail photo first, but make a bigger or more detailed picture one click away.

When it comes to your Web pages, make sure that no additional code or functions are sitting on each Web page. If you use an HTML editor like Microsoft Frontpage, sometimes they include extra HTML commands and tags that aren't necessary but make the computer think more when drawing the page, and therefore slows down the presentation of your Web store to your customers. If your pages are taking too long to load (more than a few seconds), have someone who's tech-savvy go through your Web page source files and look for content that isn't necessary.

Combine Text and Graphics to Convey Your Message

The power of the Internet today is the way you can combine text and graphics to tell a richer story. It's no longer a text-only world, but you don't want to overwhelm your users with too many pictures as well. Therefore, each Web page within your store should be a careful mix of text and graphics to tell your story or convey your message. If you can use a graphic to illustrate a process and save yourself a few paragraphs of boring text, do so. Additionally, make sure the graphics have the appropriate labels, so people don't have to guess what the graphic represents.

If you find a Web page within your store that has way too much text, consider adding some graphics to break up the text, act as category headers or text dividers, or provide a visual example to what the text is explaining. While a graphics-only Web store may seem appealing because it seems language-independent, sometimes the graphics may not load properly, and without text explanations, your customers are lost.

Make Your Product Detail Pages Only about the Product

There are a lot of things you can do with your Web store, as I have mentioned in this book. Some owners want every single Web page within their store to achieve as many options as possible, and this thinking will overload your customers quickly. One example is the product detail page. When a customer is looking at one specific product and reading about the details or functionality, they don't need to be bombarded with quick links to the rest of your Web store, or inundated with too many cross-selling or up-selling possibilities. They just want to read about that product and have a clear option to either add the product to their cart or go back and browse.

In other words, there should be only *one* focus on the product detail page — the product. Limit your cross-selling and up-selling to the checkout phase, or follow-up e-mails. Let your navigation bar provide the options for your customer to see the rest of the site, but don't overwhelm each product detail page. This page should only represent the product.

Limit Your Use of Flash Animation

Ah, no Top 10 Web store design list is complete without this one. Several years ago, Flash animation started popping up (pun intended) on all kinds of Web pages as Web site owners wanted to impress their customers with the latest and greatest technology. Flash technology is still being used today on the Internet, but it's nowhere near as abundant as it used to be, for several reasons:

- It can be incredibly distracting for the customer

- The load time of the Flash animation would slow down the Web site and increase waiting time

- The Flash animation would serve as an "Introduction screen" to the Web site, further separating your customers from your products (which separates you from potential sales)

- It adds no value to the customer experience and actually makes your store look less professional

Therefore, think long and hard about including any Flash animation on your Web store pages. If you've got a content section to your store, or want to use a Flash animation as a how-to or helpful guide, that could work. The golden rule on Flash has become this: When in doubt, don't add Flash to your Web site.

Chapter 21

Ten Traps to Avoid While Building and Running Your Store

....

Sometimes, the best advice you can give someone isn't the specific steps to take, but rather the specific steps not to make. In this final Top 10 list, I talk about the mistakes and traps that Web store owners can fall into when they are designing or maintaining their Web store. Like the other lists, many of these bullet points came from Web store owners and customers who vented their frustration and are pleading with you to heed this advice. Learn from the mistakes of others.

Overloading Your Home Page (or Any Other Page)

It's one of the most common mistakes an ambitious Web store owner can make: You work very hard to provide a robust e-commerce site, with lots of content, functionality, and products to please even the most demanding or finicky customer. The trap is feeling like the home page has to convey *everything* that the store has to offer. After all, if it's not mentioned or featured on the home page, how will the customer find it? The result is that these owners pack all sorts of content, pictures, and links, onto the home page, and the result is so thick with content that most customers give up and never enter.

Your first goal is to make sure that all the vital information or links appear "above the fold," meaning that the first screen of information that someone sees, at the top of your home page, has the vital links or info that any customer would need. This screen becomes the focus for your customers, as most of them won't take the time to scroll down, regardless of whatever messages or prompts you give them.

Secondly, remember that you don't have to display everything on the home page — you can make secondary category pages or feature pages that point people to a plethora of options. There's only one page on your Web site that should mention every single Web page you have, and that is the Site Map page. Make the most important options visible on the home page, and make everything else one or two clicks away.

Lastly, there is a hidden benefit from not overloading your Web pages, and that has to do with the search engines. If there is too much information or too many links on a page, the search engine can't figure out what the most important thing is for each page, and by definition, if everything is important, then nothing is important, and nothing stands out. By limiting the message and options on each page, you focus each page to communicate one or two messages, which improves your standing in the search engines.

Putting Too Much Animation on the Page

As the Internet and World Wide Web mature, Web site owners have an ever-changing array of ways to capture people's attention, from the simple blinking text and animated pictures, to full-blown Flash animation, audio, and video. Some Web site owners think their Web page needs to be full of activity, so the user can't help but notice the Web page. The effect is that the user's eyes get worn out and they have to stare away from all that activity on the page.

Therefore, if you plan on using any animation or moving imagery on your Web store, think carefully and use it sparingly. If you want one item to be the focus of a particular Web page, then animating that one item is sufficient. If you want to give your customers a splitting headache, then by all means, fill that Web page with dancing babies and yellow smiley face icons.

Optimizing Your Store for One Web Browser

In their quest to get as many users browsing the Internet using their software only, some Web browsers have built in special commands that work only for their software. They offer Web site developers the chance for faster load times, advanced functionality, and other perks for "optimizing" the Web site for a certain technology. The risk of doing that is that your "optimized" Web store may not look right to customers who use a competing Web browser.

Let's face it, if customers don't see your Web store properly, and perhaps certain functions don't even work on other Web browsers, they can't shop with you. Do you really want to turn away a potential section of your audience before they have a chance to buy? Try using different Web browsers to place orders, and make sure your Web site is available to anyone who wants to shop from you, regardless of the technology they're using.

Having Music Play Automatically on Any Visit

I remember the first time I went to the Monte Carlo Las Vegas Web site. As the fancy home page was loading, suddenly I heard this music and wasn't sure where it was coming from. It took me a minute to realize that the music was coming out of my computer speakers and it was a part of the Monte Carlo Web site! Over the past few years, Web site owners have added music as a way to distinguish themselves from the competition, in hopes that a soothing classical tune will improve the customers' state of mind and increase their enjoyment of the Web site.

Sadly, this technique has backfired on a lot of Web site owners, especially those who don't make it clear how to turn off the music. Many customers now use work time to browse the Web, and nothing tips off a boss more than music suddenly emanating from Mr. Smith's cubicle. Even if your Web site sells music, you shouldn't automatically have the music load and play when someone comes to visit, but rather offer the music as a link someone can click on if they choose to listen.

Mixing Personal Opinion with Your Business

For many entrepreneurs their store is their livelihood, and they see their store as a way to do good and promote their own personal beliefs. The trap is assuming that your customer's beliefs are the same as yours, and that your beliefs cannot offend anyone else. The truth is that your customers have a wide range of beliefs, ideologies, and customs, and they're shopping from you because you offer a good product or excellent customer service, not because you have the same affiliations.

Accepting Only One Payment Method

Customers love the Internet because of the convenience offered, and credit cards make the ordering process much more convenient than other payment methods. However, it doesn't mean that 100 percent of your customers will have an available credit card and feel comfortable giving it to a complete stranger. Heck, there's not even one dominant credit card out there. It's never "Visa?" or "Mastercard?" but rather "Visa or Mastercard?" And then there's American Express, Diner's Club, Discover, Carte Blanche, other credit cards, PayPal, checks, money orders, wire transfers, and so on. Are you going to limit your customer base to only one payment method?

Even if 90 percent of your customers use the one payment method you offer, you're instantly losing 10 percent of your potential customer base. As a new Web store owner, you can't afford to isolate a chunk of your audience if you can help it. Just as customers want selection of products, they want a choice in payment methods too, if for no reason other than it signals flexibility and concern for the customer experience.

Forcing Your Customers to Register Before They Shop

Years ago, I walked into a Radio Shack and asked the clerk how much a pack of batteries cost, only to get the question, "Uh, what's your zip code?" Zip code? What does that have to do with the cost of batteries? I ended up storming out and going somewhere else. Some Web stores are set up where the customer has to register, put in all their information, and in some cases, create a customer account first before they're allowed to add items to a shopping cart or check out. In some cases, the customer can't see the total price, including shipping and handling, until they add the item to the cart and register for an account.

In most cases, making it that difficult to proceed will result in lots of abandoned shopping carts. Let the customer browse as much as possible, give as much information as possible before they place their order, and make it as easy as possible to place an order first. Your "customer" isn't even a customer until they have consciously decided to pay for a certain basket of items and check out. Once they have made that decision, then you can start asking them questions and encouraging them to sign up for a customer account. Get them comfortable about the product and your prices first, then get their information.

Forgetting to Consistently Refresh Your Content or Store Look

You've gone through all the steps, you've double-checked all your Web pages, and you've uploaded everything to the Internet. Whew, you're done! Well, not exactly. As your customers decide whether to place repeat orders with you, they'll come back to your Web site on a regular or irregular basis. While it's important to be consistent, if your customers see the same Web pages, with the same color scheme and layout, month after month, year after year, they begin to wonder if anybody is actually "minding the store" or someone built the store and walked away.

If you've used any of the big Internet retailers, like Amazon, eBay, or Overstock.com, you'll notice that, on average, every 12 to 18 months they unveil an almost completely different look to keep up with the times and tastes of the Internet, and in smaller intervals, unveil updates or slight changes to their page. This makes the business seem fresh and current, as customers are craving to do business with stores that will keep up with their needs and wants.

You should reserve a big re-design of your Web site for an anniversary or special product launch, but every few months, consider changing a small element of your Web site. Perhaps you roll out a new color scheme after 6 or 12 months. Definitely change any promotion boxes or announcements on your home page after a set period of time. Of course, whenever you make any changes, make sure every page is still consistent. Otherwise, you end up with a jumble of different designs after a year, and that conveys an unstable, unprofessional, unprofitable store.

Letting Discussions or Questions Go Unanswered

Your Web site look and feel isn't the only thing that should be touched up or refreshed as time goes on. Many Web store owners add a discussion board or chat room to their Web store, or implement comments on their blog section. But then they forget to go back in regular intervals, read what customers or visitors have written, and respond to any open questions. The quickest way to show your customers that you don't care about them is to ignore their questions and pleas for help. Answer any posted questions as soon as possible. Even if one customer answered another customer, post a reply and give additional information, even if it's to say, "Yep, Jeff is right, that's how we do business. Thanks for your question."

Along the same note, if you provide an area for discussion, don't assume that "if you build it, they will come." You'll need to start the conversation, and in the beginning, perhaps have a discussion with yourself by posting multiple times, and encouraging others to take part in the discussion. Stop in on regular intervals, add any postings or announcements to show everyone that new content will be available there, and perhaps design a promotion to encourage usage of this area. If you add this functionality to your Web store, factor in some time for you (or an employee) to manage this area, as it won't manage itself effectively.

Neglecting to Test or Optimize Your Web Page Load Times

You've tested your Web store for accuracy, for functionality, and for completeness. Every link works, every function works, every page has the same navigation bar. You post your Web store and get to work fulfilling orders. But there's one thing you neglect to test for — how quickly the Web store loads in the Web browser. Typically, it will load fast for you because you're developing the site, so perhaps the graphics are locally stored, requiring less load time. If you have a fast connection or are working directly on your storefront provider's account, then the store will load quickly for you.

The test comes by going to someone else's computer and loading your Web store on their system. Make a note of the first time it loads on their screen, and if any elements load slower than the rest, like a picture that is drawing itself one line at a time on the screen. While lots of people now have a fast connection into their home, not everyone does, so if possible, test your Web store on someone's computer that has a dial-up connection to the Internet. Hopefully you've designed your Web pages to load as quickly as possible, but you should check for it at some point just to be sure.

Index

• T •